STOUR VALLEY RAILWAY PART 2

THROUGH TIME

CLARE TO SHELFORD & AUDLEY END

Andy T. Wallis

AMBERLEY PUBLISHING

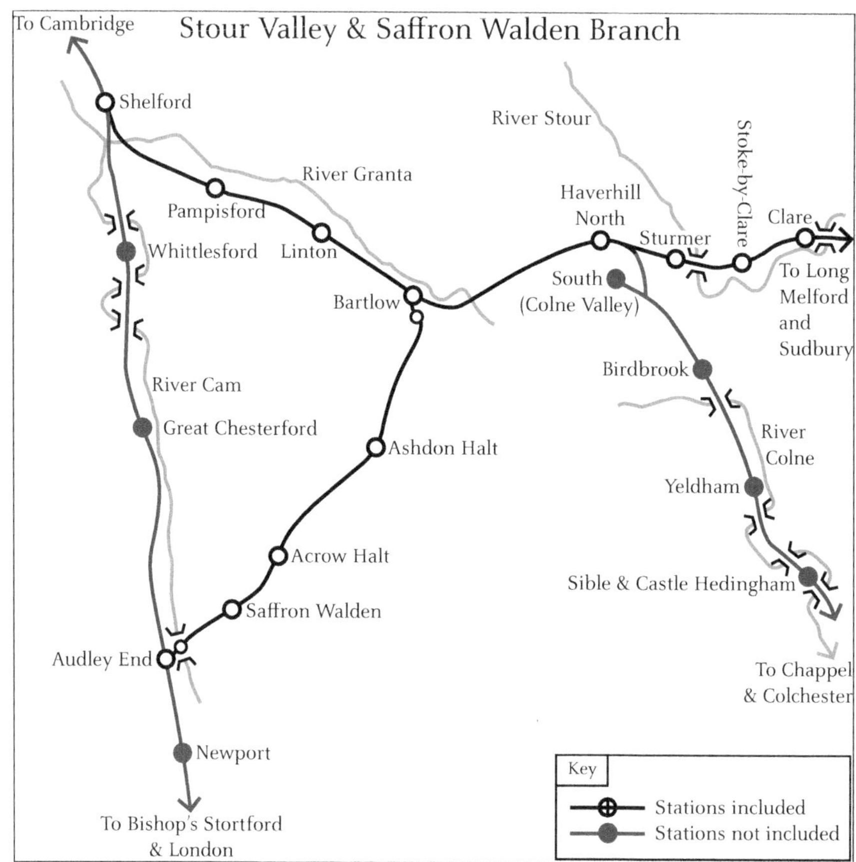

To Ray, Paul and all the photographers without whose help there would be no book.

First published 2011

Amberley Publishing Plc
The Hill, Stroud
Gloucestershire, GL5 4EP

www.amberley-books.com

ISBN 978 1 4456 0473 2

British Library Cataloguing in Publication Data.
A catalogue record for this book is available from the British Library.

Typeset in 9.5pt on 12pt Celeste.
Typesetting by Amberley Publishing.
Map illustration by User Design.
Printed in the UK.

Introduction

The Great Eastern Railway completed the construction of its new line from Shelford, junction with the London to Cambridge main line, to Haverhill in 1865 and the line duly opened in June of that year; this included a connecting spur to the Colne Valley line at Haverhill. The remainder of the line through to Sudbury was opened on 9 August of that year.

The branch between Audley End and Saffron Walden was authorised by Act of Parliament on 22 July 1861 and was extended to Bartlow by a further Act of Parliament on 22 June 1863. The line between Audley End and Saffron Walden was duly opened on 23 November 1865; the Great Eastern Railway worked the line from the outset. Meanwhile, work continued on the extension to Bartlow, which duly opened on 26 October 1866.

Under the Great Eastern Railway the fortunes of both lines had reached their zenith by the earlier part of the twentieth Century. The Great Eastern Railway passed into the new London & North Eastern Railway (LNER) on 1 January 1923 and the new owners started a cost saving programme which saw the closure of some duplicate signal boxes on the line and reduction of the single-line sections, and also included upgrading of the final section between Clare and Haverhill to Key Token working.

During the late 1920s and '30s, special summer excursion trains ran from the Midlands and Cambridge via both the Stour Valley and Colne Valley lines to Clacton and Walton. Traffic over the line peaked again during the war years and for a short time afterwards passenger and freight traffic was heavy, especially during the period after the war, when petrol rationing was in force. By the mid-1950s traffic receipts for both lines were dwindling due to road competition.

From 1 January 1959, steam traction was replaced by diesel locomotive-hauled trains for both freight and excursion traffic, local services being worked by DMUs and rail buses. Unfortunately, this did not slow down the losses being made by the Stour Valley and Saffron Walden branches.

When the Beeching Report was published in March 1963, the complete closure of both lines was proposed. A short while later, British Railways published plans to close the Saffron Walden branch; there was strong opposition to the closure plans, principally led by the local authorities. The Saffron Walden branch closure hearing took place over two dates in December 1963; withdrawal of the passenger service was recommended, despite numerous objections. British Railways announced that the branch would close to passenger traffic on and from 7 September 1964, the last trains being on Sunday 6 September.

The neighbouring Stour Valley line was also under threat, with the withdrawal of freight facilities from Sturmer, Cavendish and Bartlow having already taken place by the end of 1964.

In April 1965, British Railways published plans to close the whole of the Stour Valley line; in August a public hearing, where all parties could object to the proposals, was held into the closure plans at Sudbury. The decision to close only the line between Sudbury and Shelford, but retain the line south to Marks Tey, did not placate the local authorities. British Rail demanded a subsidy to keep the line open during 1966, which was duly considered by the local councils.

Meanwhile, the freight services had been withdrawn from the remaining threatened stations by October 1966. In January 1967, BR demanded the subsidy be increased by 100 per cent and the local authorities withdrew their objection to the closure. BR announced a closure date of 6 March 1967; the last passenger trains would run on the previous Saturday, 4 March 1967.

This book will show you what has happened to the Stour Valley and the Saffron Walden branch stations on the line over the last forty-plus years since the closure of both routes.

ATW

August 2011

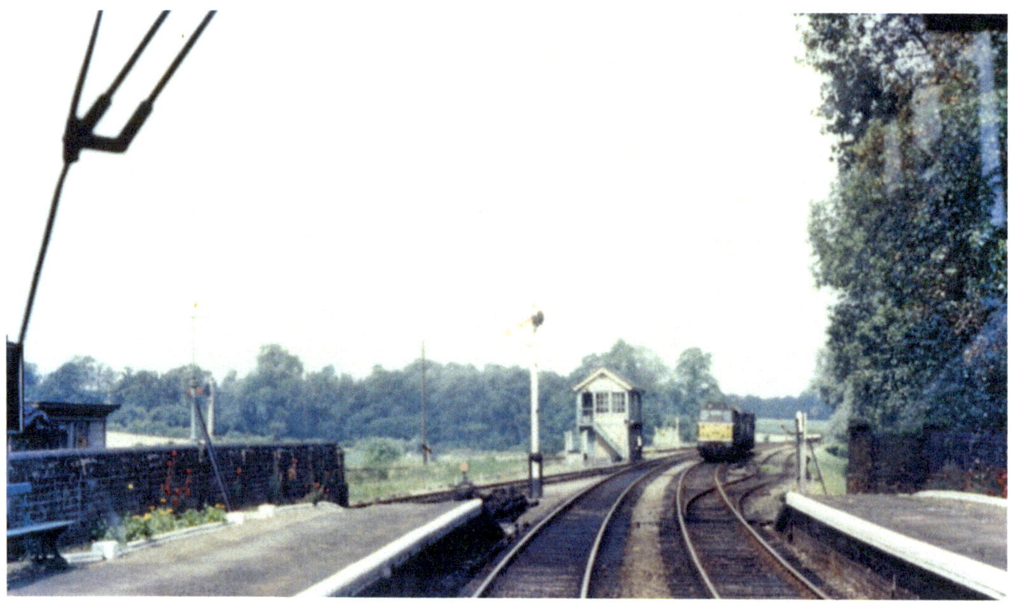

A Class 31 diesel and brake van wait at Bartlow Junction signal box for the single line tablet to proceed towards Haverhill. This view was taken from the cab of a DMU waiting in the loop – HMRS ABB656.

Clare

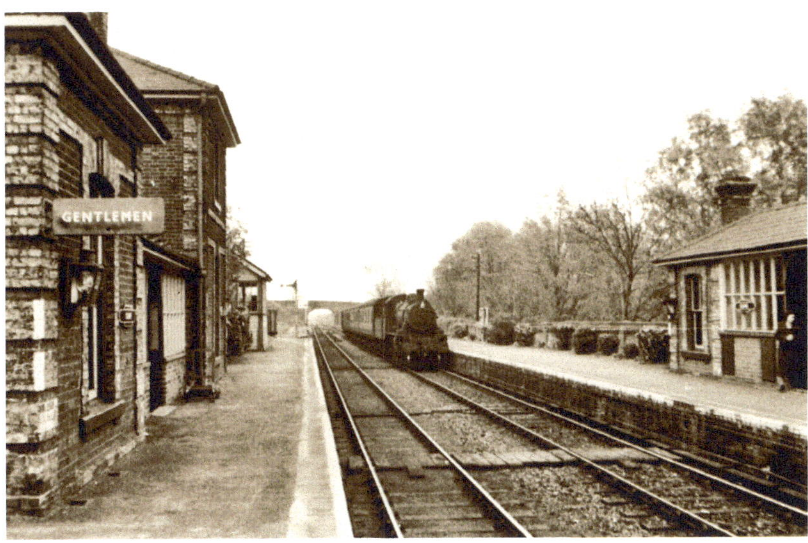

Steam local passenger service arrives in the down loop platform at Clare in the spring of 1955. The Ivatt-designed 2MT locomotives took over most of the passenger work on both the Stour and Colne valley lines in the early 1950s when five new-build locomotives were allocated to Cambridge and Colchester depots. (Stations UK)

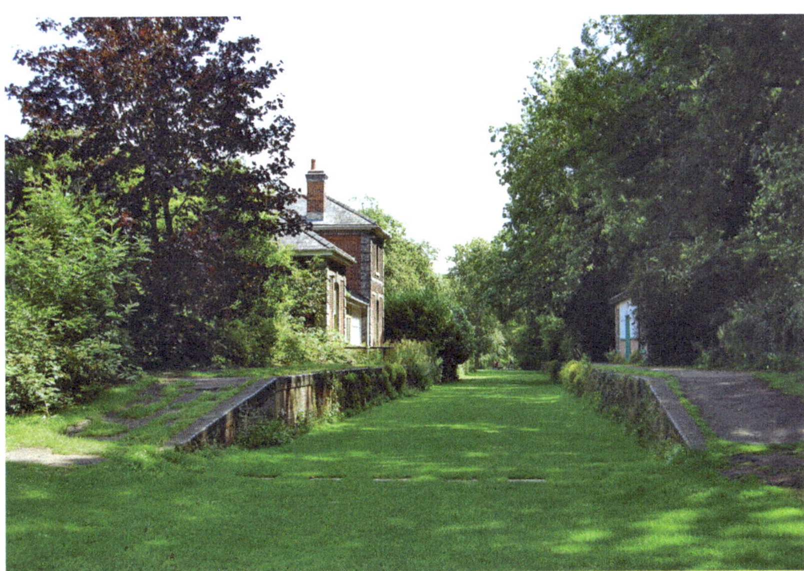

Today the rails have long gone, to be replaced by grass and walkways. Clare station and goods yard has been turned into a country park; the former stationmaster's house is used by the park warden. (Ray Bishop)

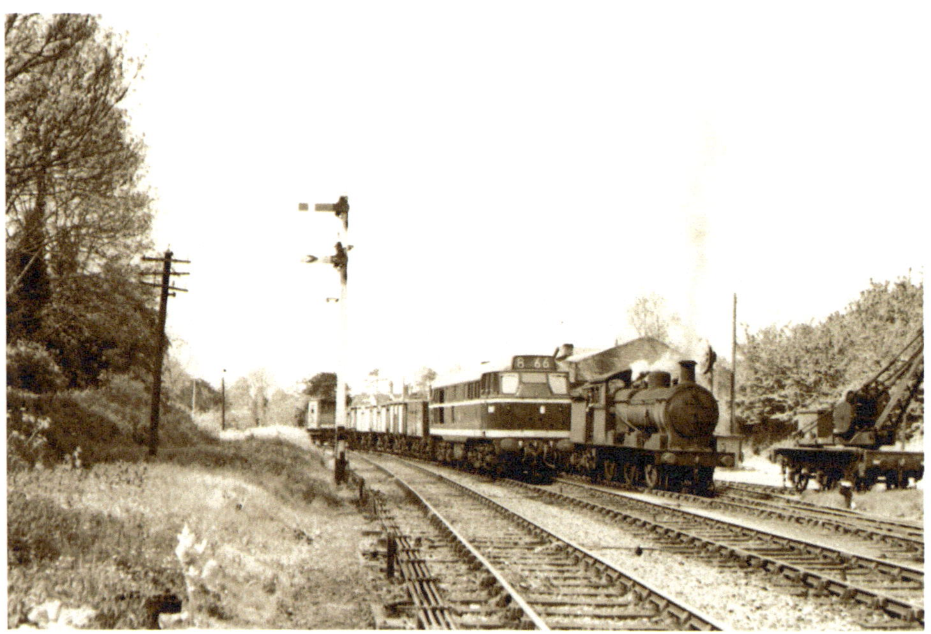

A Brush type 2 diesel, later designated Class 31 by BR, hauls a local Class 8 goods train into Clare station; meanwhile, a Class J17 steam local of the previous generation waits in the yard. This view was taken from the down platform. The signal on the left is Clare's down starter, with the gate distant for Ashen level crossing underneath. (Dr I. C. Allen/Transport Treasury)

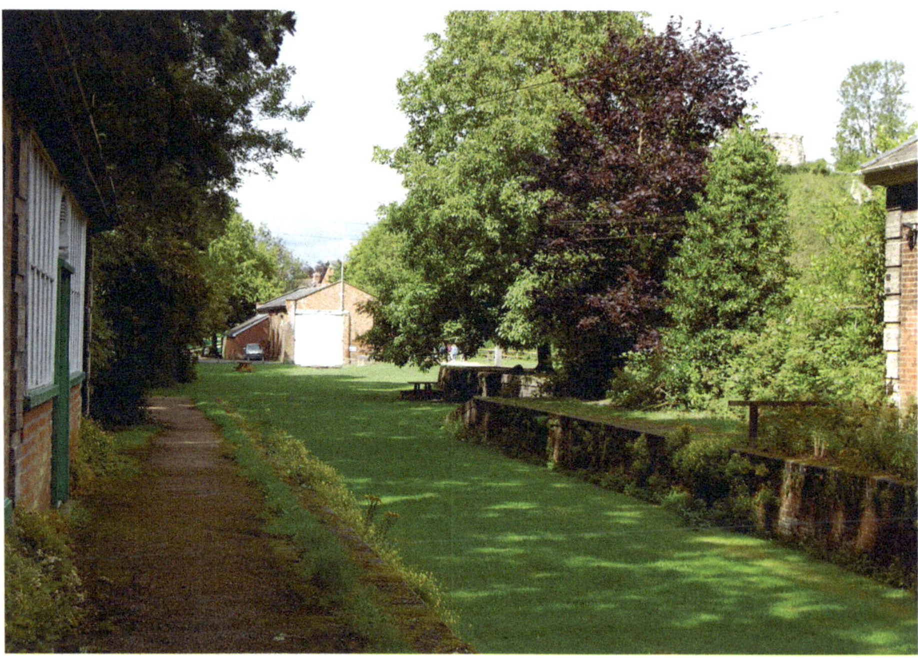

Standing on the former down platform, looking at the old goods shed, also preserved in the country park. The goods shed can be seen above the steam locomotive in the top picture; it contains some railway artifacts and is open for viewing on certain days. (Ray Bishop)

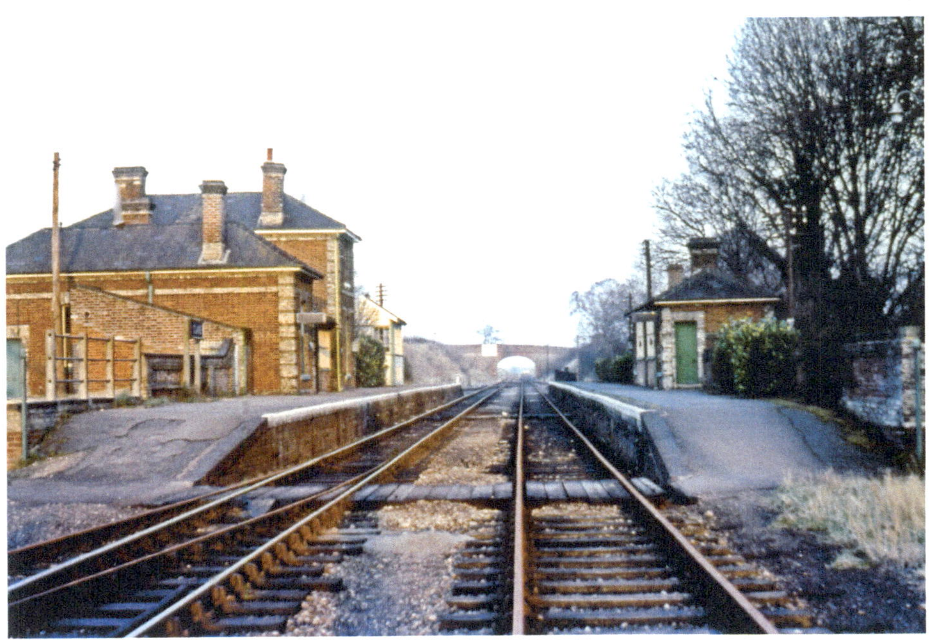

A sad view of Clare station taken on Sunday 5 March 1967, the day after the railway had closed completely; the signalling had already been removed when the signal box closed in January 1967. For the final two months of the passenger service, all trains used the up platform. The goods yard had been closed on 12 September the previous year. It would be late 1969/70 before the track was recovered for scrap. (Brian Pask)

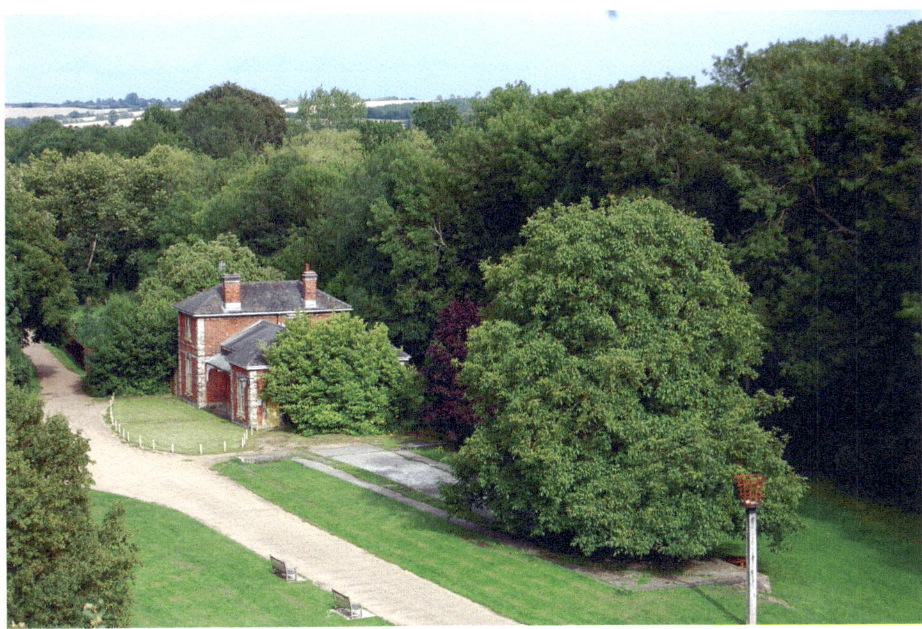

The redundant railway land was sold to the local authority, which turned the whole area into a country park. This elevated view shows the station's buildings surrounded by grass and walkways; the main line ran to the right of the tree in the foreground. (Ray Bishop)

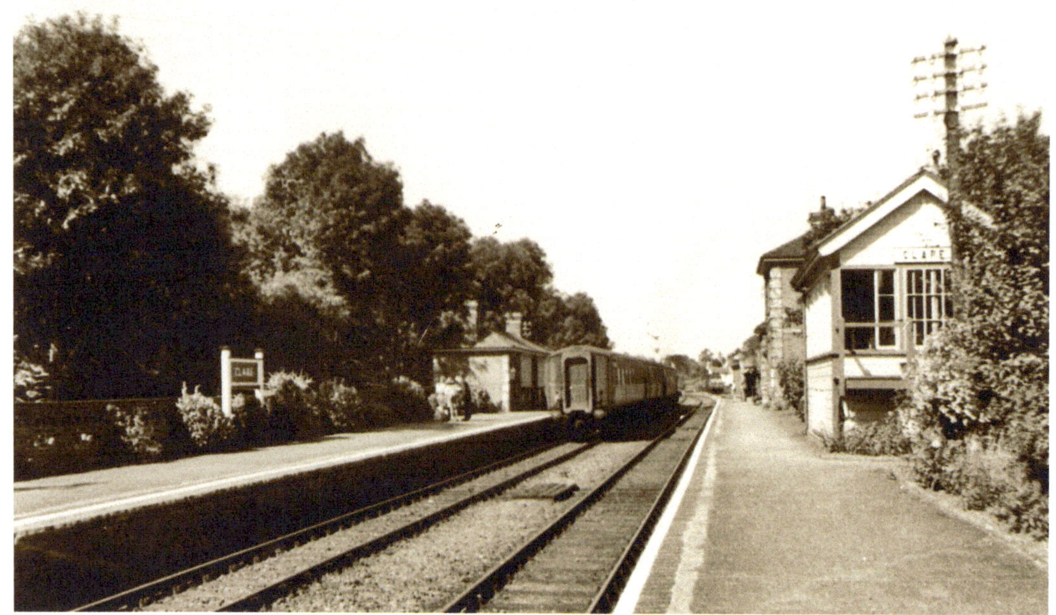

A view looking towards Haverhill from the up platform at Clare with a local passenger train departing; the signal box on the right controlled the passing loop on the single line and contained a Saxby & Farmer twenty-five-lever frame with nineteen working and six spare levers. Note how clean and tidy the station was kept. (Stations UK)

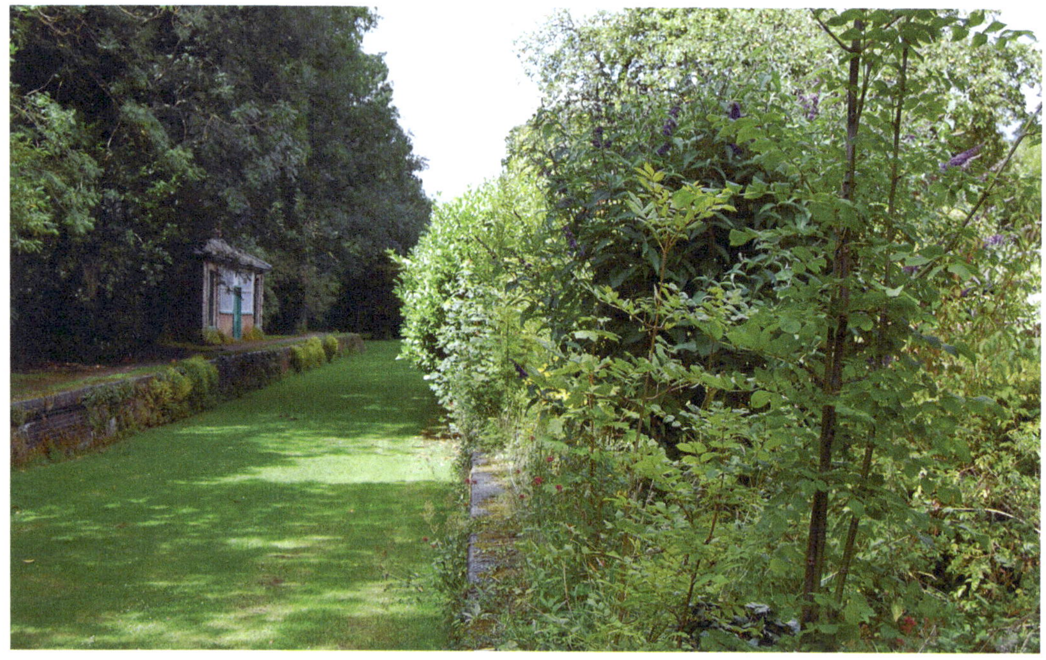

Standing in a similar position today, the site of the old signal box and the main station buildings are completely hidden by trees and bushes. Common to both pictures is the down side platform building; the track bed has been grassed over. (Ray Bishop)

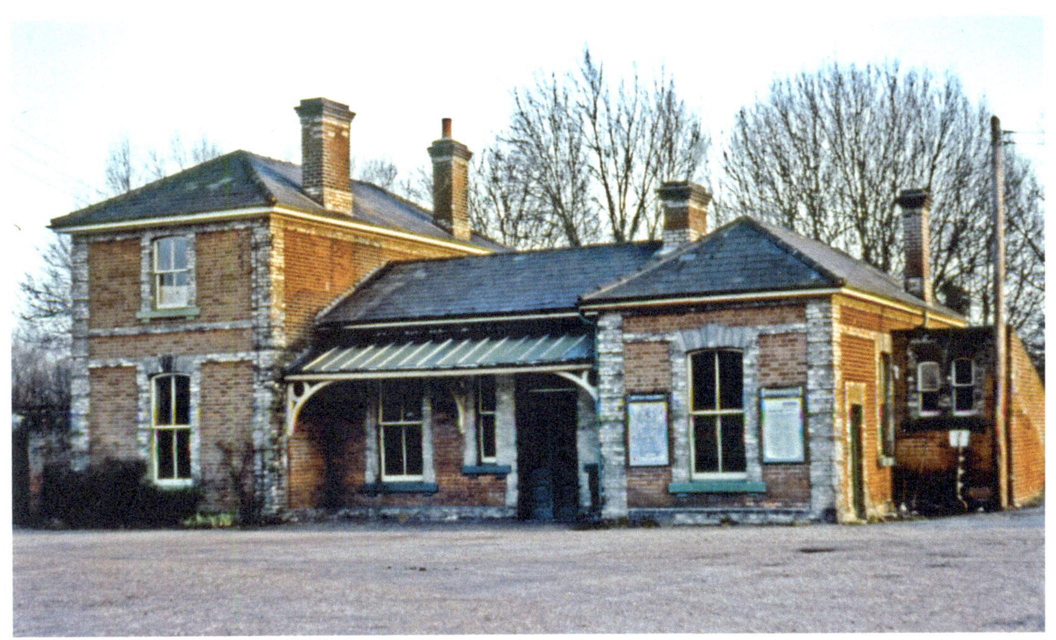

The main station buildings at Clare as seen from the approach road on Sunday 5 March 1967, the day after the closure of the station. The stationmaster's accommodation was to the left, with the booking office, parcels office and waiting rooms on the right. The station is of the standard GER 1865 design, which features regularly on this line. (Brian Pask)

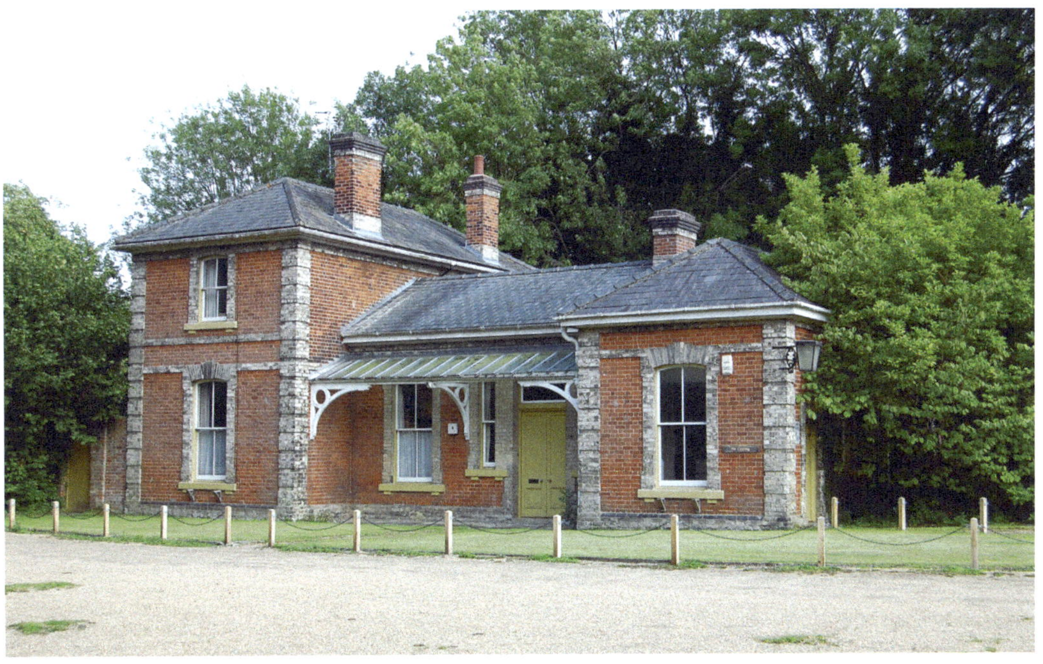

A similar view of the main station buildings as seen in July 2011, in use as accommodation by the country park warden. The only difference seems to be the small building on the extreme right of the top view, and the notice boards attached to the walls. (Ray Bishop)

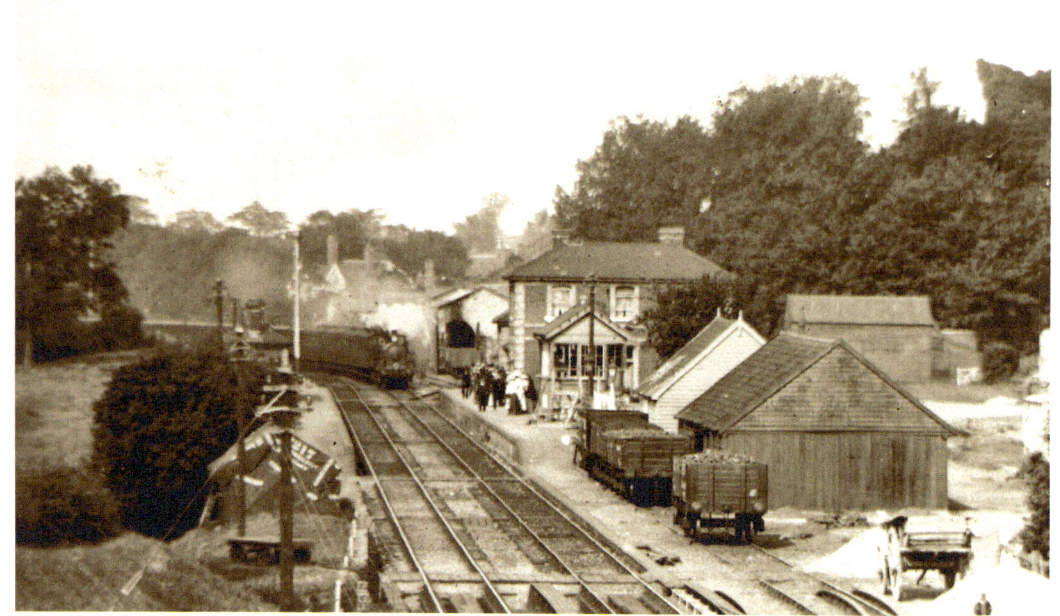

An early Great Eastern Railway view of Clare station looking towards Haverhill, taken from the over bridge at the Sudbury end of the station. A local passenger train is seen arriving in the up platform. There seems to be plenty of trucks waiting to be loaded or emptied in the sidings and goods yard. (Lens of Sutton Association)

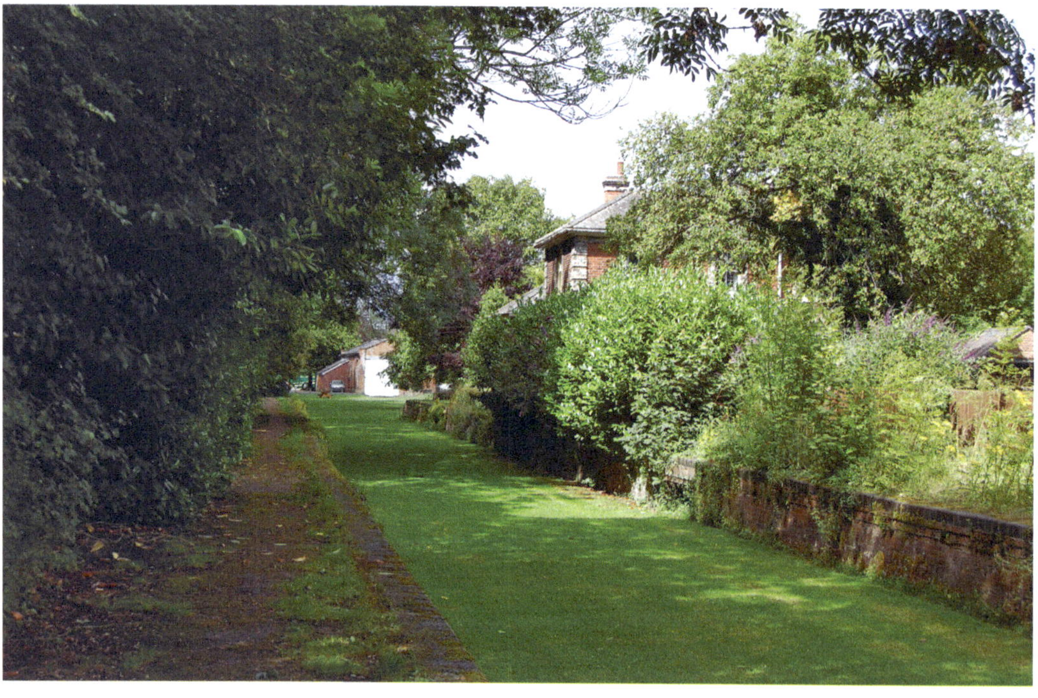

Due to tree growth, this view had to be taken nearer the station. The edge of the main building is common to both views. (Ray Bishop)

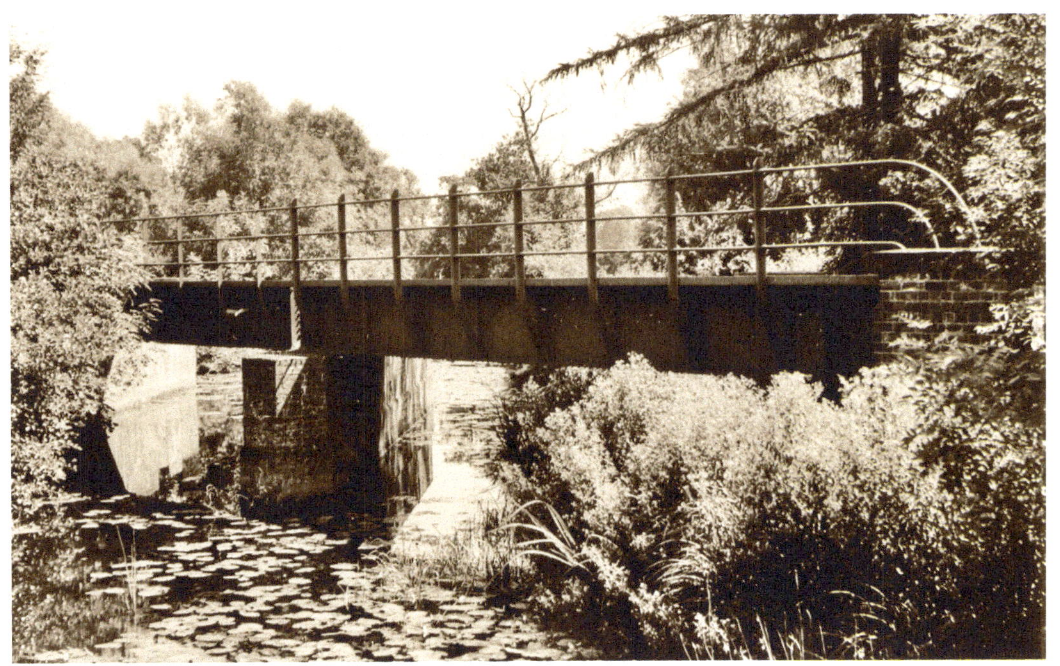

The railway bridge over the river on the approach to Clare station. The abutments were clearly built for two tracks, but only one span was in use. The railings are common to both pictures. (Brian Connell/Photos from the Fifties)

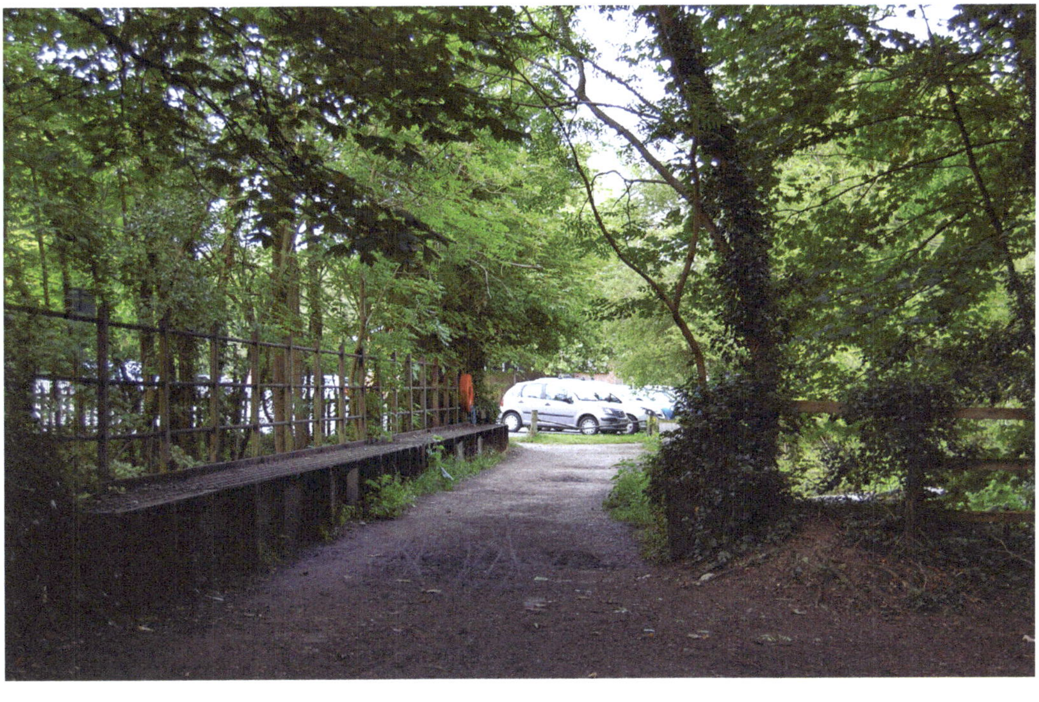

Today, the bridge is used as a walkway leading away from the car park to the other end of the park, which runs out at the former Ashen level crossing. (Ray Bishop)

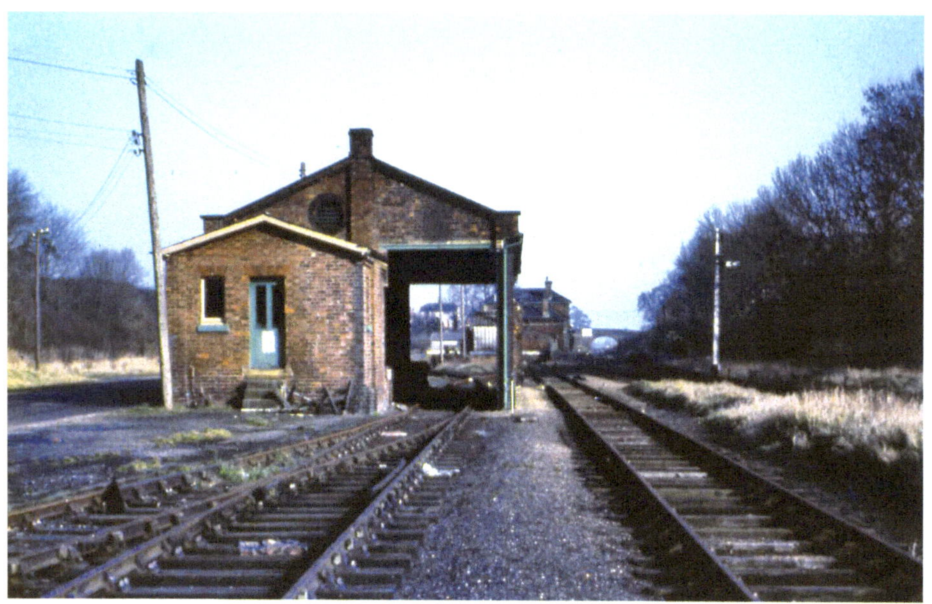

A view from the goods yard, looking through the deserted goods shed at the main station buildings. The freight service had been withdrawn from Clare on 12 September 1966; the passenger service continued until the following March. The crossing loop was taken out of use in January 1967, the local DMUs using the former up platform in both directions for the remaining few weeks until closure. The token/tablet sections were modified to be Haverhill to Cavendish, with the former Clare/Cavendish tablets over-stamped with Haverhill. The former key token section between Clare and Haverhill was abolished and the machines were recovered. (D. J. Plyer)

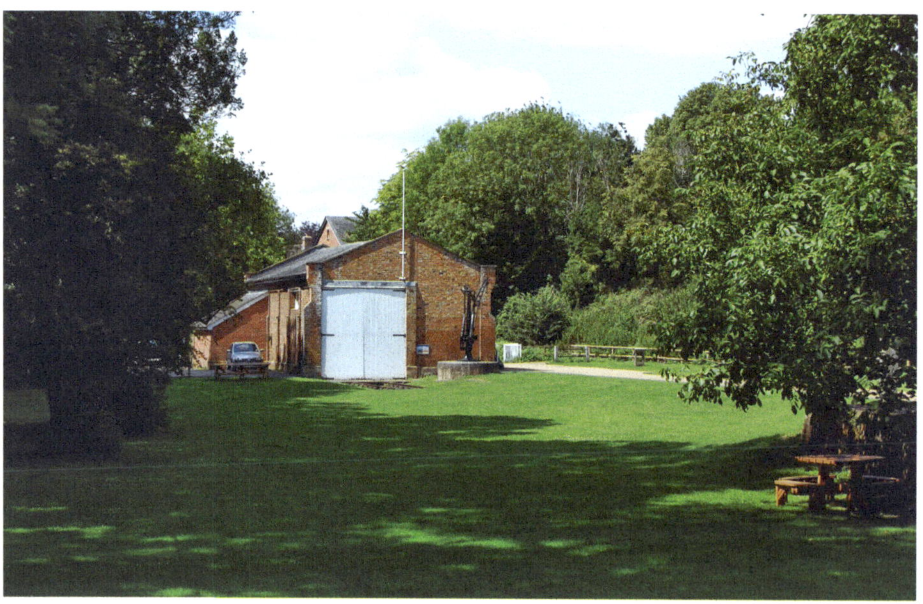

A view of the opposite end of the former goods shed, showing the small loading crane to the right. An extension has been added to the main goods shed. (Ray Bishop)

Stoke-by-Clare

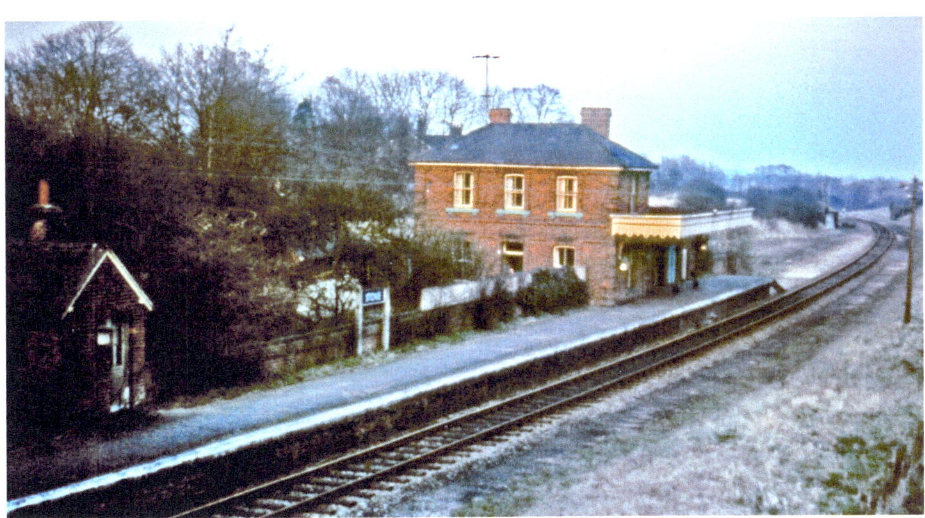

Stoke-by-Clare station, as viewed from the road bridge looking towards Sudbury on Sunday 5 April 1967, the day after the last passenger service had run. The goods loop and yard track had already been lifted, but it was to be nearly another three years before demolition commenced. The station had the standard GER 1865 station buildings; booking facilities had been withdrawn on 28 January 1963 as an economy measure. (Brian Pask)

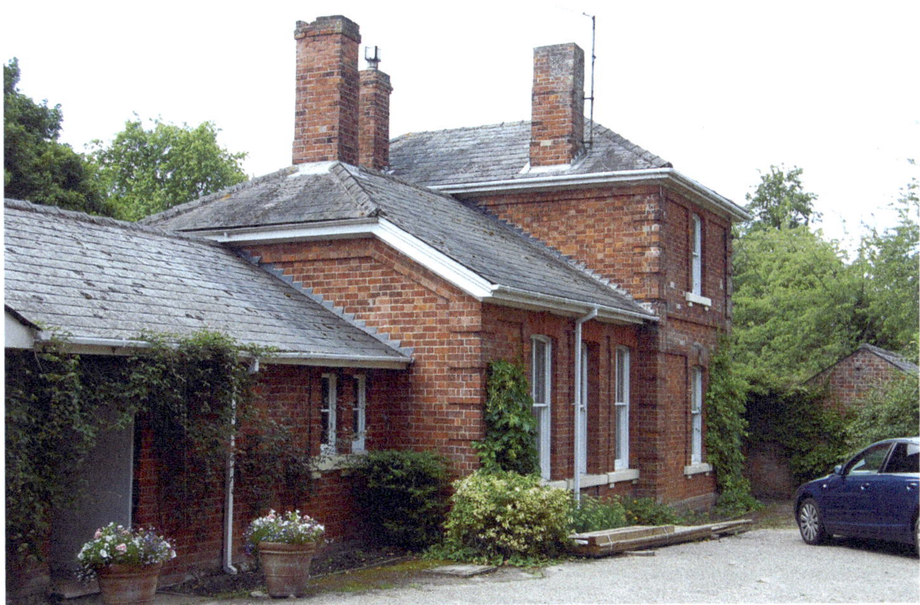

Today, the front view of the former station clearly shows its origins; the former buildings have been turned into a fine house and have been well looked after. (Ray Bishop)

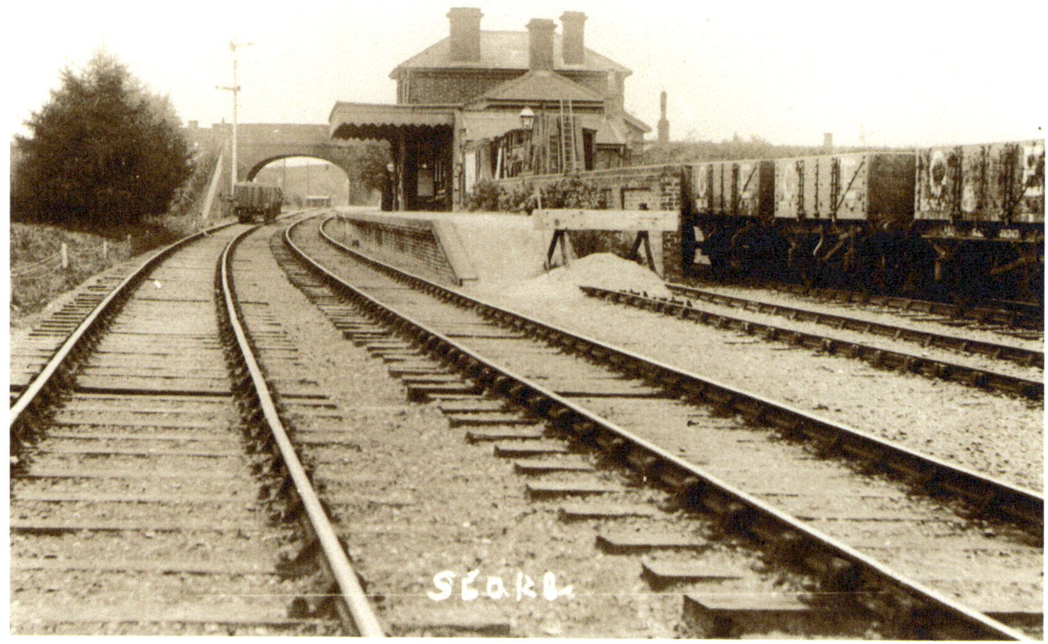

An early Great Eastern Railway view taken from the opposite end of the station, looking towards Haverhill; plenty of trucks in the yard indicate a healthy traffic flow. From the 1920s until the withdrawal of the freight service the station handled large amounts of sugar beet traffic being shipped to the processing plants at Bury St Edmunds or Felstead. (Lens of Sutton Association)

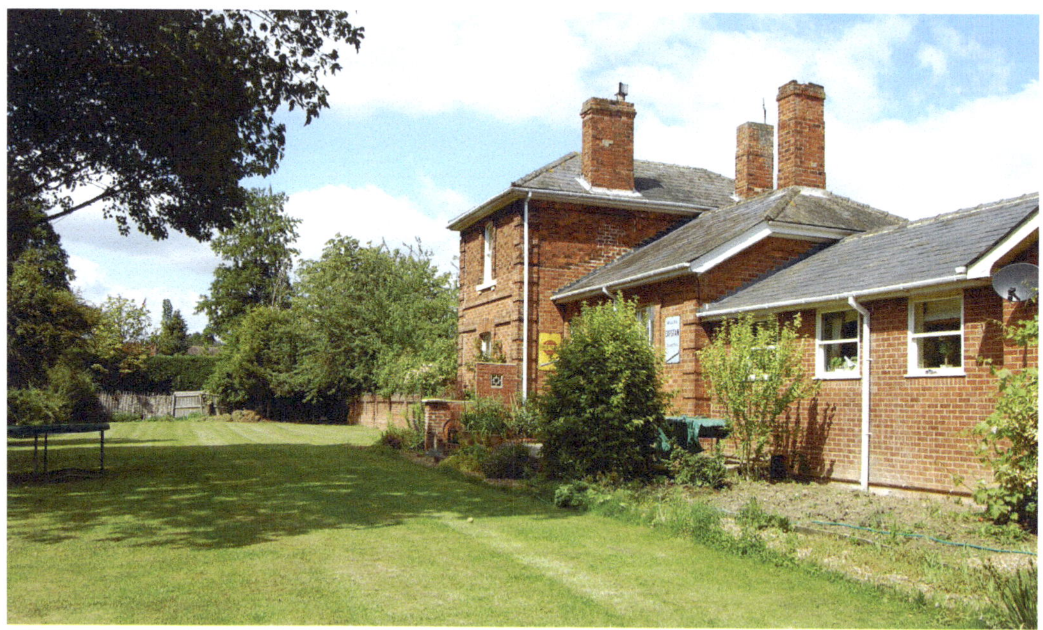

Today, the view from the garden shows the old station, with its canopy removed but an extension added at one end. The track bed has been filled in and grassed over. The three chimneys are common to both pictures. (Ray Bishop)

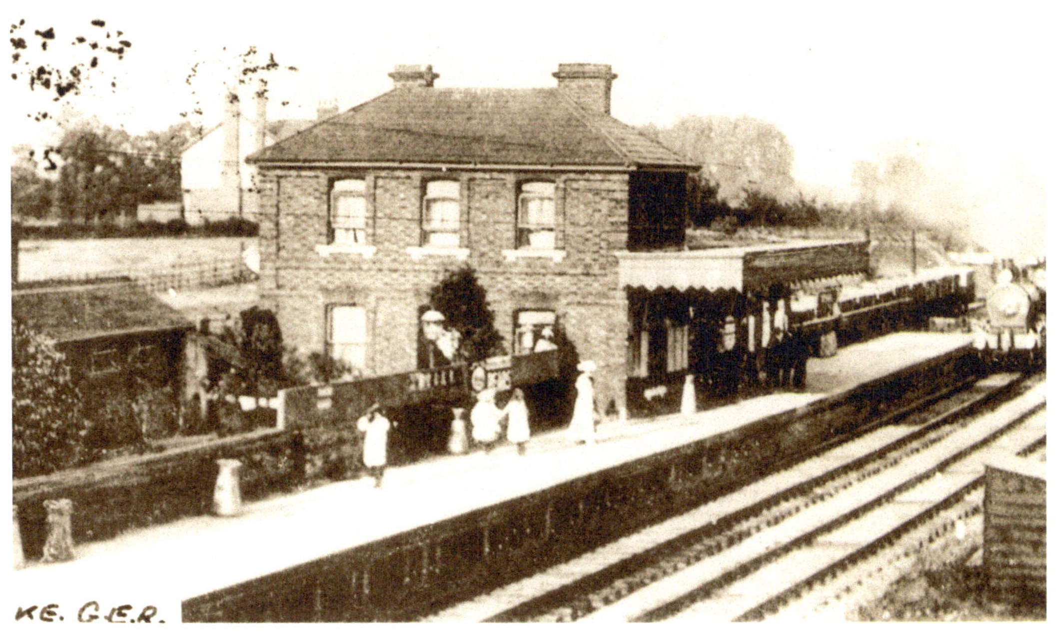

Another early GER view of the station taken from the road bridge, with a few passengers waiting the arriving train to take them to Haverhill and Cambridge; again the goods yard looks busy, with plenty of wagons awaiting dispatch. The trees behind the station buildings had yet to grow. (Lens of Sutton Association)

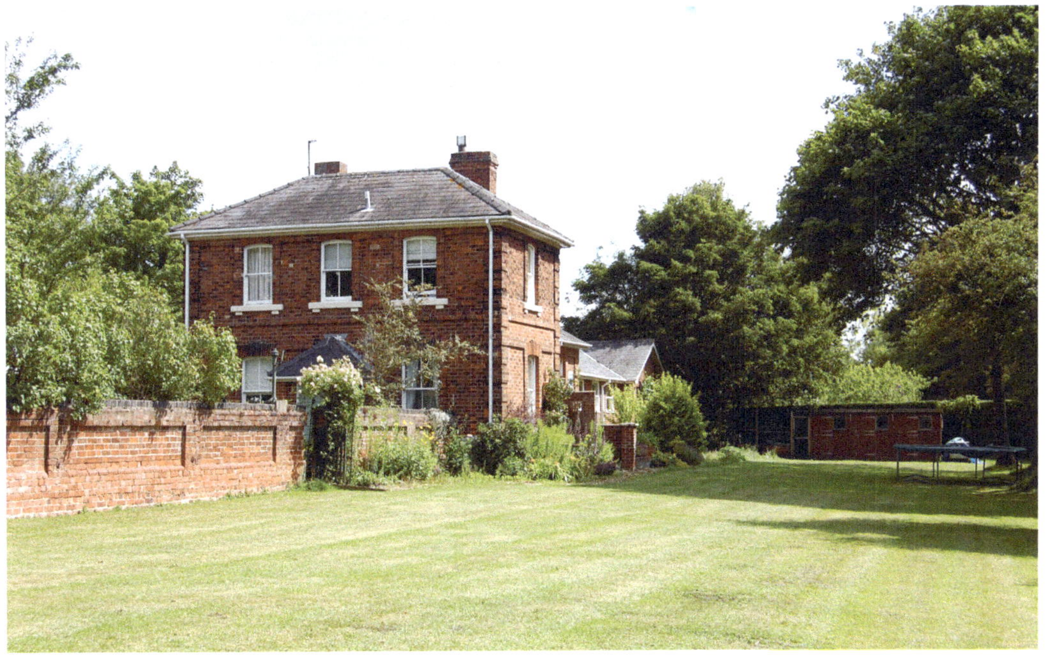

The same view today, but this time from the gardens. The wall is common to both views. Beyond the end of the garden, the former goods yard has had new housing built on it. (Ray Bishop)

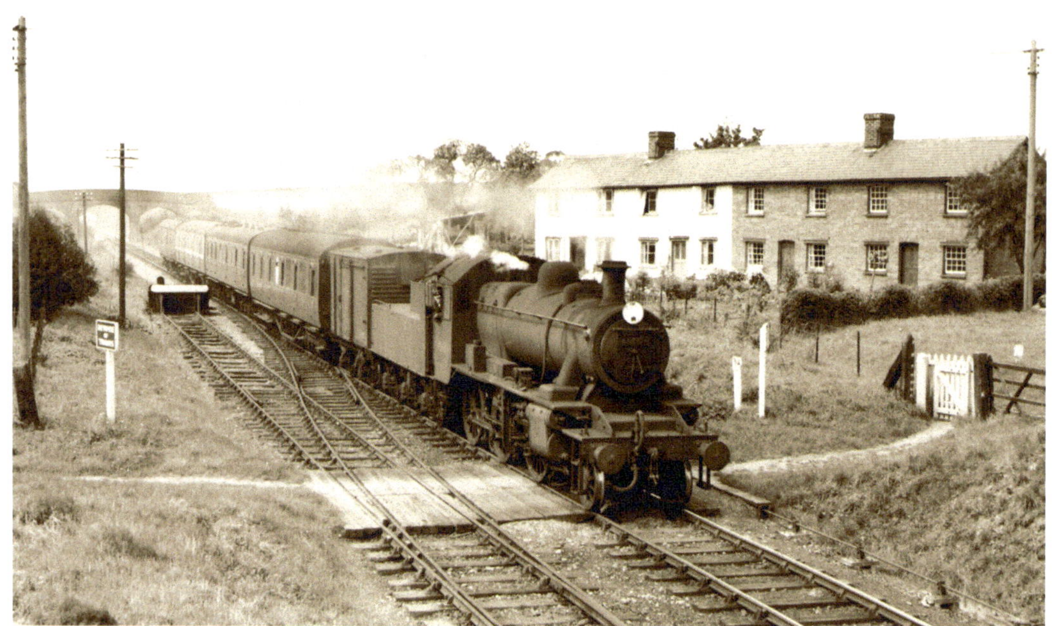

An Ivatt-designed Class 2MT locomotive on a local passenger working arrives at Stoke-by-Clare, as viewed from the road bridge sometime in the 1950s. The green at Stoke was severed by the building of the railway, a right of way and occupational crossing being maintained for the purposes of crossing the line. After the signal box closed in the 1930s, the points from the goods loop were worked from a ground frame located behind the engine. (Dr I. C. Allen/Transport Treasury)

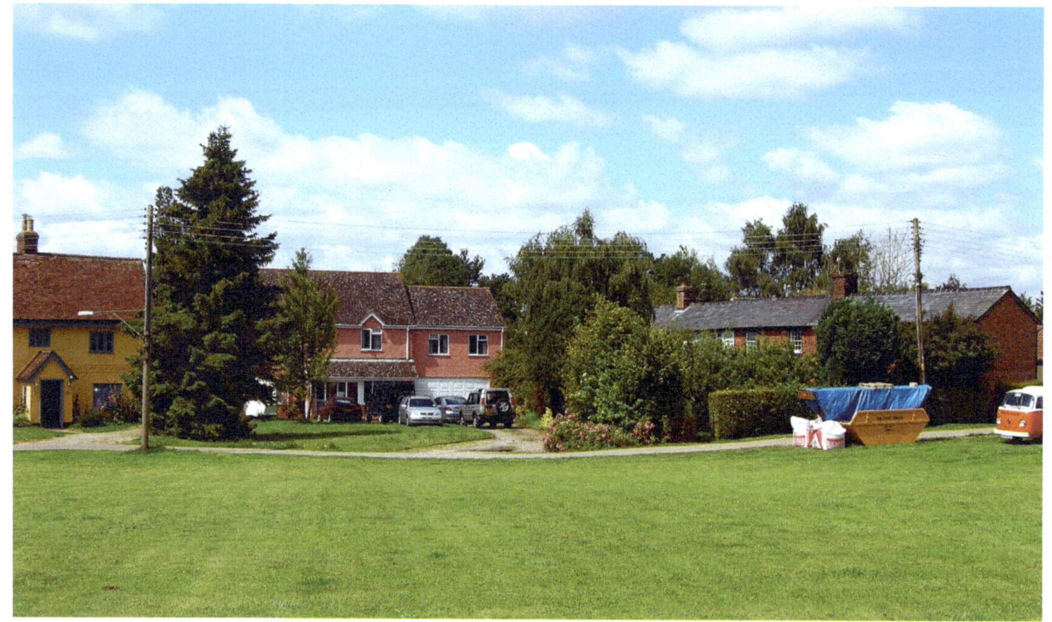

Today, the bridge has been demolished and the road realigned – the green is all one again. The cottages on the right are the common view; the railway used to run through the new house in the centre of the picture. The electricity power cables also feature in both views. (Ray Bishop)

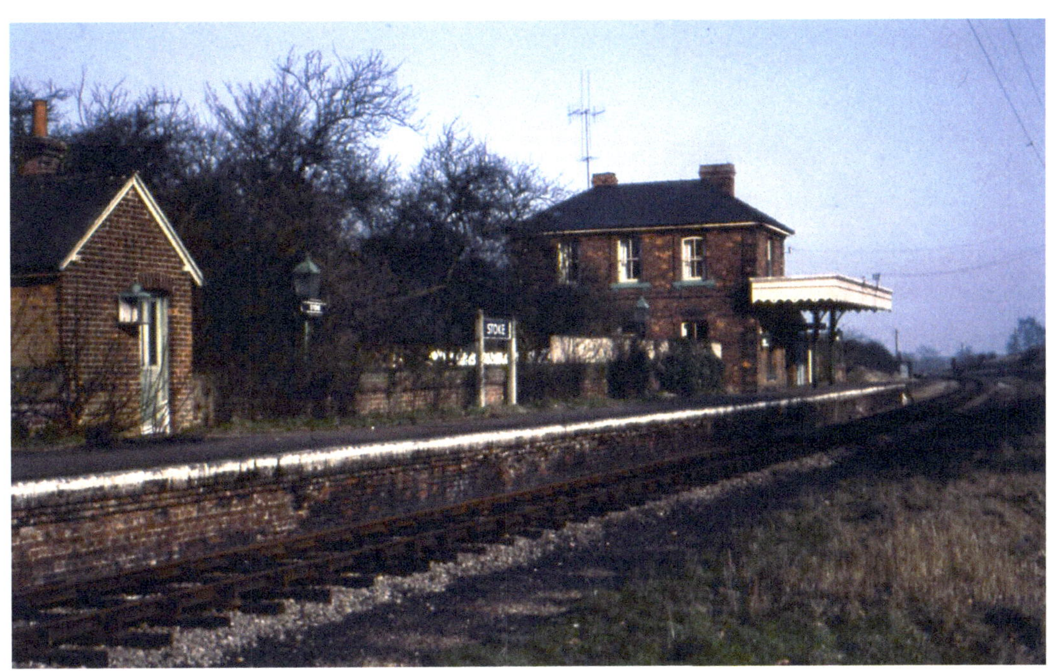

A rare colour view of Stoke-by-Clare taken in February 1967, just a few weeks before the closure of the line to passenger traffic; by this time, all the sidings and the loop line had been recovered. Later, the station buildings were sold to be converted into a private dwelling. (D. J. Plyer)

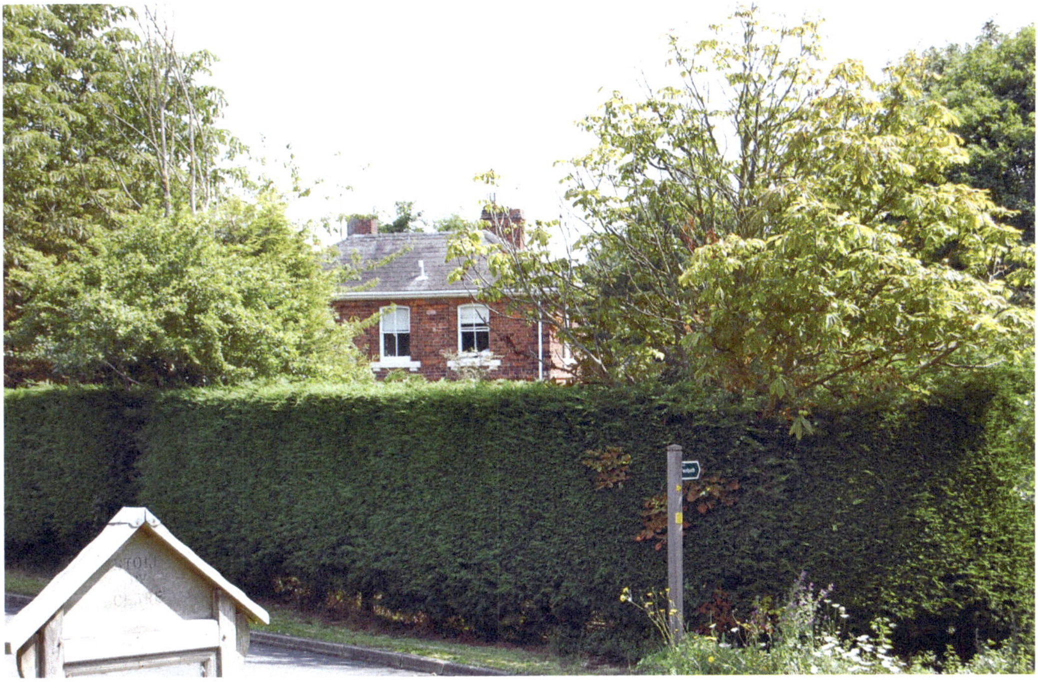

Today, hedging and trees give the former station an enclosed private view. Note the 'Stoke-by-Clare' board in the bottom left of the picture. (Ray Bishop)

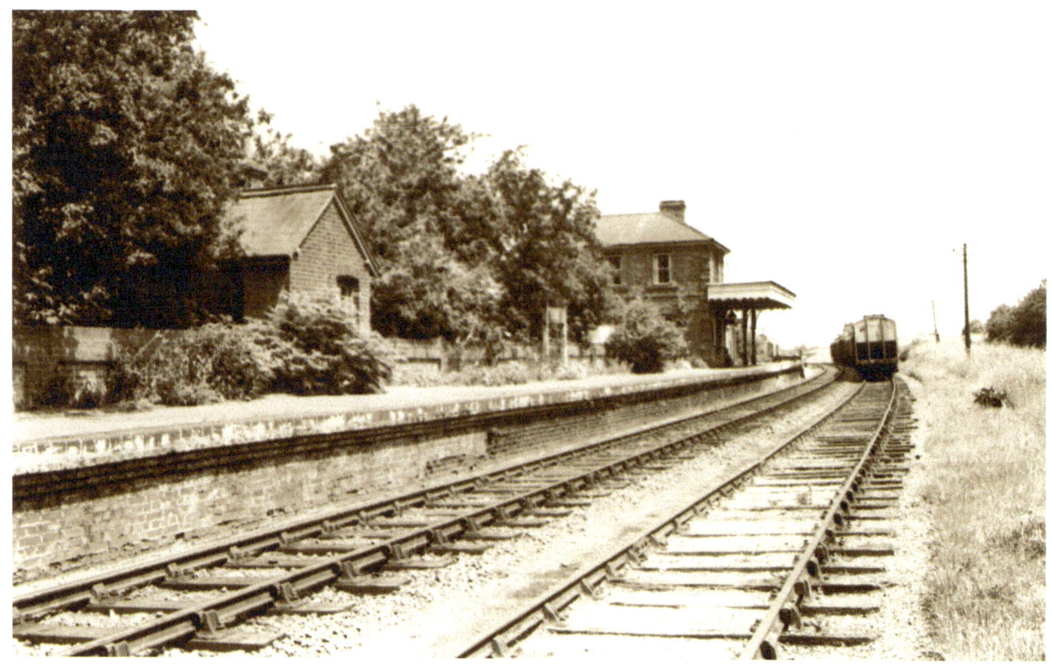

Stoke station in happier times, with traffic on the loop line. This view was taken at ground level from the Haverhill end of the station. The former signal box was located on the right-hand side, at the Sudbury end of the station; it was closed in the 1930s and replaced with two ground frames. (Stations UK)

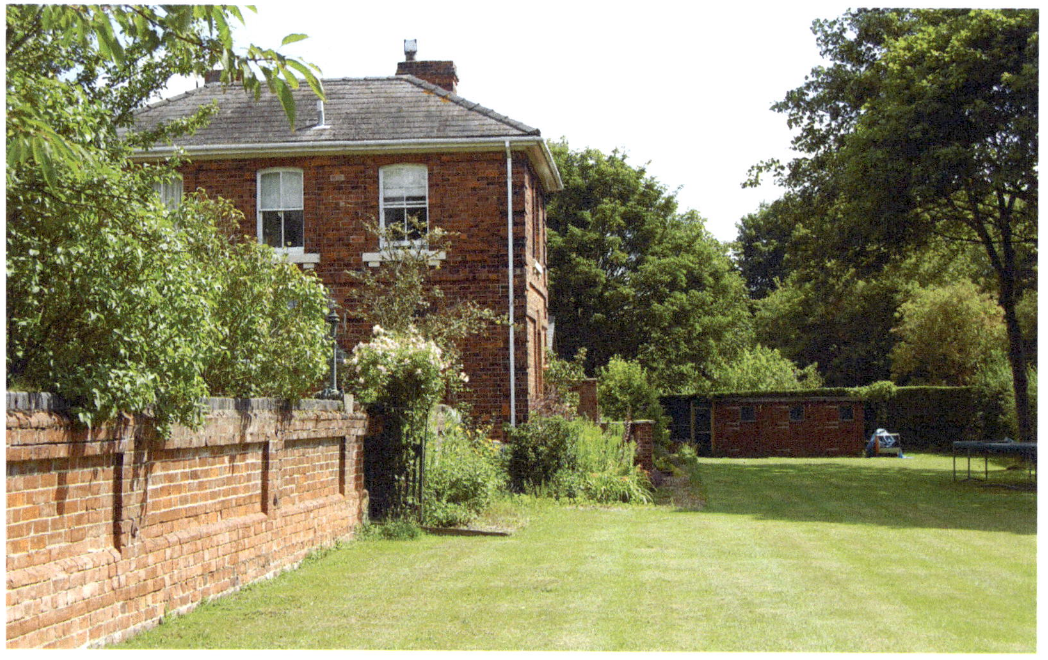

A modern view, looking towards Sudbury; the garden wall is original and would have separated the platform from the stationmaster's garden. (Ray Bishop)

Sturmer

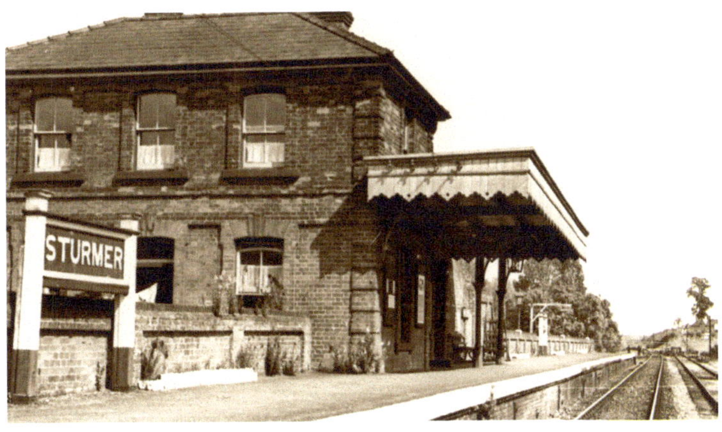

Sturmer station was very similar to Stoke, in that there was the standard GER-type station building on the single platform, a level crossing at the Haverhill end of the station and, until the 1930s, this was protected with a full range of signals controlled from the adjacent signal box. After the signal box closed, it was replaced with three ground frames; the first was a two-lever controlling entry into the down siding, and the second was four levers, controlling the level crossing gate lock, distant signals and the trap points in the down siding. The third ground frame was at the Clare end of the layout and controlled access to the up siding, the two sidings' ground frames being released by the Haverhill North to Clare Key tokens; an auxiliary token machine was provided at the Haverhill end of the down siding to shunt away goods trains if required. (Stations UK)

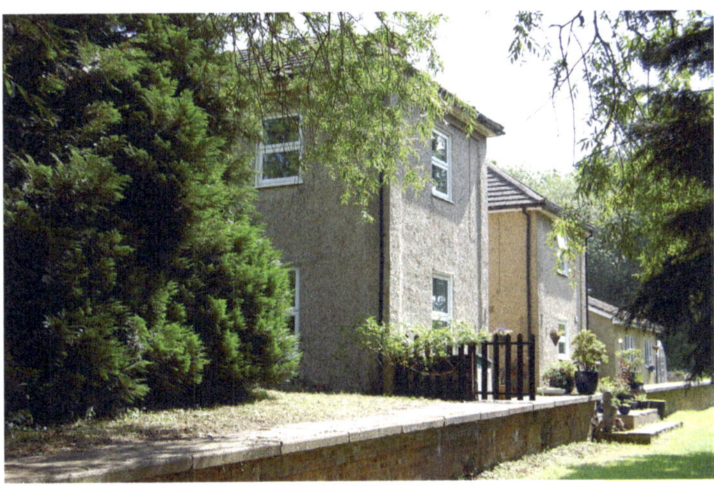

Today, the station has been much improved and extended; the platform still exists, with steps down to the lawn. (Ray Bishop)

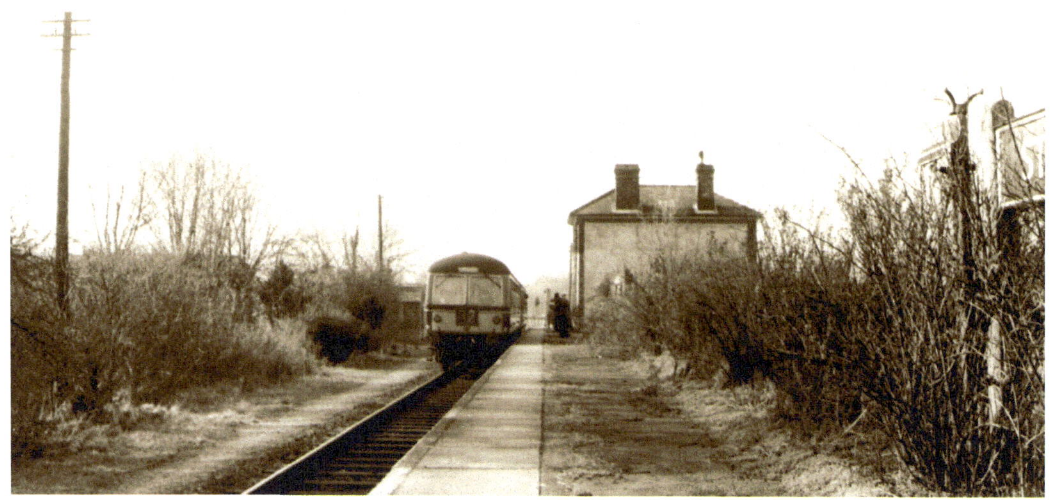

A Craven-type diesel multiple unit at Sturmer station in the mid-1960s. The station had lost its booking facilities in January 1963 as an economy measure; a crossing keeper was retained to work the level crossing gates and signals. Freight services at the station had been withdrawn in June 1962 and the up and down sidings were then recovered. Following the withdrawal of freight and booking facilities, the station took on an air of neglect. (Stations UK)

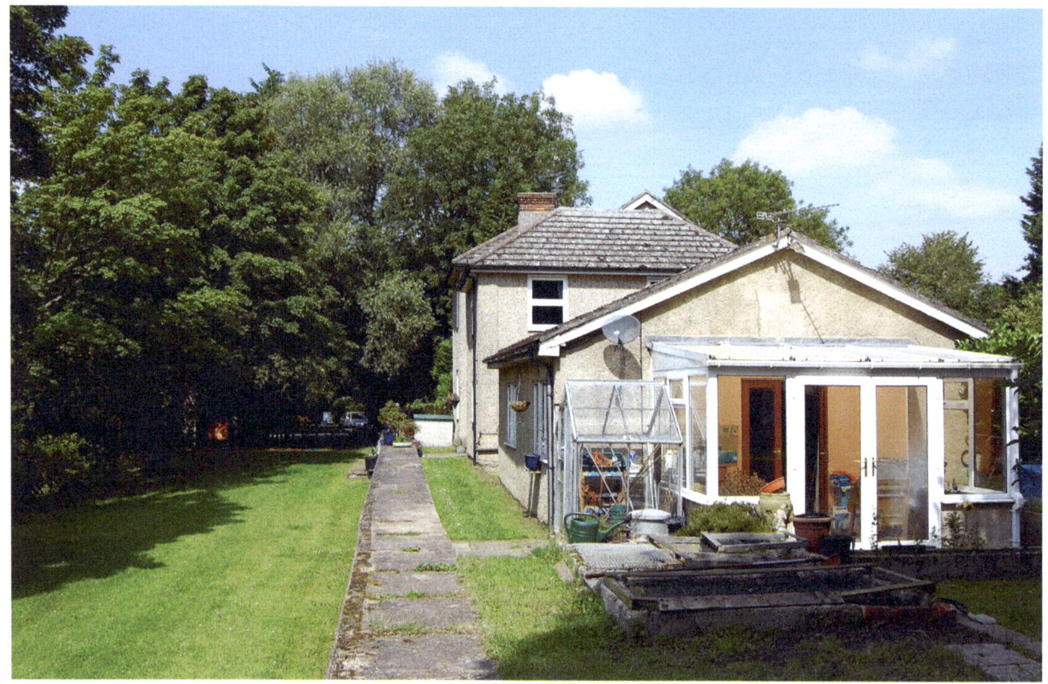

Today's similar view sees a large two large extensions to the accommodation, together with a conservatory; the platform edge is clearly visible. (Ray Bishop)

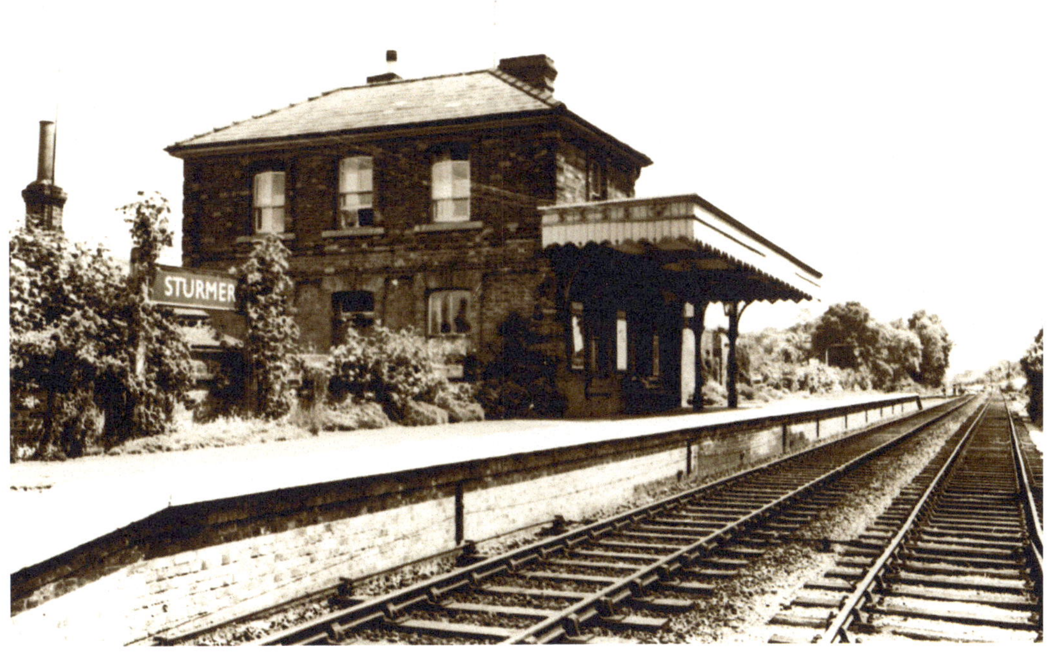

Sturmer station, with all its facilities. Both the siding and running line passed over the level crossing; the siding was fitted with trap points to prevent wagons fouling the crossing. On the Haverhill side of the level crossing, a short additional siding was provided for a number of years. (Stations UK)

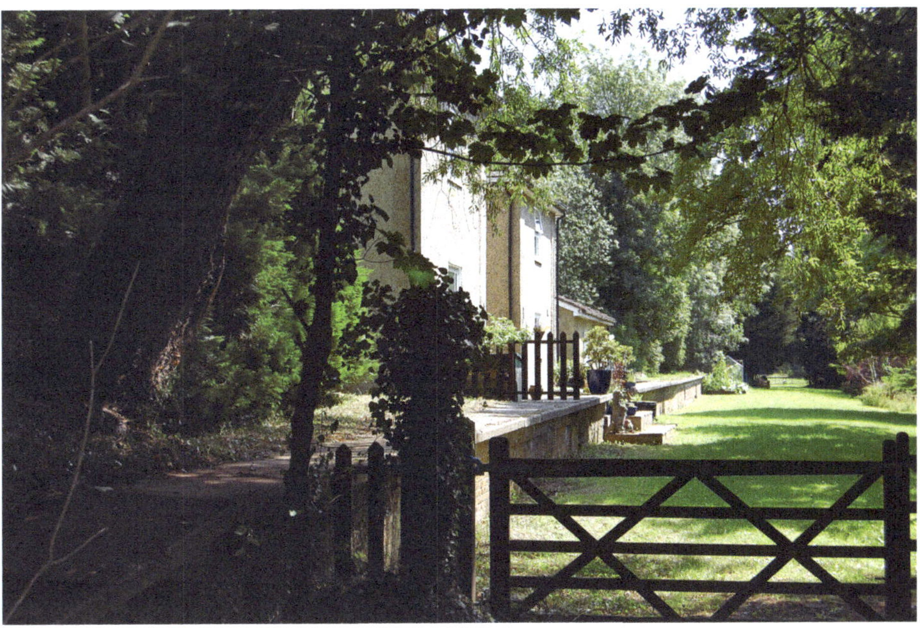

The view from the road today, showing the platform ramp and double gate across the former track bed. During the last forty years, a large tree has grown at an angle from the back of the platform. (Ray Bishop)

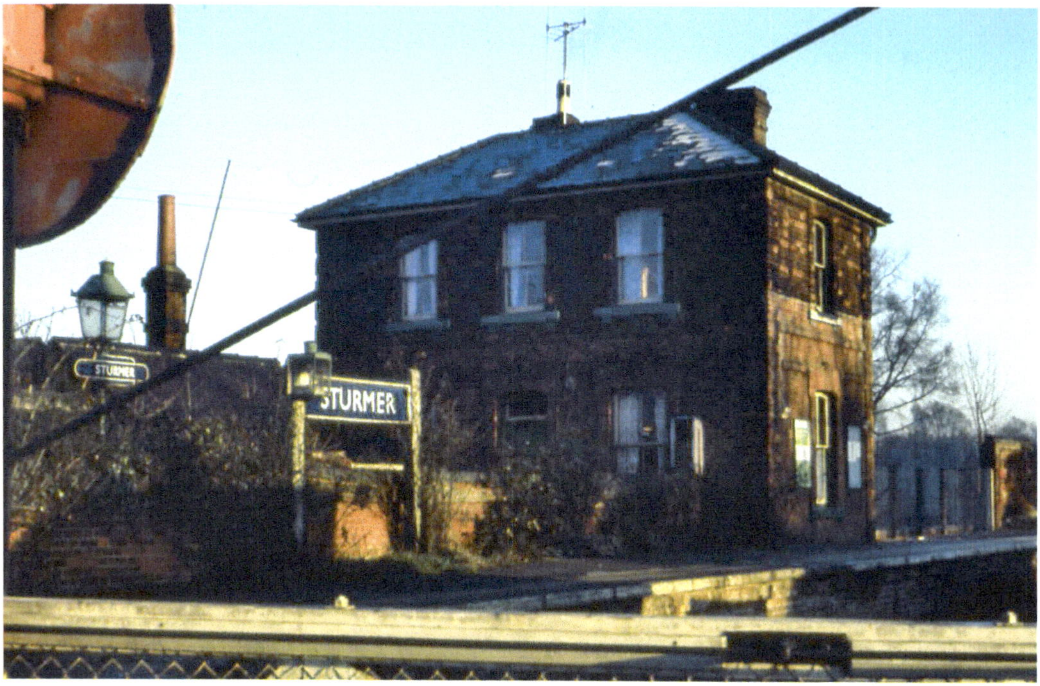

A colour view of Sturmer station taken from the road looking over the level crossing gate, on 26 December 1965. By this time the line was already under threat of closure, freight and passenger booking facilities having already been withdrawn (D. J. Plyer)

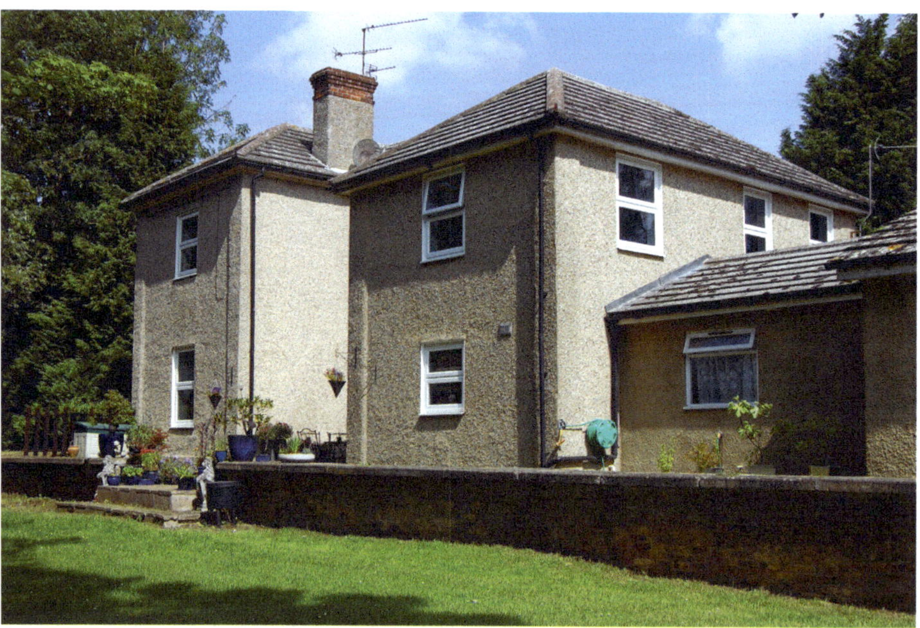

A modern view from the 'track bed' looking at the original building on the left, with the new buildings on the right. All the buildings have been coated with pebbledash; they also have had replacement windows fitted. (Ray Bishop)

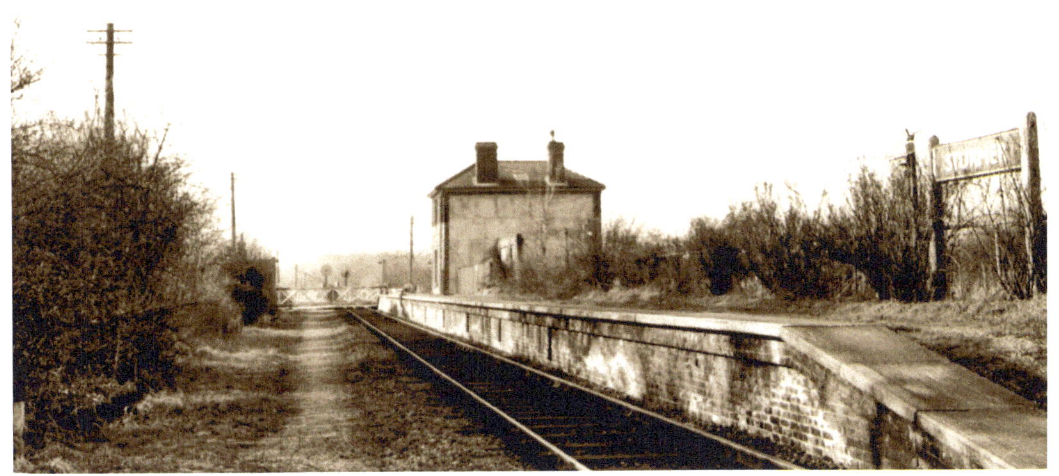

Sturmer station viewed from the lifted down siding at the Clare end, with the level crossing gates in the distance. The gates were fitted with extended large red targets with the lamp mounted in the middle as an aid to rail drivers in sighting the crossing. Protection of the crossing was by working distant signals operated by the crossing keeper. (Stations UK)

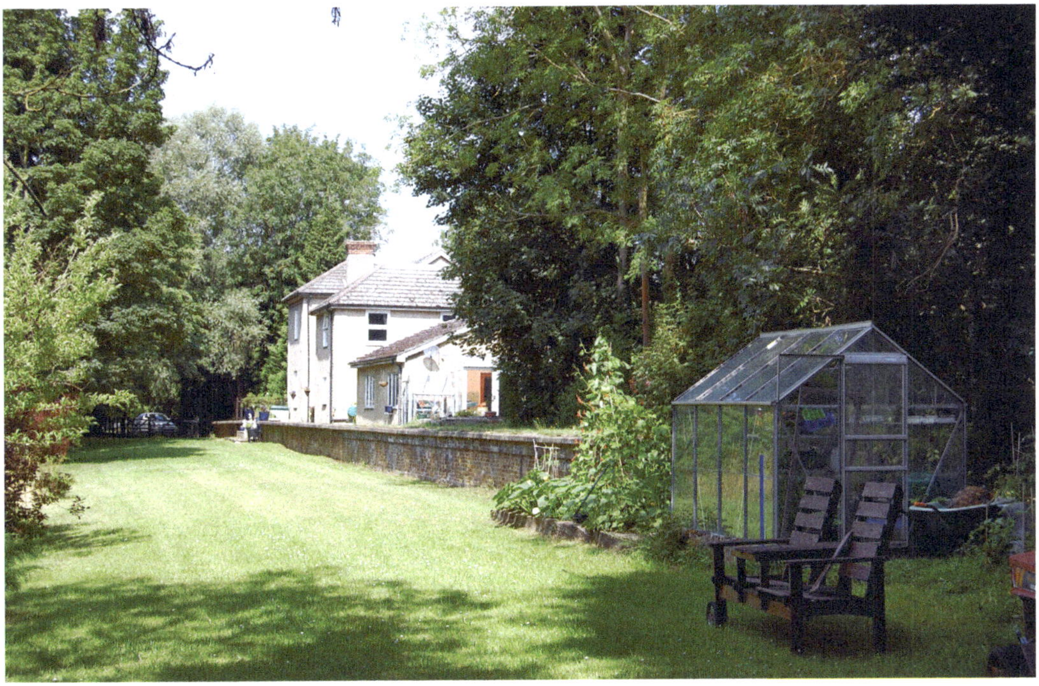

The same view today shows a very nice private house and gardens; the platform ramp shown in the top picture is hidden behind the greenhouse. (Ray Bishop)

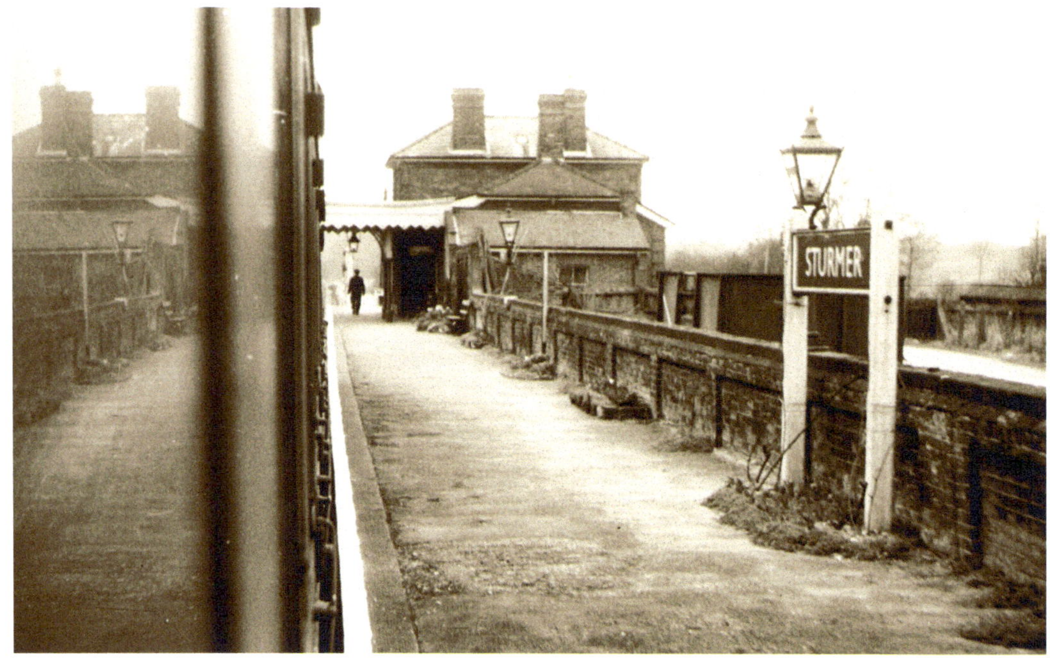

Sturmer station buildings and platform as viewed from the train on 6 April 1956. Note the coal truck behind the platform wall standing on the up siding. At this time, the gardens look well kept. (R. M. Casserley)

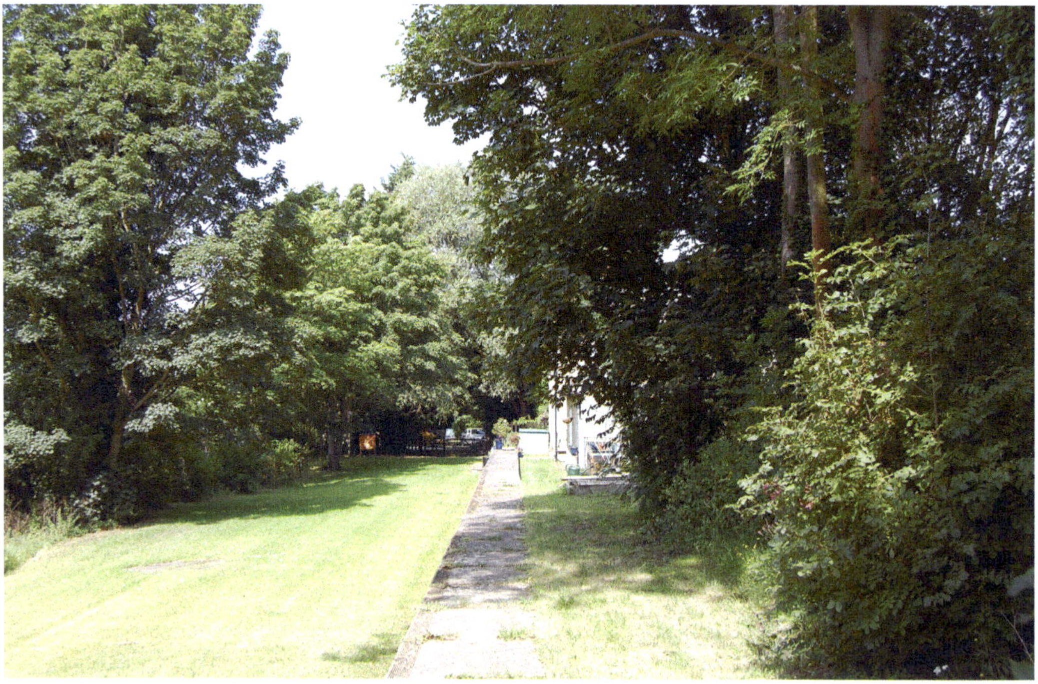

Today, mature trees and shrubs hide the former platform wall and most of the house, although the concrete coping stones of the former platform edge can be clearly seen. (Ray Bishop)

Haverhill Junction

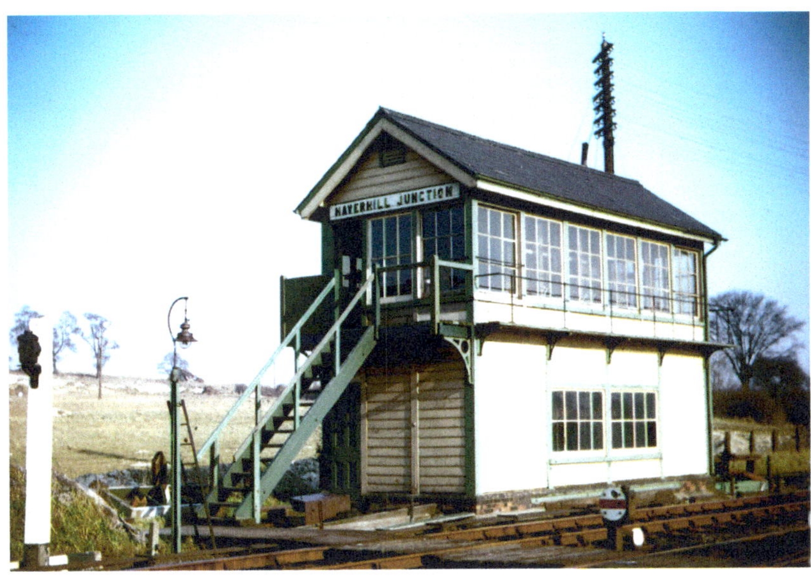

A colour view of Haverhill Junction signal box taken in 1966. The signal box was fitted with a forty-two-lever Saxby & Farmer frame and by the date of this picture the former Colne Valley line had closed completely, making some thirteen levers spare in the frame. The box remained open until the last day of the passenger service on 4 March 1967. (N. L Cadge)

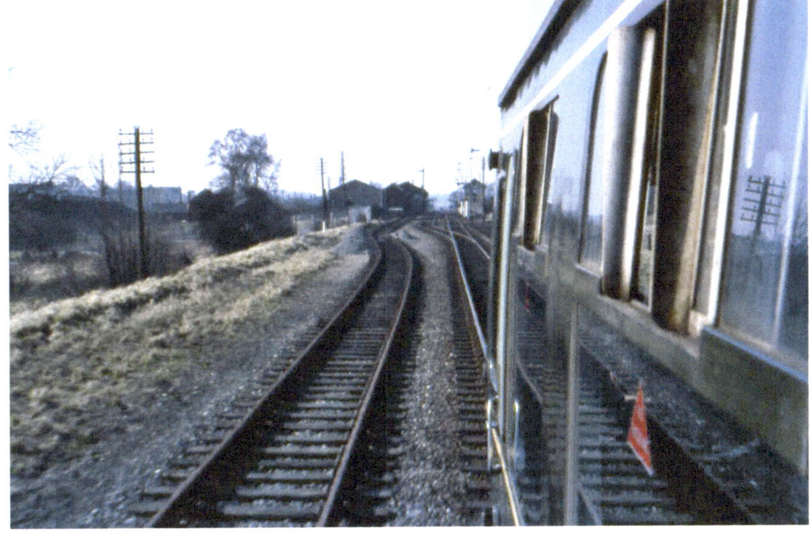

An alternative view of Haverhill Junction taken from a train, with the signal box in the middle of the picture. The line to the left is the former Colne Valley line, which by this time was out of use. (D. J. Plyer)

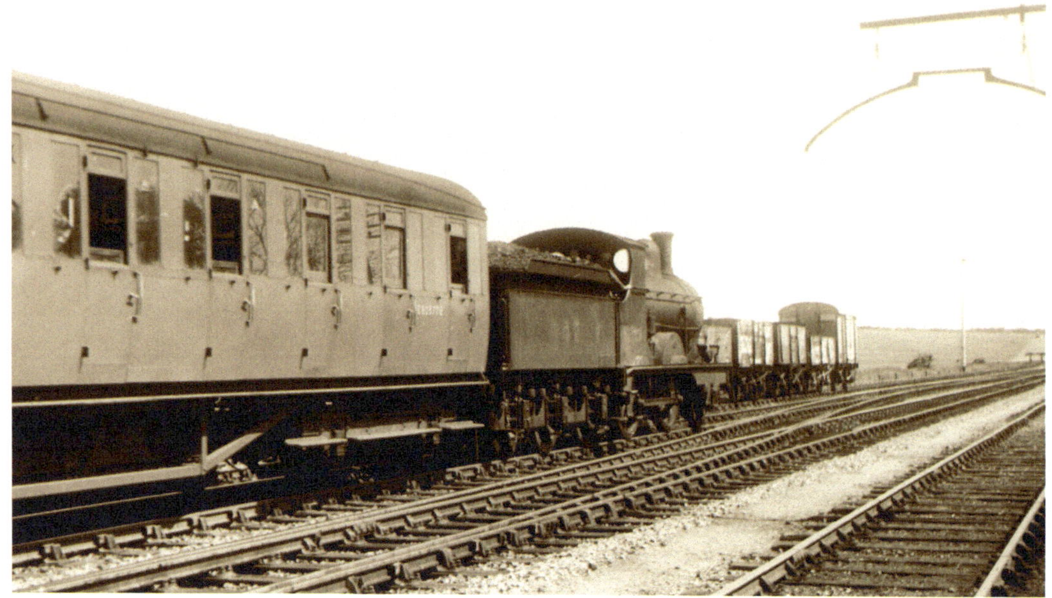

LNER class E4 locomotive 62789 takes the Stour Valley line at Haverhill with a three-coach local service on 27 May 1957. The line seen on the left is the up siding and next to the locomotive is the Colne Valley single line and another track known as the long siding. (R. C. Casserley)

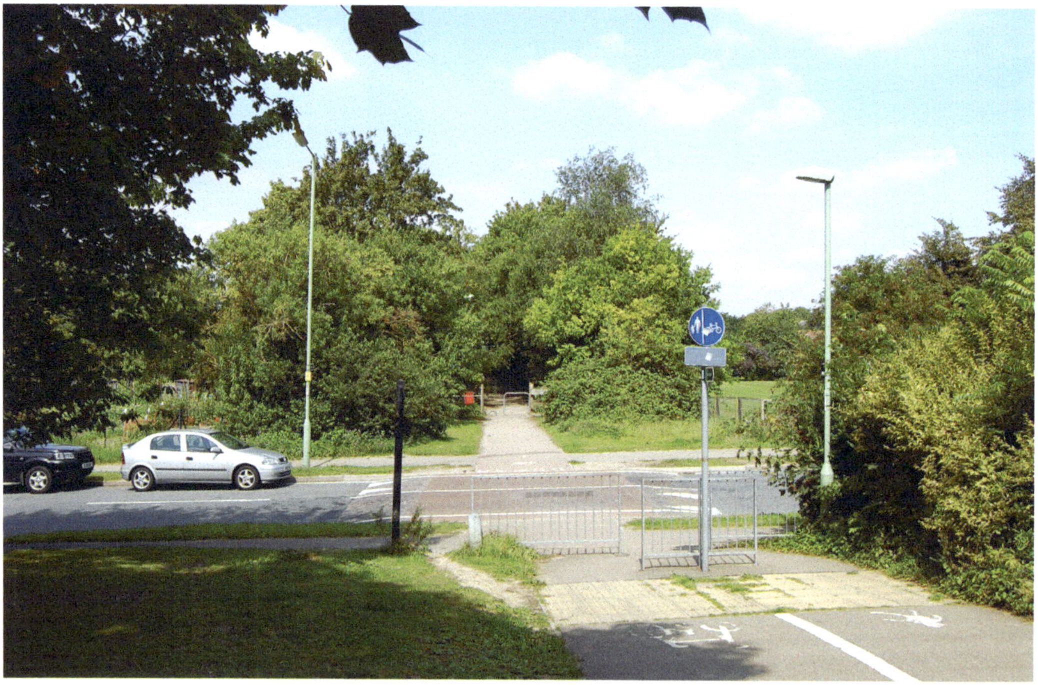

Today, the old railway formation has been turned into a pleasant footpath within the town's boundaries. Since closure, two new roads cross the old railway – these lead to new housing developments. (Ray Bishop)

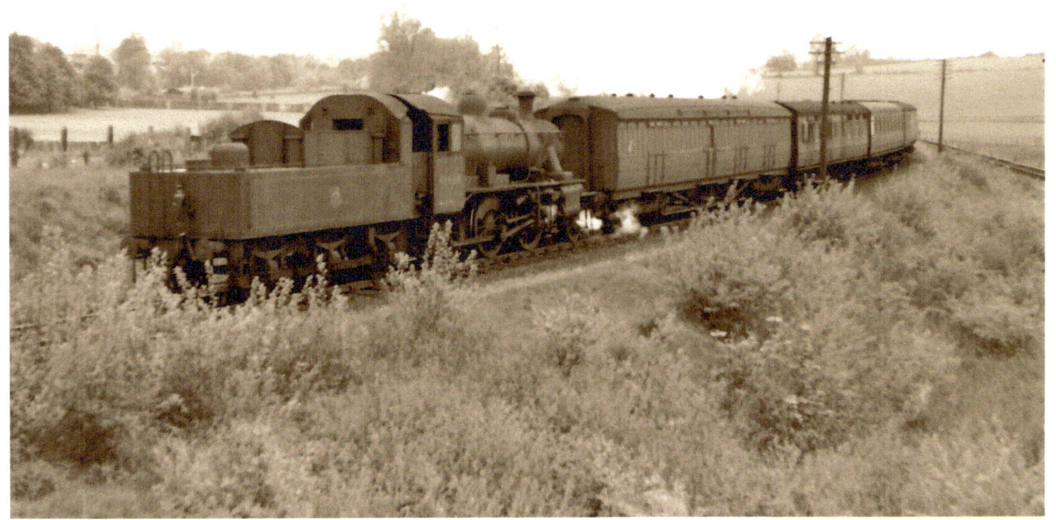

Turning now to the Colne Valley line, we have Ivatt-designed Class 2MT number 46468 hauling a passenger service towards Birdbrook and Halstead. The date of this picture is around the mid-1950s; the Ivatt 2MTs saw service on the Colne and Stour Valley lines between 1952 and 1960. (Dr I. C. Allen/Transport Treasury)

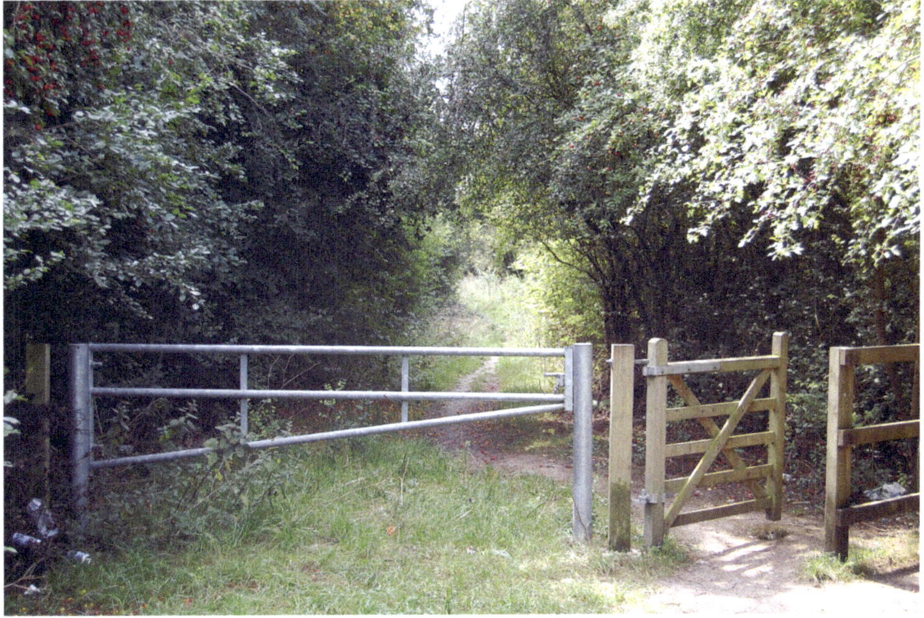

Today, the area around the former junction is a small wildlife conversation area. Footpaths created on the former track bed allow one to walk around to the site of Colne Valley Junction, or along the route towards Sturmer station. (Ray Bishop)

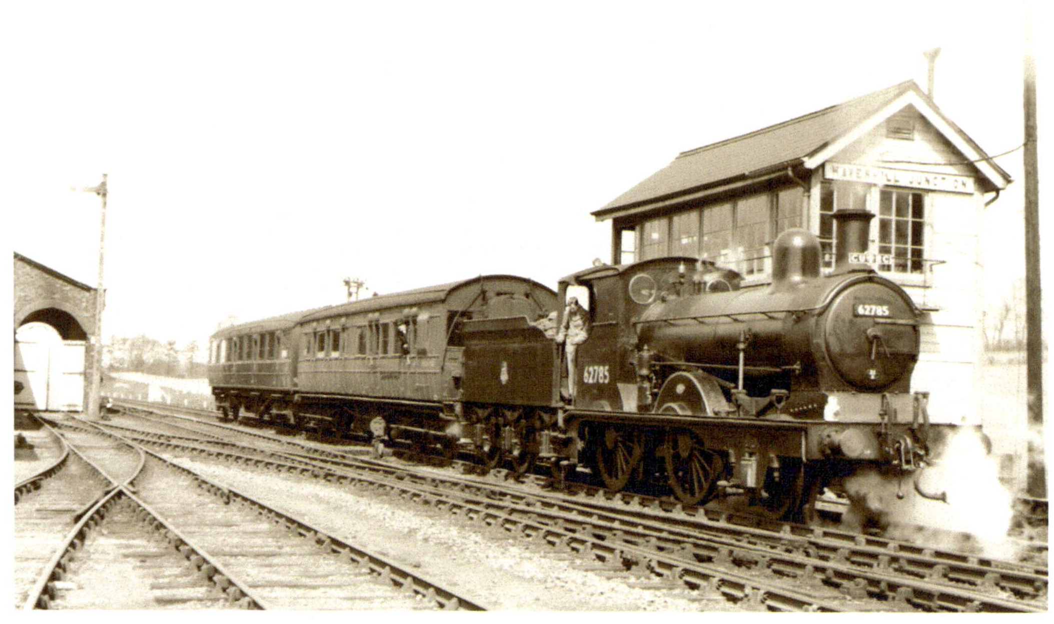

Former GER/LNER E4 locomotive number 62785 passes Haverhill Junction signal box on a two-coach Cambridge University Railway Club special service on 27 April 1958. (R. C. Riley/Transport Treasury)

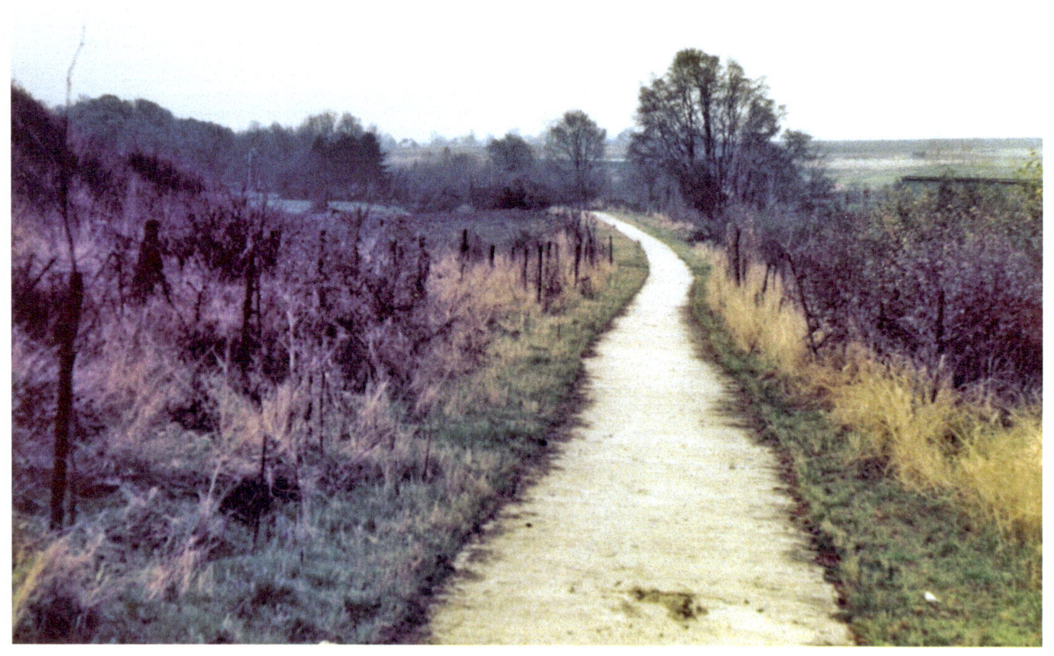

Back in 1978, the new footpaths look a bit bare; the new trees had all just been planted. This view is looking towards Sturmer. (Andy T. Wallis)

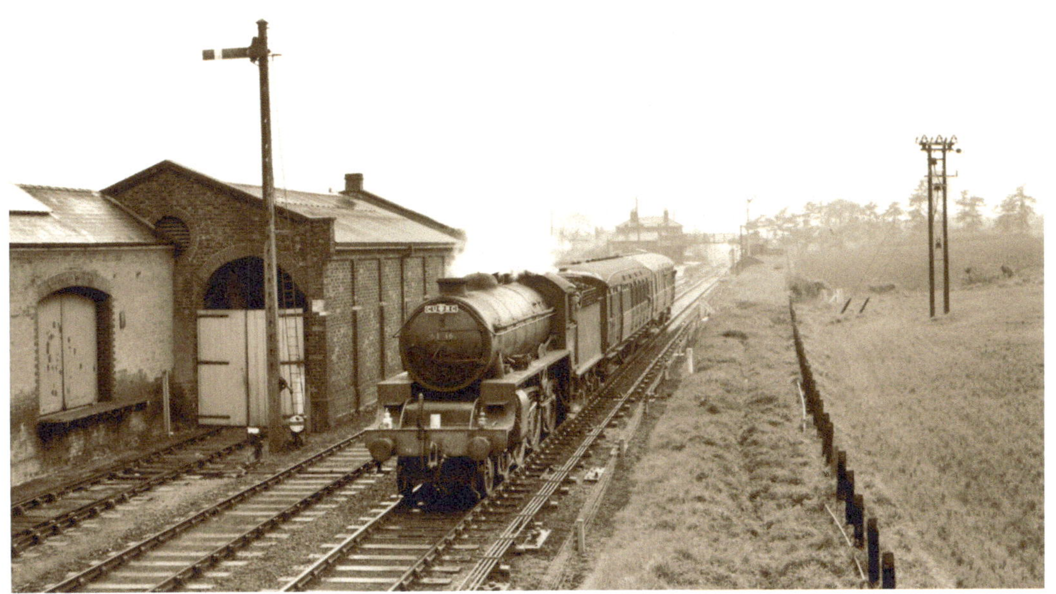

A Cambridge University Railway Club special service hauled by B2 61616 is seen approaching Haverhill Junction signal box on 3 May 1959; the goods shed and granary can be seen on the left. The tall concrete home signal was an LNER replacement for a wooden-posted lower quadrant example. (R. C. Riley/Transport Treasury)

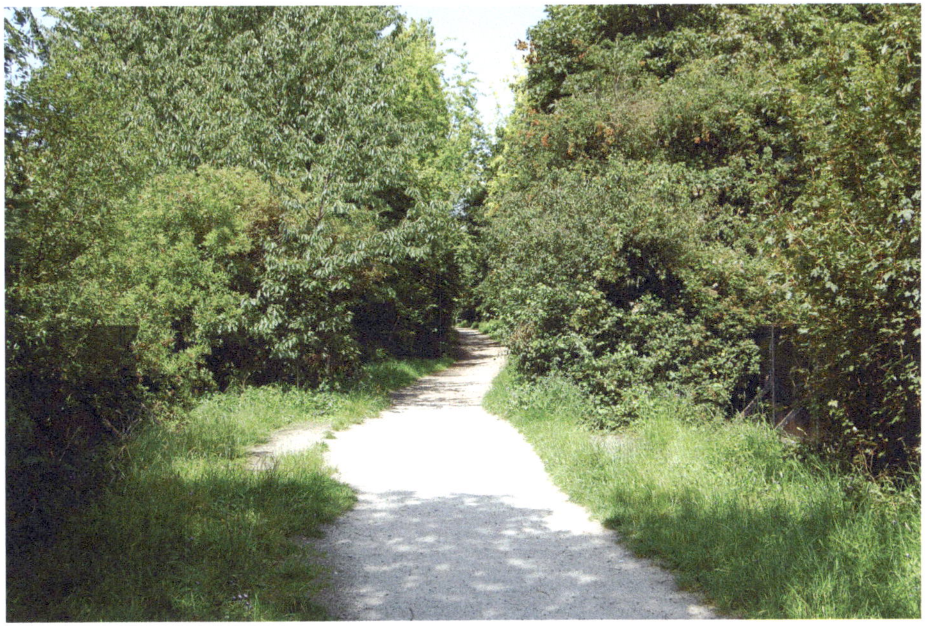

Between the former junction signal box, the goods shed and the station there was a footpath subway under the railway; today, the old brick retaining walls of the old subway can be seen among the trees. (Ray Bishop)

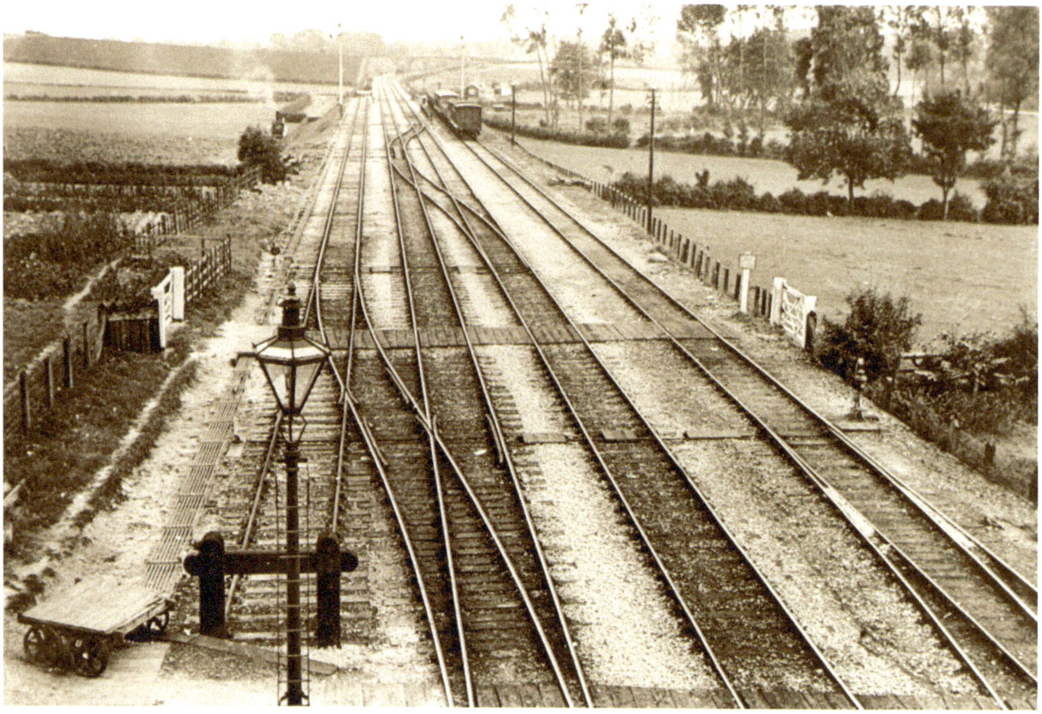

A 1911 view of the line looking towards Sudbury from the operating floor of Haverhill Junction signal box; the lines from left to right were the up refuge siding, Stour Valley single line, Colne Valley single line and the 'long siding'. (HMRS ABB314)

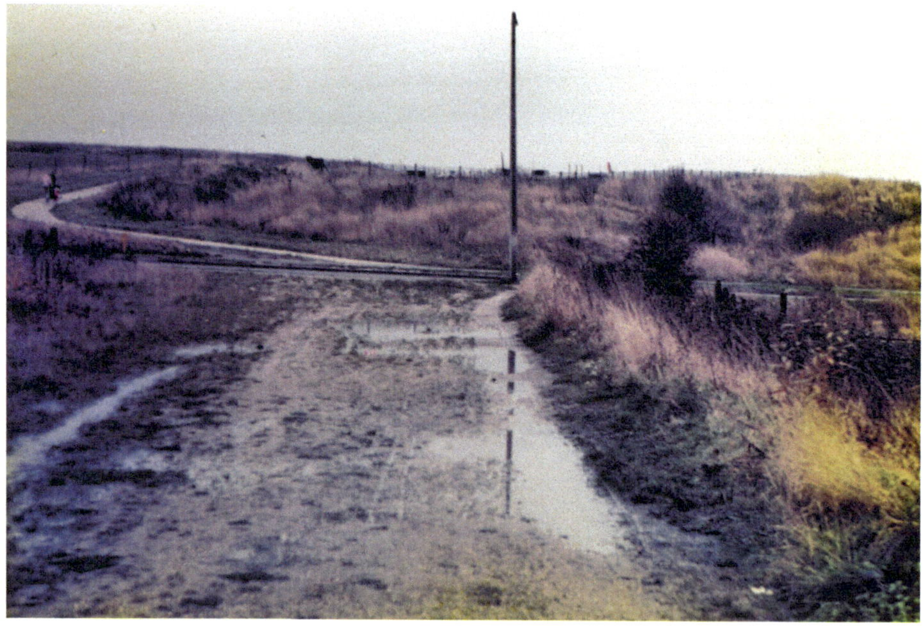

A 1978 view taken near the site of Haverhill Junction signal box looking westwards to where the two former railways parted company. (Andy T. Wallis)

Haverhill (North)

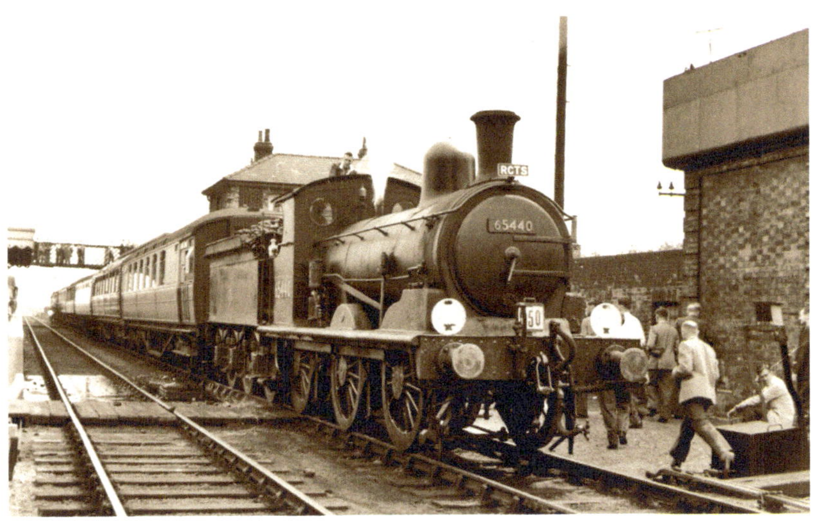

Haverhill 'North' station opened in June 1865 when the line from Shelford junction opened to all traffic; it was provided with a large GER 1865-style station house and associated buildings, the main buildings being on the down platform. In this view we see an RCTS (Railway Correspondence & Travel Society) special train being hauled by ex-LNER J15 locomotive 65440 standing at Haverhill having just taken water; the date was 10 August 1958. The main buildings can be seen in the background. (Leslie R. Freeman/Transport Treasury)

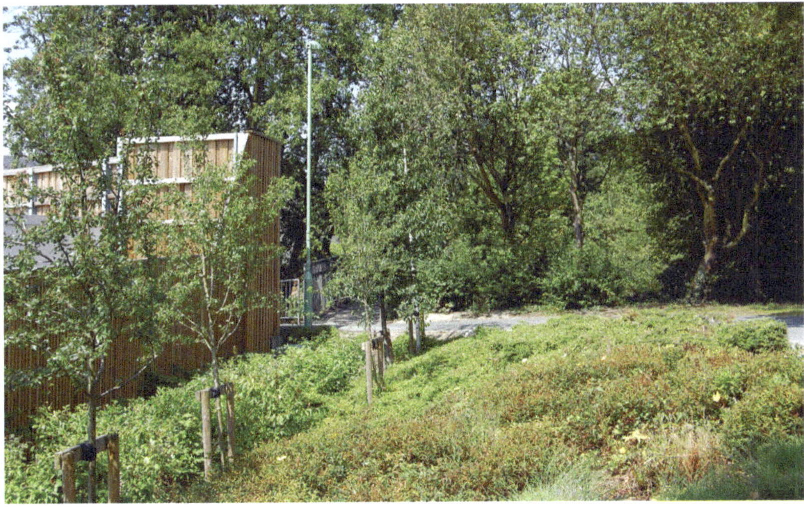

Today, Tesco occupies the whole station site. This view is looking west over the replacement footbridge towards Bartlow; the wooden fence is the back of the Tesco delivery yard, which occupies the site where the steam engine is shown in the top picture. (Ray Bishop)

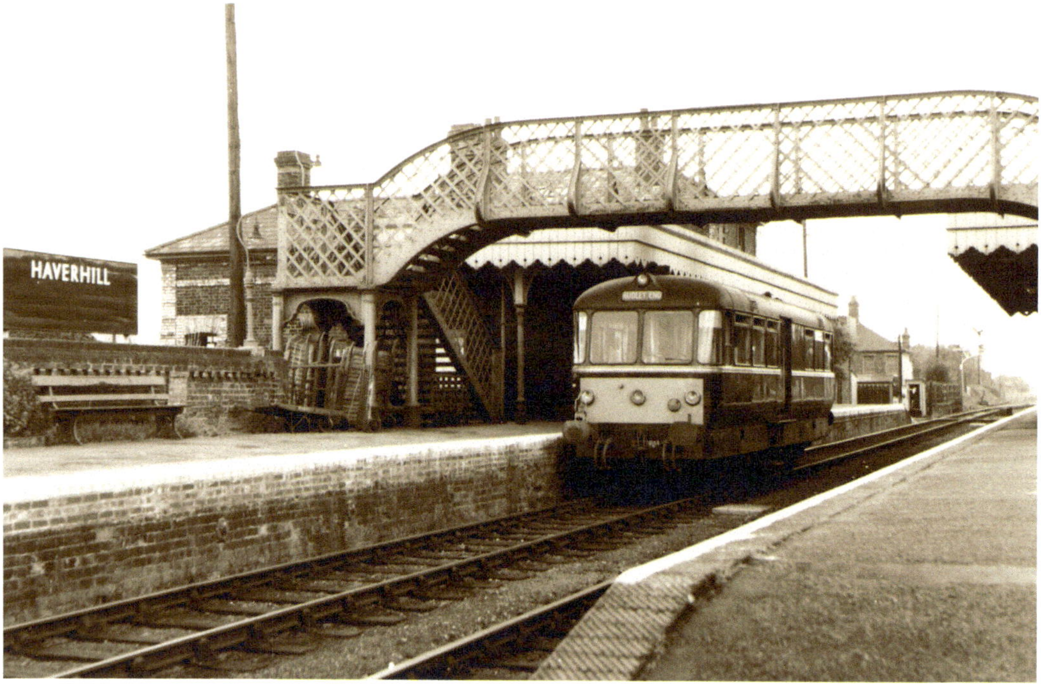

Modern motive power in the form of a diesel rail bus standing in the down platform awaiting departure. Until 1964, the Saffron Walden branch services that served Bartlow were extended to Haverhill. Imagine today being able to take the train from Haverhill to Audley End for the London connections; unfortunately, this was not to be. (Dr I. C. Allen/Transport Treasury)

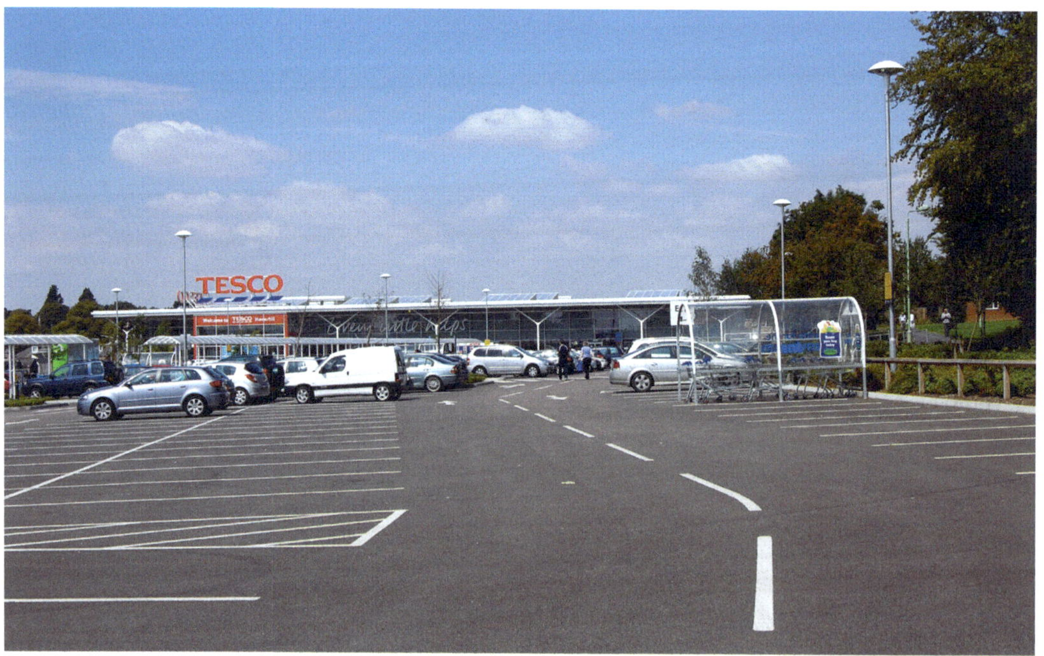

The same view today is of the supermarket and car park. (Ray Bishop)

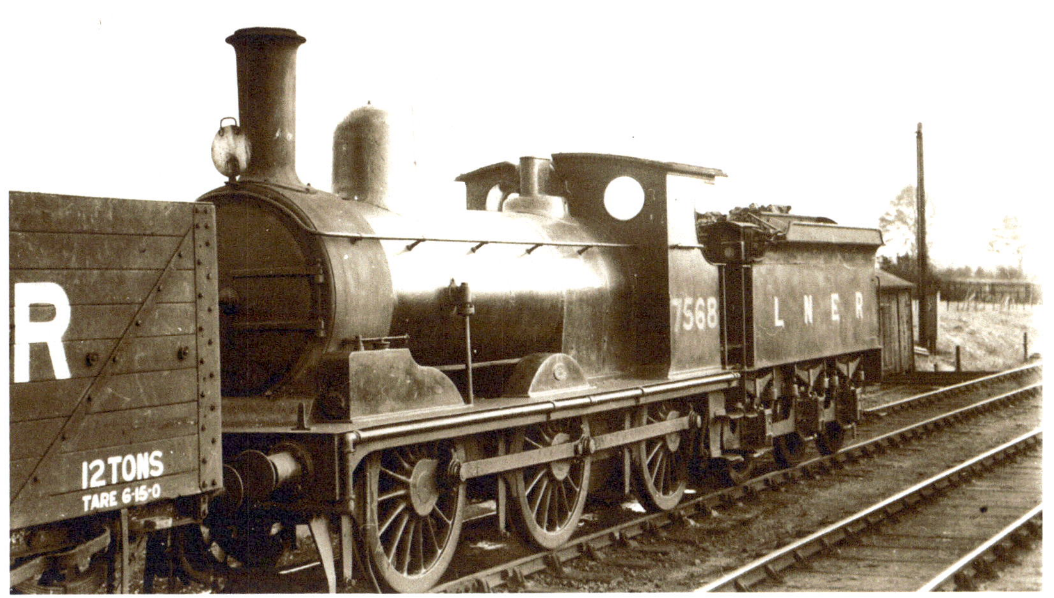

Class J15 locomotive 7568 shunts wagons at Haverhill on 19 October 1935. The goods yard was located between the station and the junction signal box; there were also additional sidings on the Bartlow side of the station. (H. C. Casserley)

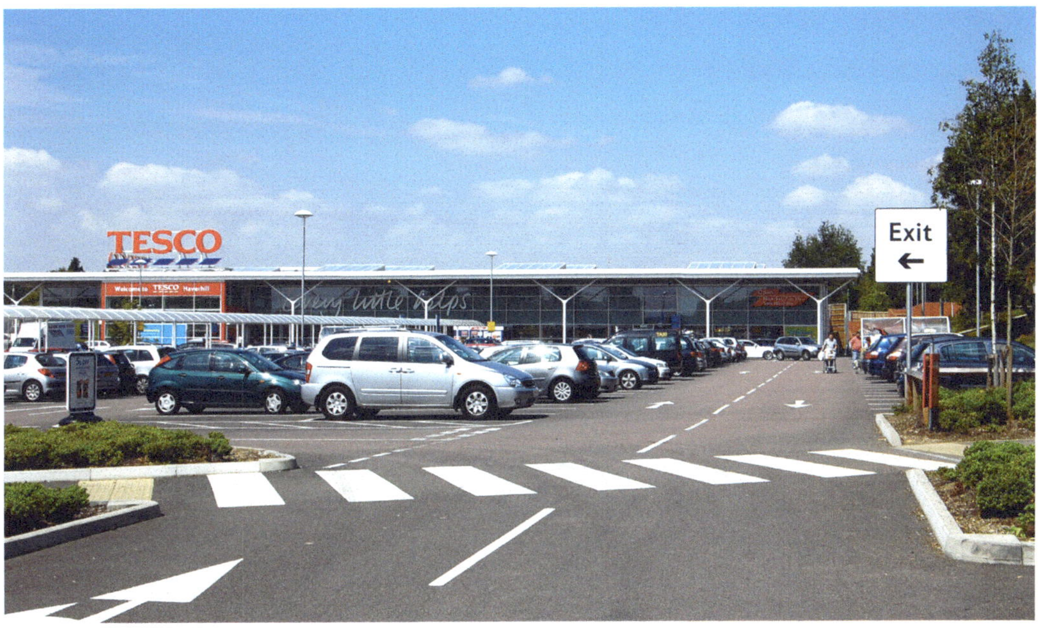

A close up view of the supermarket and car park which now occupy the former station site; a footpath which used to run through this site has now been moved to run down the boundary. (Ray Bishop)

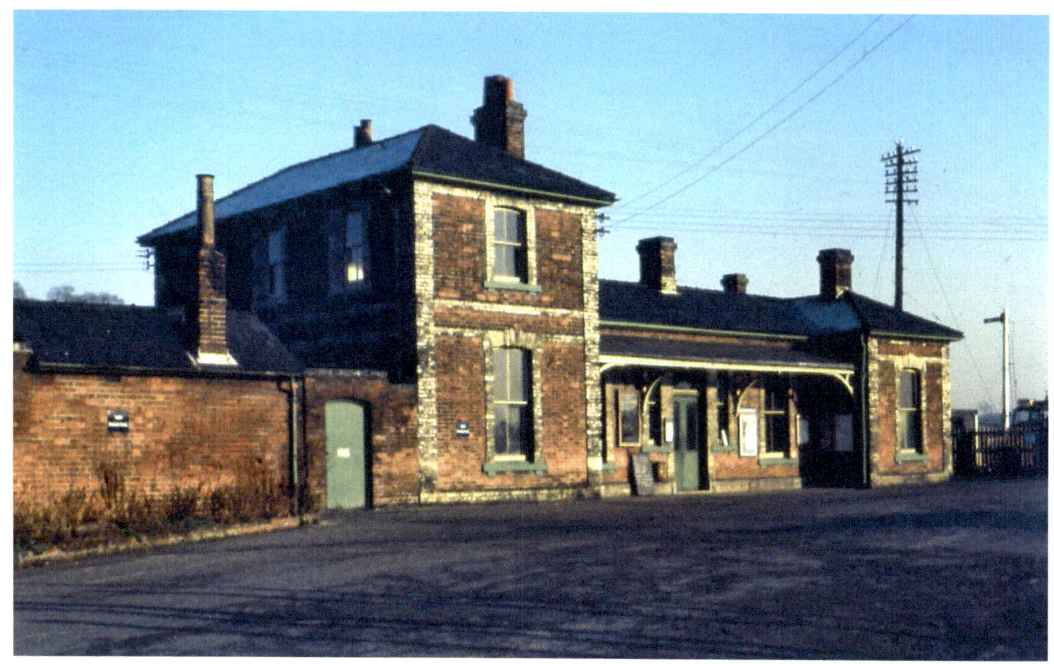

Exterior view of Haverhill 'North' station taken on a clear winter's day, 26 December 1965; the main station buildings were on the down platform. Haverhill station was known Haverhill GE from opening in 1865 to 31 January 1925; then, under the LNER, it was renamed Haverhill North until 1952, when British Railways dropped the 'North' suffix. (D. J. Plyer)

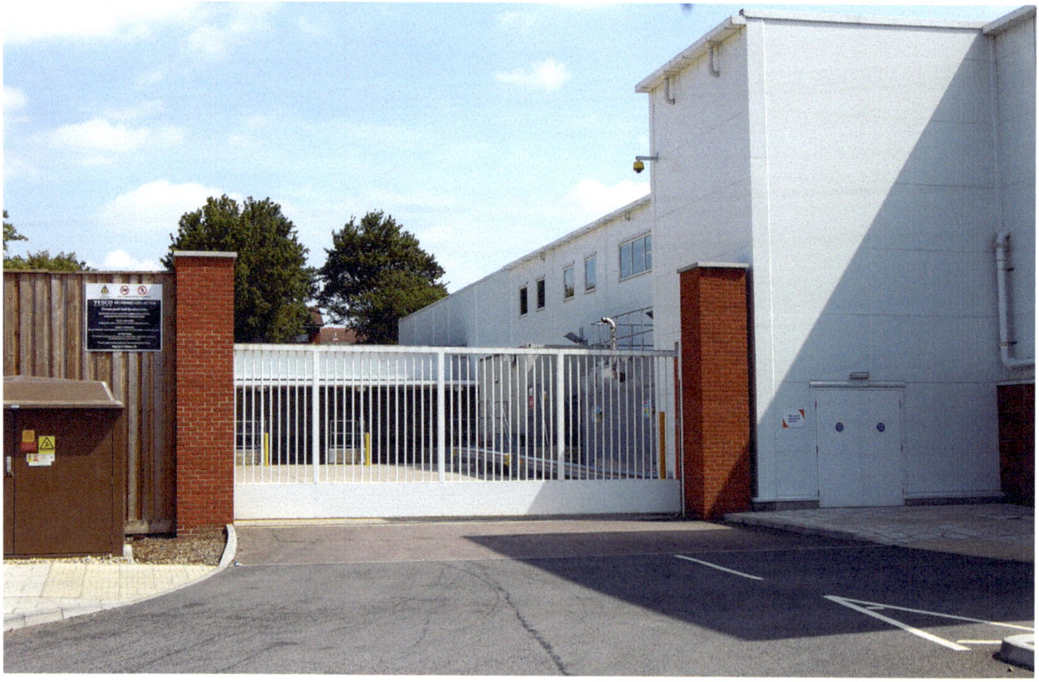

The same view today is the back of the supermarket and the delivery yard. (Ray Bishop)

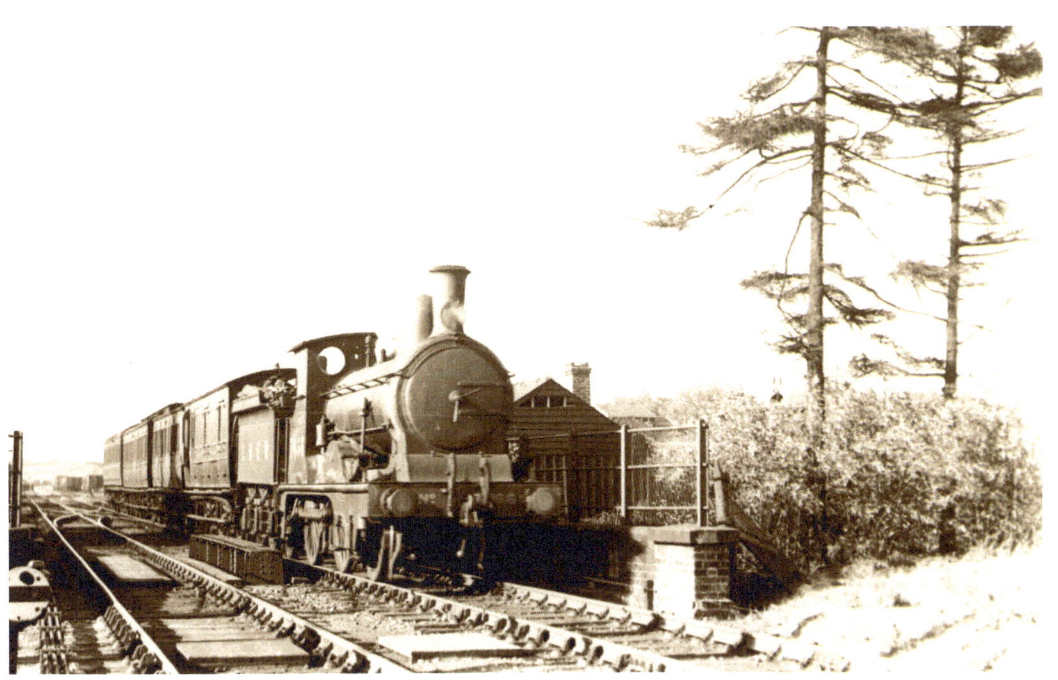

The 13.05 Cambridge to Colchester passenger train arrives at Haverhill North on 19 October 1935; the locomotive is one of the former GER machines inherited by the LNER and designated Class E4. The former station signal box was located on the extreme right of this view; it had closed a couple of years earlier and was replaced by two ground frames released from the junction signal box. (H. C. Casserley)

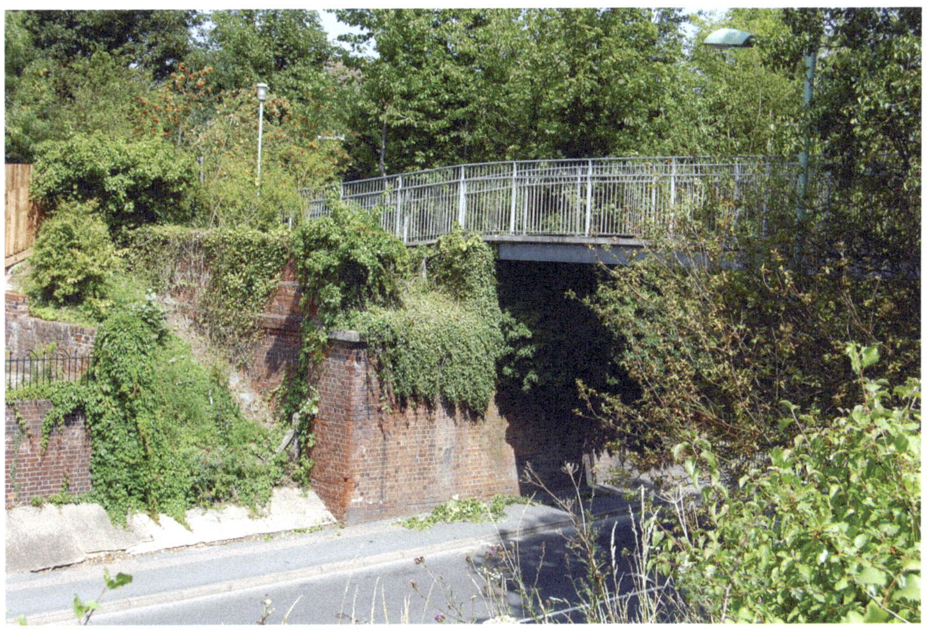

Today, the rail bridge has long since been demolished, to be replaced by a footbridge linking the footpath over the main road. The old abutments can clearly be seen. (Ray Bishop)

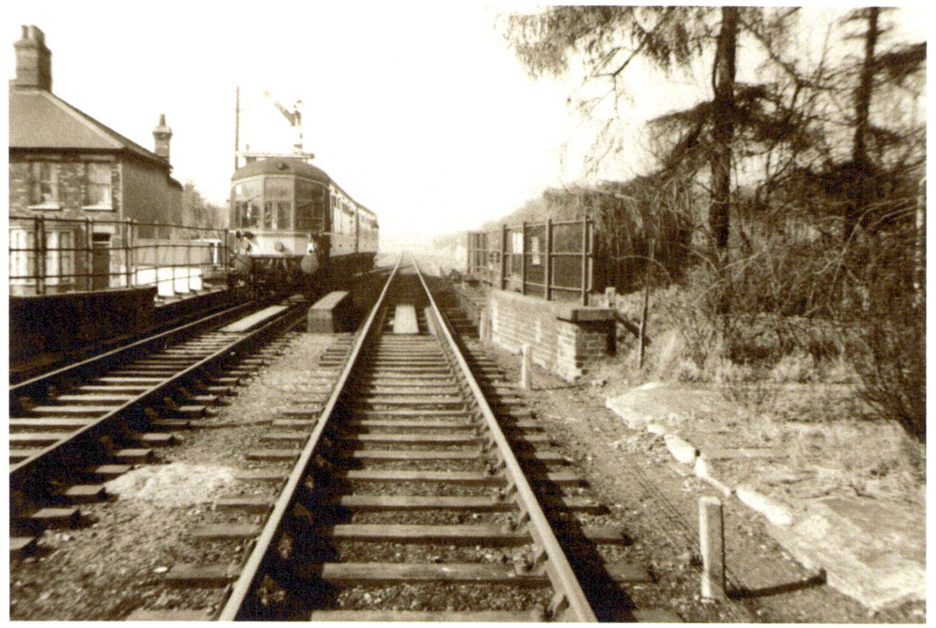

Wind forward thirty-two years at nearly the same location, but this time with a departure going towards Cambridge, and we have a photograph of a Derby lightweight diesel multiple unit passing Haverhill's down starting signal taken in 1967, on the last day of the passenger service over the Stour Valley line. Even on the last day the station looks cared for and has a tidy feel about it. (Dickie Pearce)

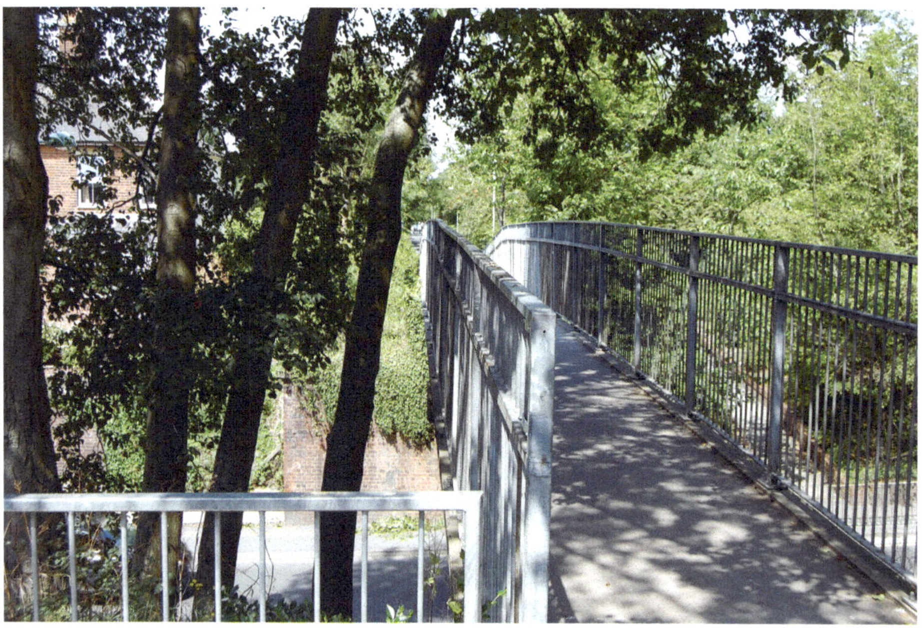

This view of the replacement footbridge shows the former track bed now in use as a footpath; the house in the top picture can just be seen through the trees in the lower view. (Ray Bishop)

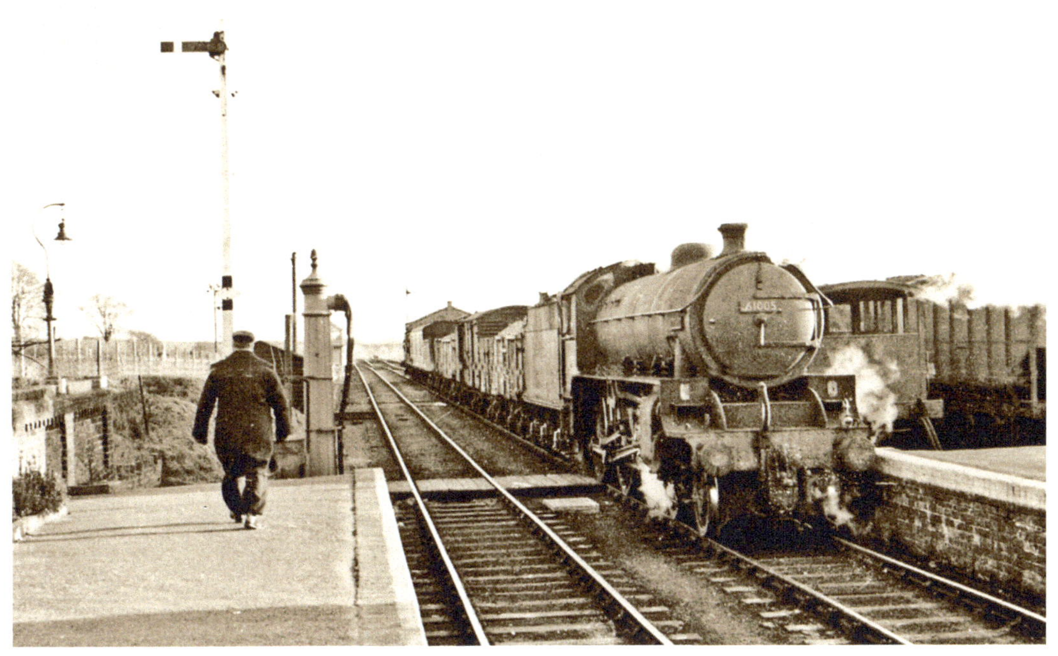

On the same day as the previous photograph, B1 locomotive No. 61005 arrives on a mixed freight working, this time approaching from the Sudbury direction. Plenty of wagons in the goods yard would indicate healthy traffic flows; little would the staff know that this would all be gone in six short years. (B. P. Pask)

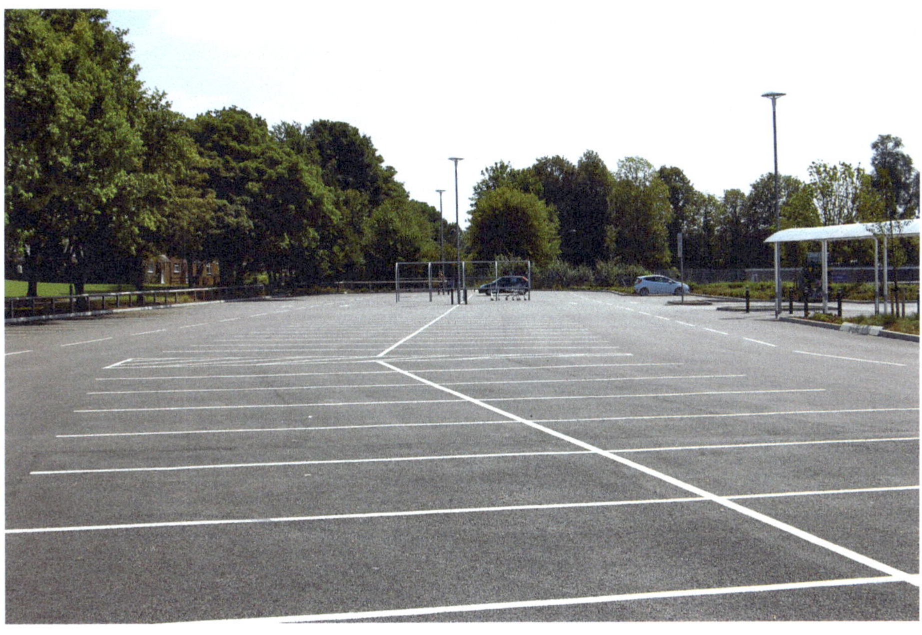

Today, we have the panoramic view of the supermarket car park looking towards Sudbury. (Ray Bishop)

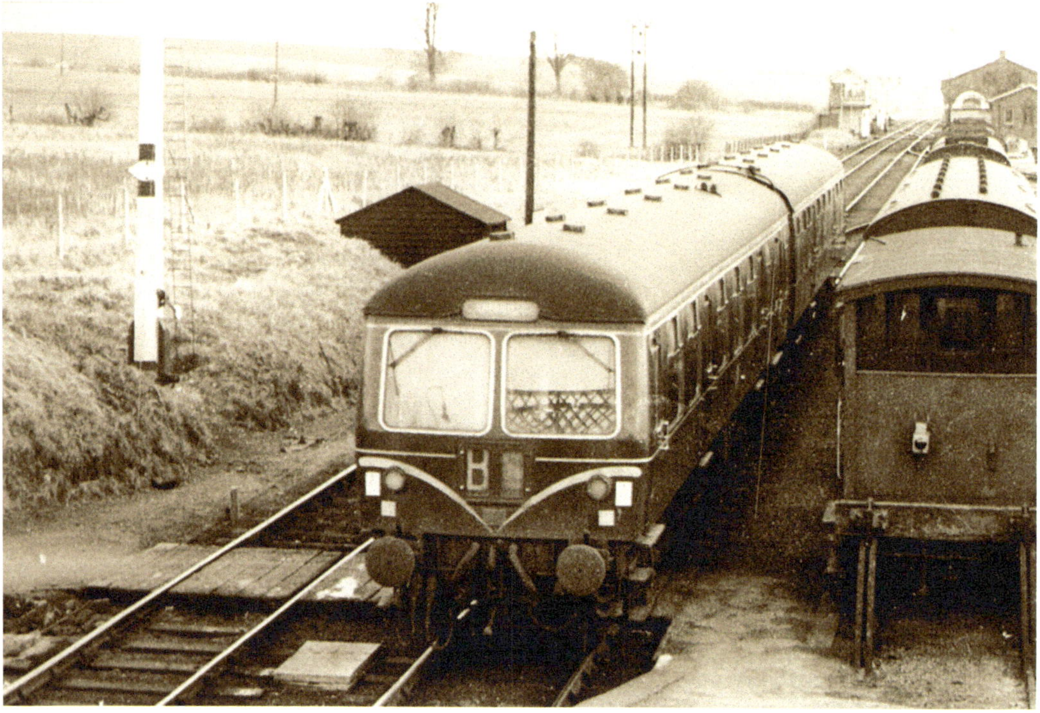

From the height advantage of the footbridge, we see a Craven-type DMU arriving at Haverhill with a local passenger working for Cambridge. In the background can be seen the junction signal box, goods shed and yard, which seem to be fairly busy; this view was also taken on 23 December 1961. (B. P. Pask)

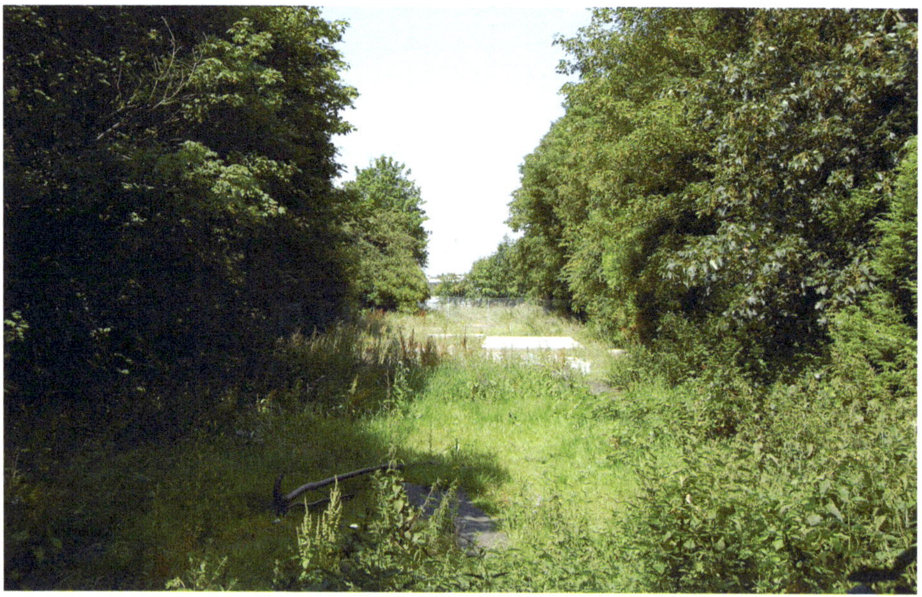

Today, there is a small portion of track bed as yet undeveloped; the tall lampposts of the supermarket car park can be seen in the distance. (Ray Bishop)

Bartlow (Stour Valley)

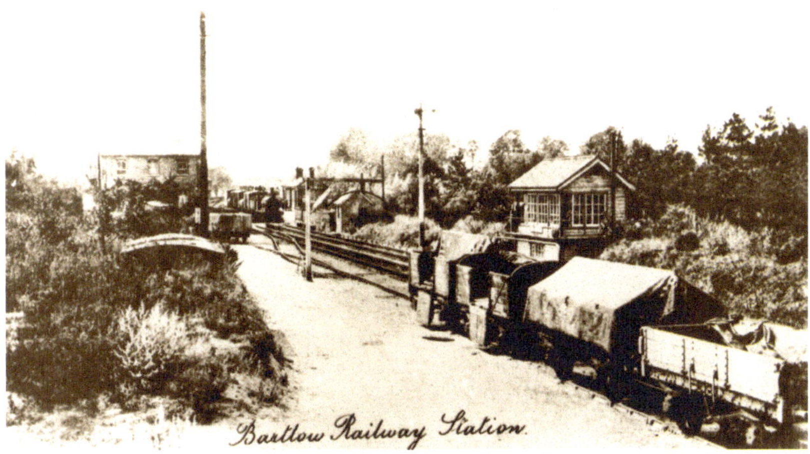

Very early GER view of Bartlow station, taken from the goods yard, showing the station signal box and station buildings on the left of the view. The LNER were always looking for ways to save costs and this was achieved at Bartlow by closing the station signal box in 1926 and transferring some functions to the junction signal box, or by putting them on a ground frame, which they duly did. The single line to double line points at the Haverhill end of the layout were too far away for mechanical operation, and so they were motorised. (Lens of Sutton Association)

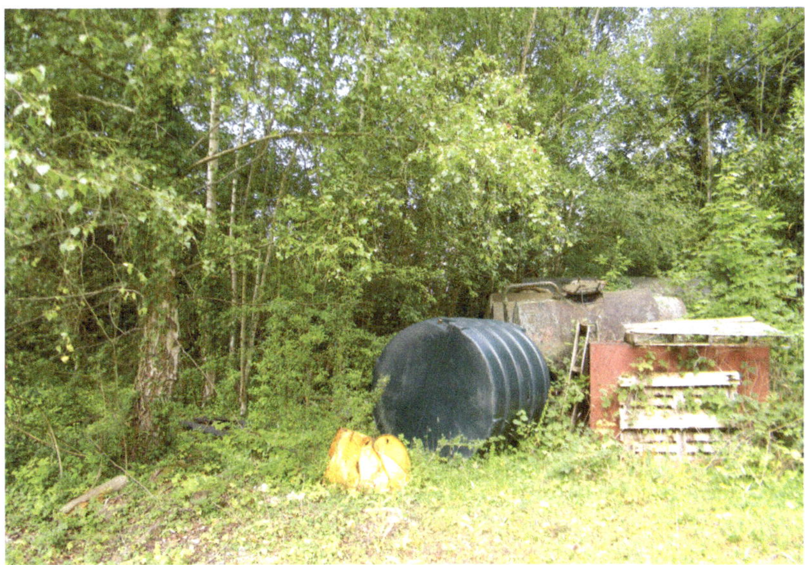

Today, the former goods yard is used as access by local farmers. The old station is hidden behind the trees, as is the main road. (Paul Lemon)

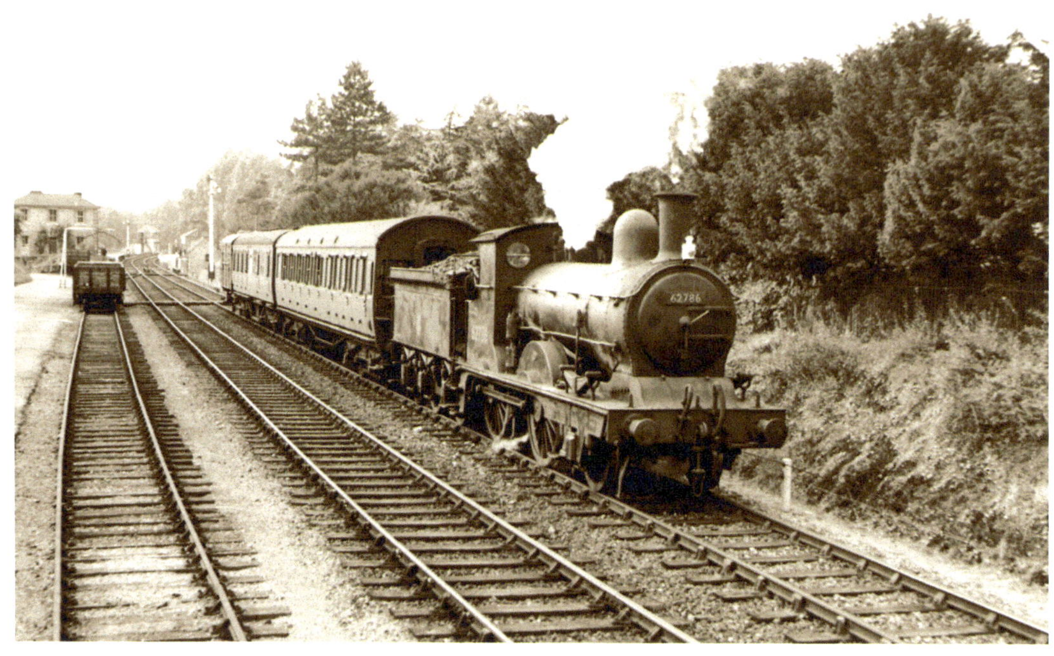

Locomotive Class E4 No. 62786 departs from Bartlow with a local passenger train. The lines from left to right were the down siding, down loop and up loop; the down and up loops merged into a single line a short distance further on. (Dr I. C. Allen/Transport Treasury)

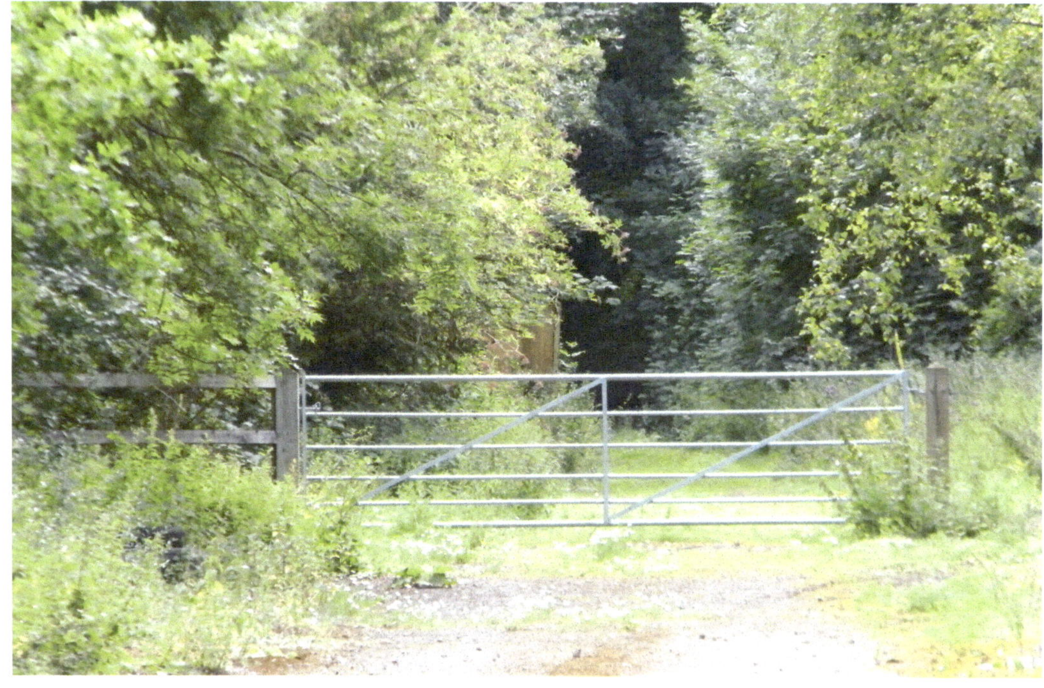

Access to the former goods yard and track bed is beyond the gate; the bridge seen in the picture on page 44 is hidden among the vegetation. (Paul Lemon)

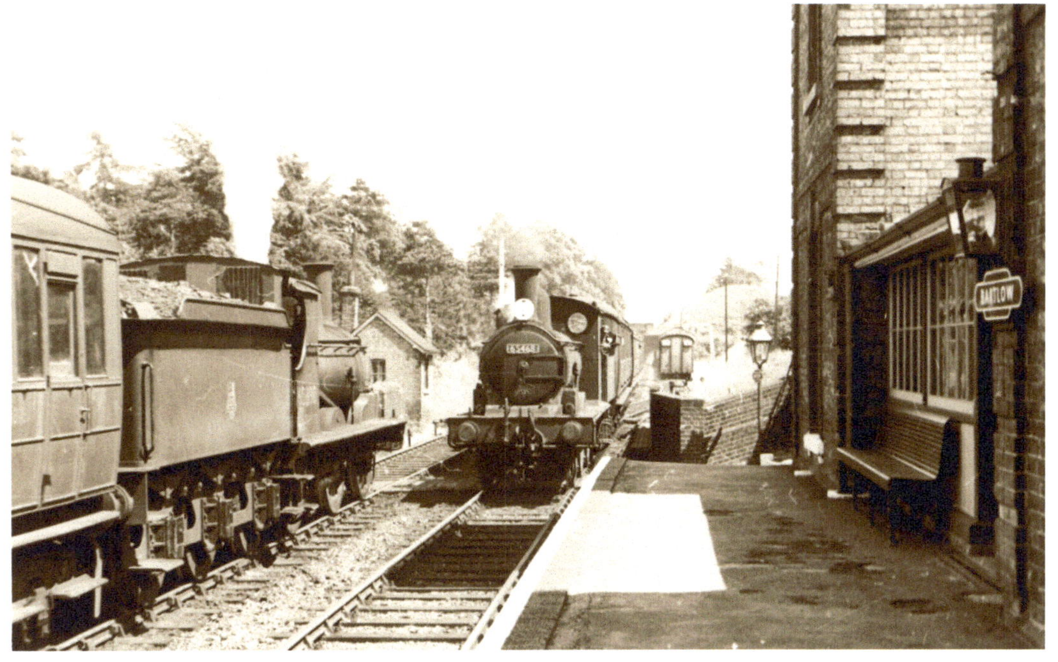

A busy scene with locomotives 65390 and 65468 passing at Bartlow on the 13.26 Cambridge to Colchester and the 12.30 Marks Tey to Cambridge services. This scene was taken on 7 July 1956; there only seems to be one thing missing and that is passengers. (H. C. Casserley)

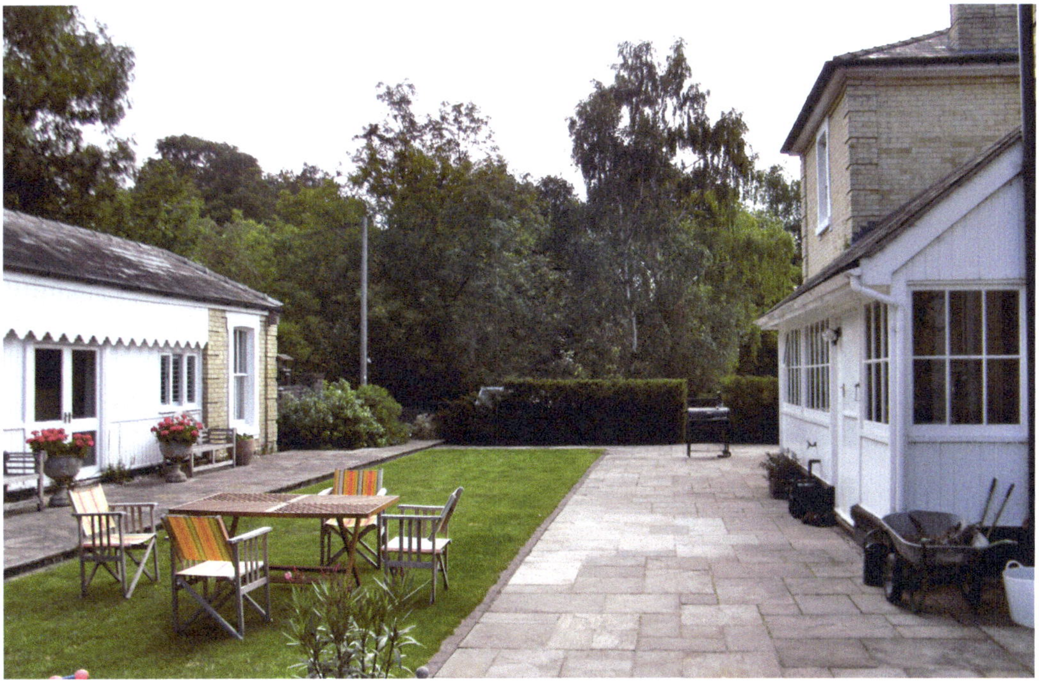

Today, the station buildings have been extended; the grassed area is where the tracks were, and the brick style on the edge of the main building is common in both photographs. (Paul Lemon)

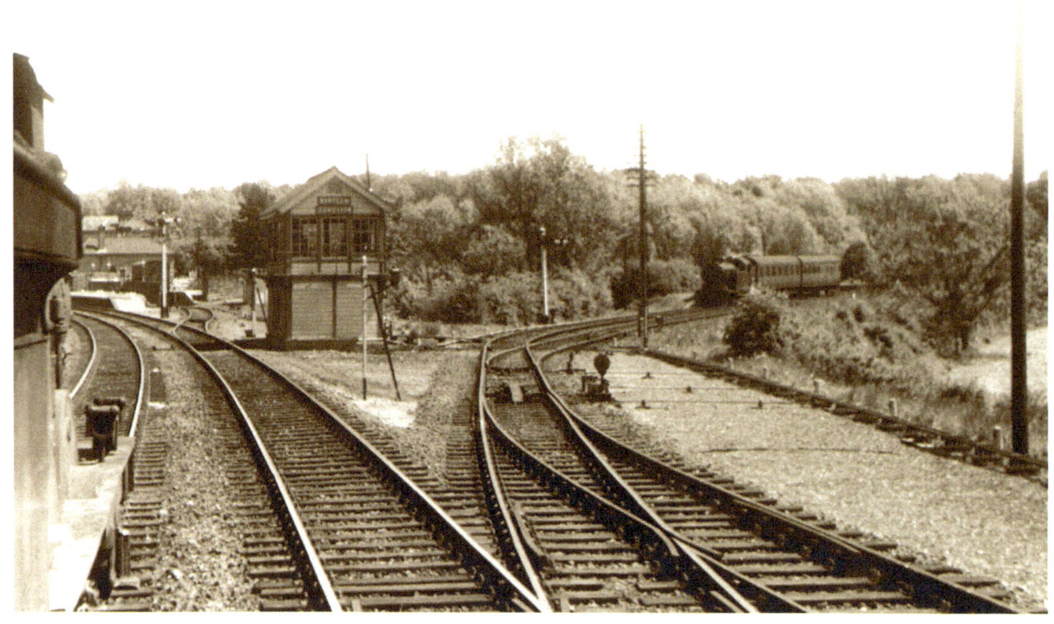

A view of Bartlow Junction from the leading coach of a steam-hauled train; the junction signal box is seen in the centre of the picture, while on the Saffron Walden branch platform can be seen a N7 class of locomotive on a push/pull branch working. (R. M. Casserley)

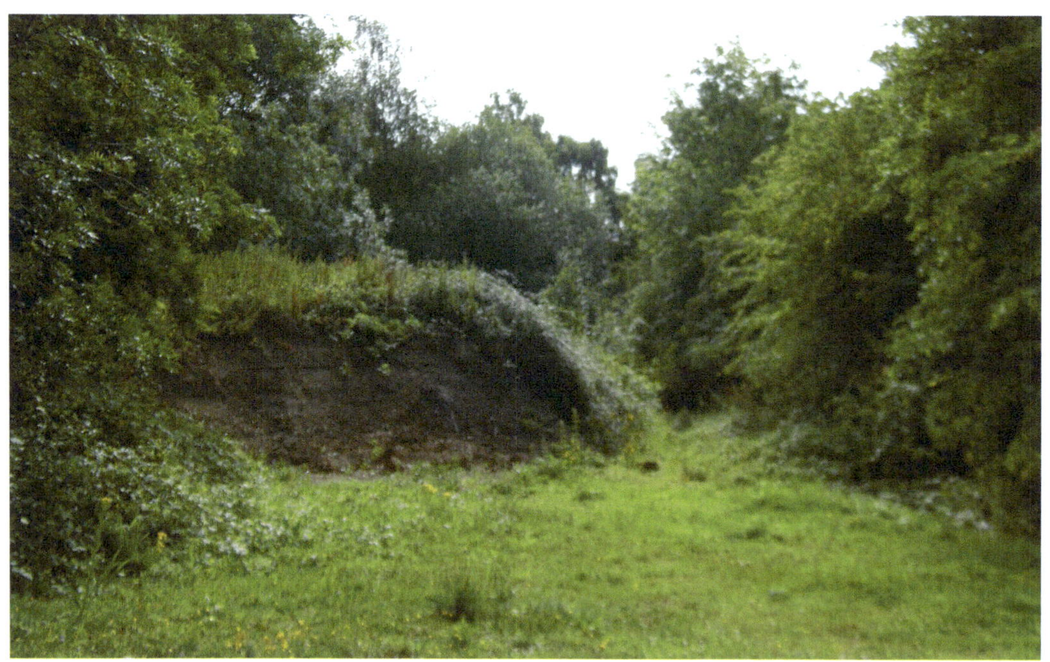

The same view today features a large mound of earth piled up and left on the track bed; trees, bushes and other shrubs have taken control of this whole area. (Paul Lemon)

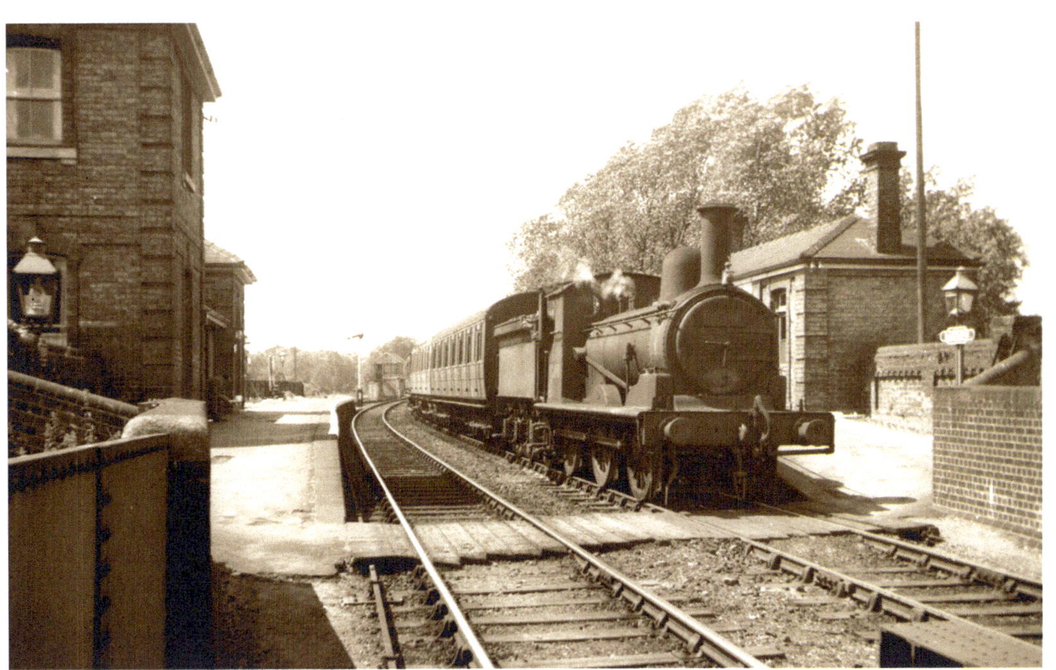

Locomotive 65390 hauling a local passenger service waits in the up platform loop at Bartlow to pass a down direction working. The main buildings at Bartlow were located on the down platform. The double span railway bridge over the road can be seen in the foreground. By this time, the junction signal box controlled all movements in the station area. (R. M. Casserley)

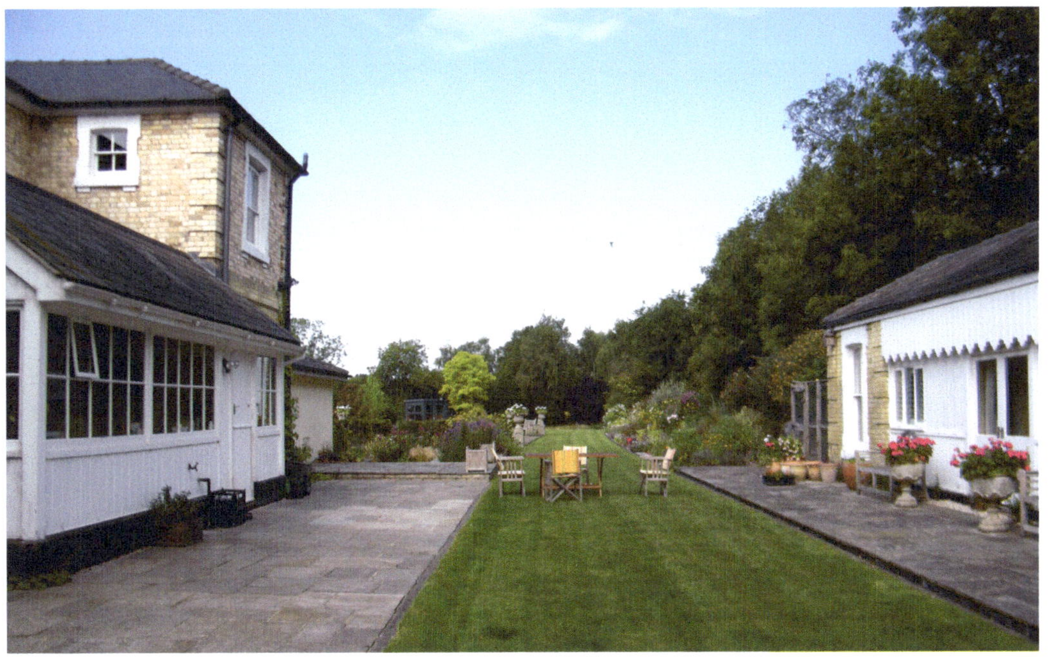

A similar view today shows the extended station building. The road bridge has been removed and a fence now guards against anybody falling over the edge. (Paul Lemon)

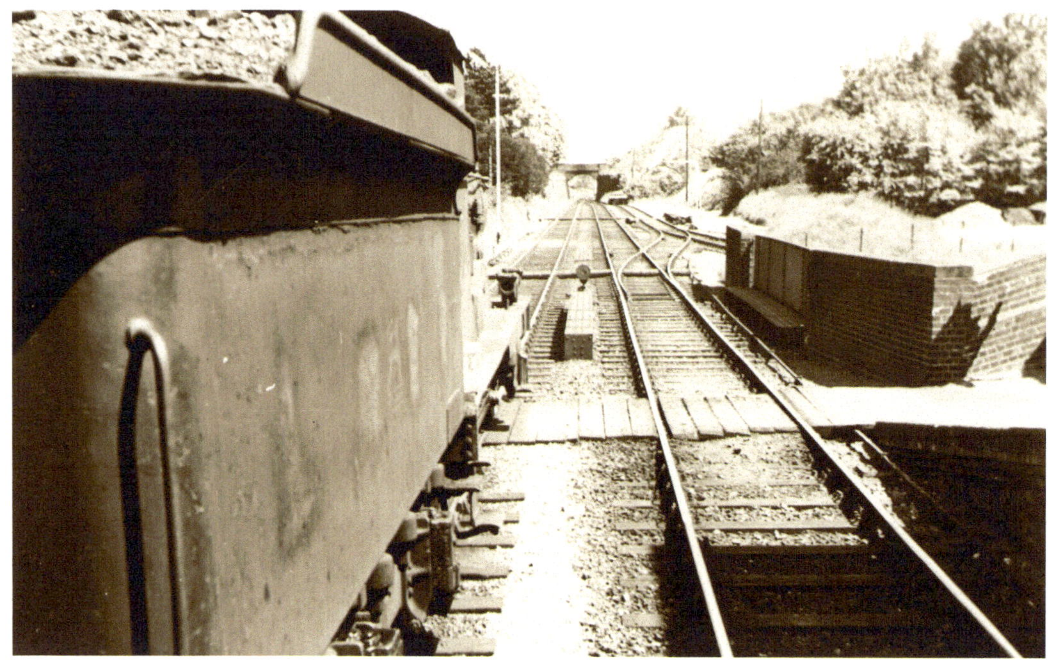

An unusual view from the first coach, looking down the side of the tender along the track towards Haverhill; the goods yard and its single siding can be seen on the right of the down loop line. A further siding on the downside was located beyond the distant bridge and was controlled by a ground frame, which was released with an Annett's key by the junction signal box. (R. M. Casserley)

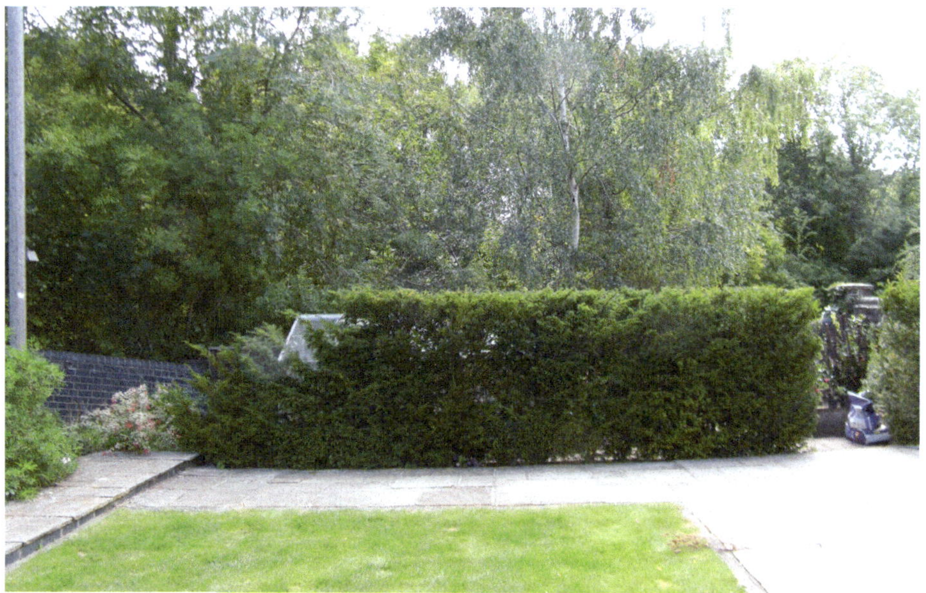

Today, hedging hides the green house and a protective wall/fence prevents one falling down into the roadway. The bridge in the distance still exists, completely surrounded by trees and bushes. (Paul Lemon)

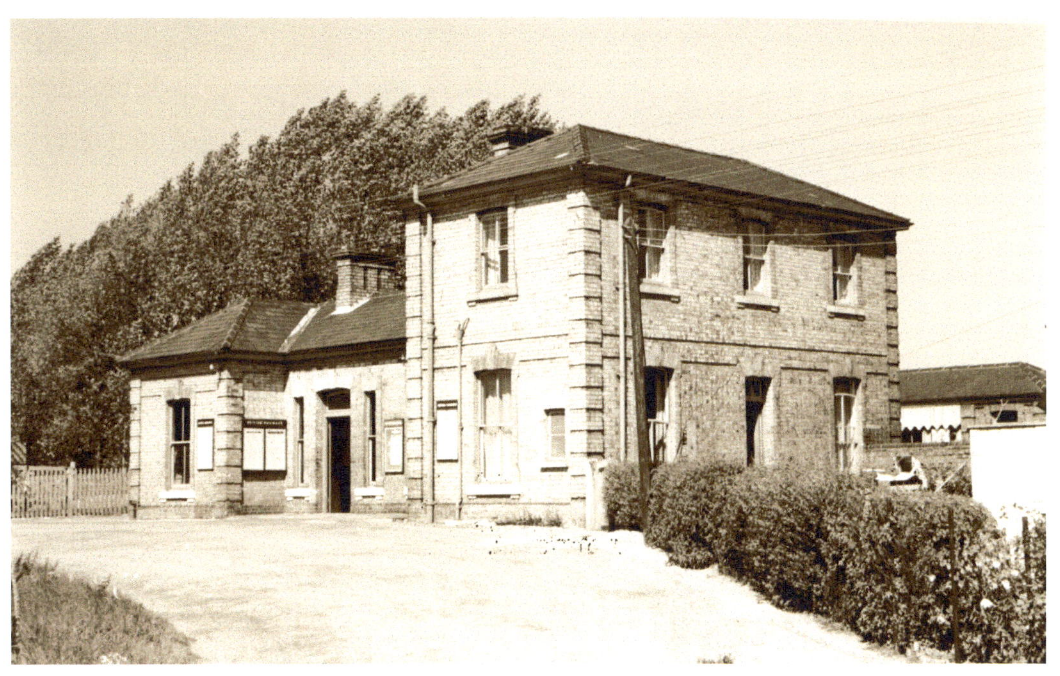

Close-up view of the main station buildings at Bartlow as seen in the 1960s, presenting a clean and tidy appearance. (A. Swain/Transport Treasury)

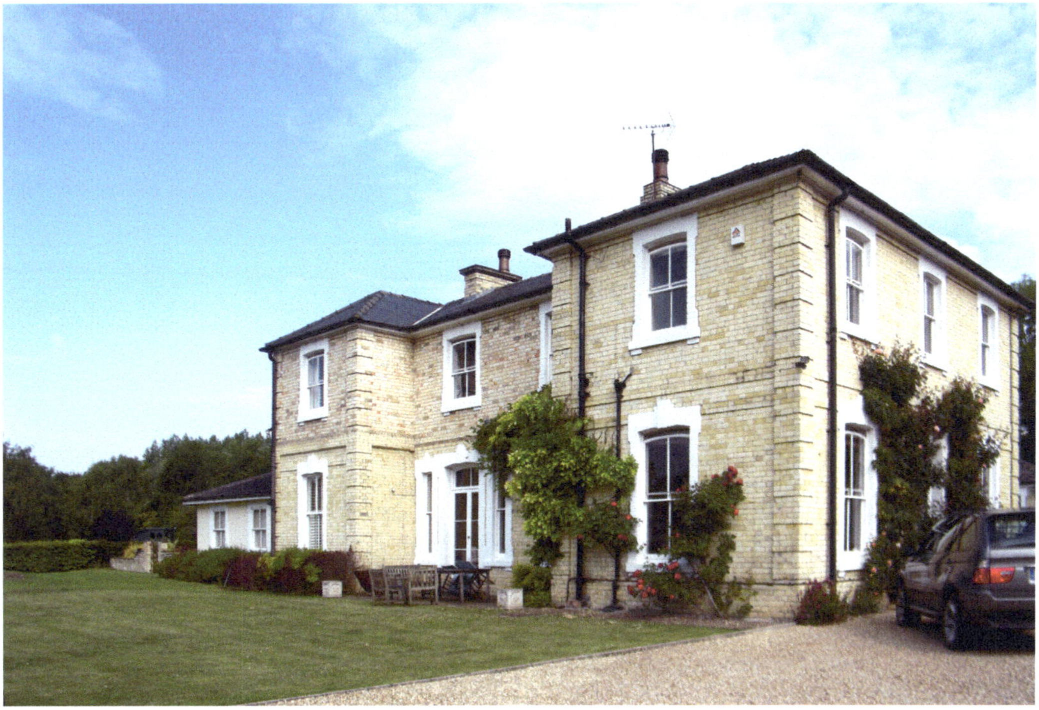

Today, the much-extended Bartlow station buildings are in use as a private house known as the 'Booking Hall'. The surrounding grounds have been turned into a lovely garden. (Paul Lemon)

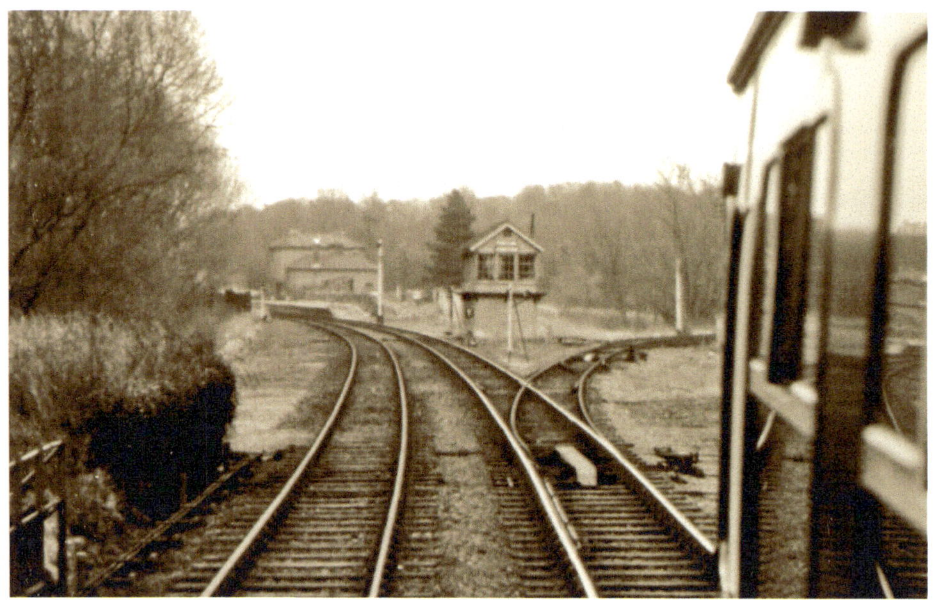

Colour view from a diesel multiple unit of Bartlow Junction, showing the then-closed signal box and the disused branch to Saffron Walden on the right. The signal box contained a thirty-eight-lever Saxby & Farmer lever frame, later thirty-nine. The line off to the right is the connection to the Saffron Walden branch, which was waiting demolition at this time. (Brian Pask)

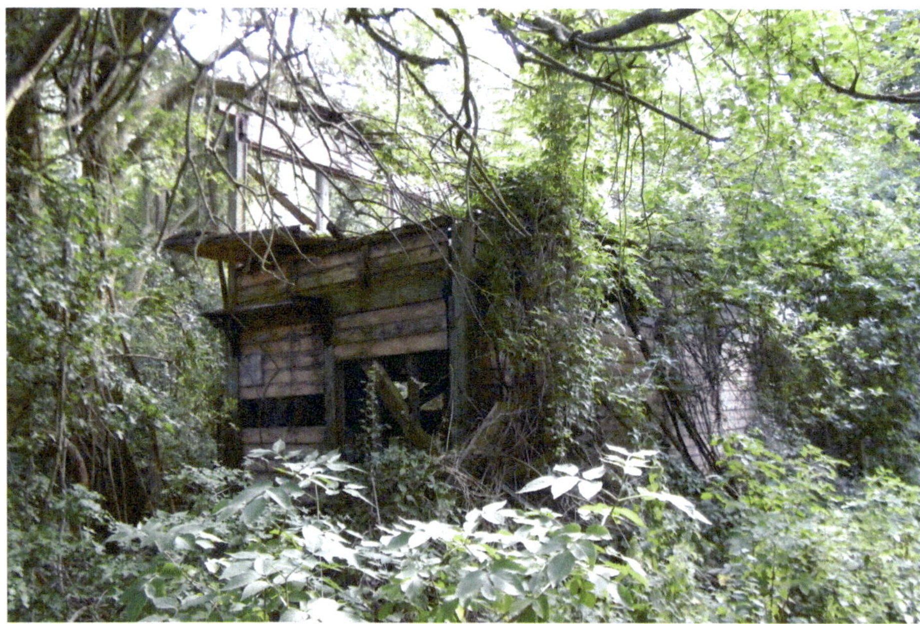

The derelict signal box is now hidden among the trees; while the roof has collapsed into the surrounding walls, the operating floor joists are still holding the lower structure together. Nature was doing its best to taken over the site some forty-five years after the signal box had closed. (Paul Lemon)

Linton

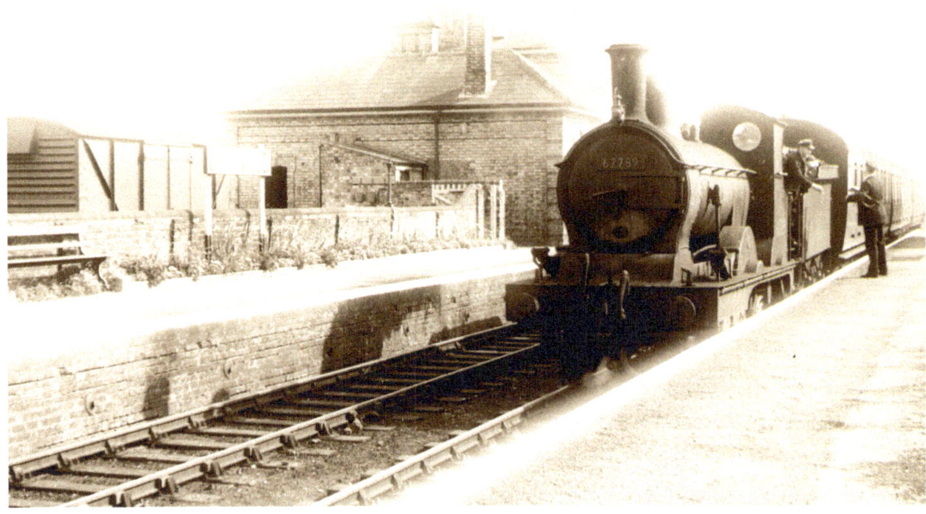

Locomotive No. 62789, hauling the 11.36 Colchester to Cambridge local service train, arrives at Linton down platform on 28 September 1957. The fireman is seen exchanging the single line tablets with the signalman. (R. M. Casserley)

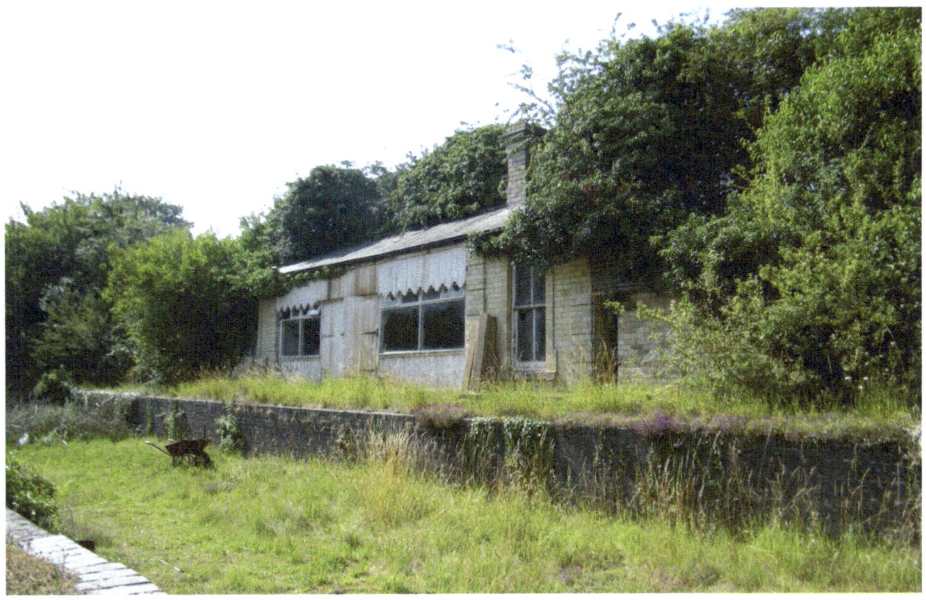

Today, the down platform and building looks in need of some care – the boundary fence shrubs and trees are slowly taking over the platform. (Paul Lemon)

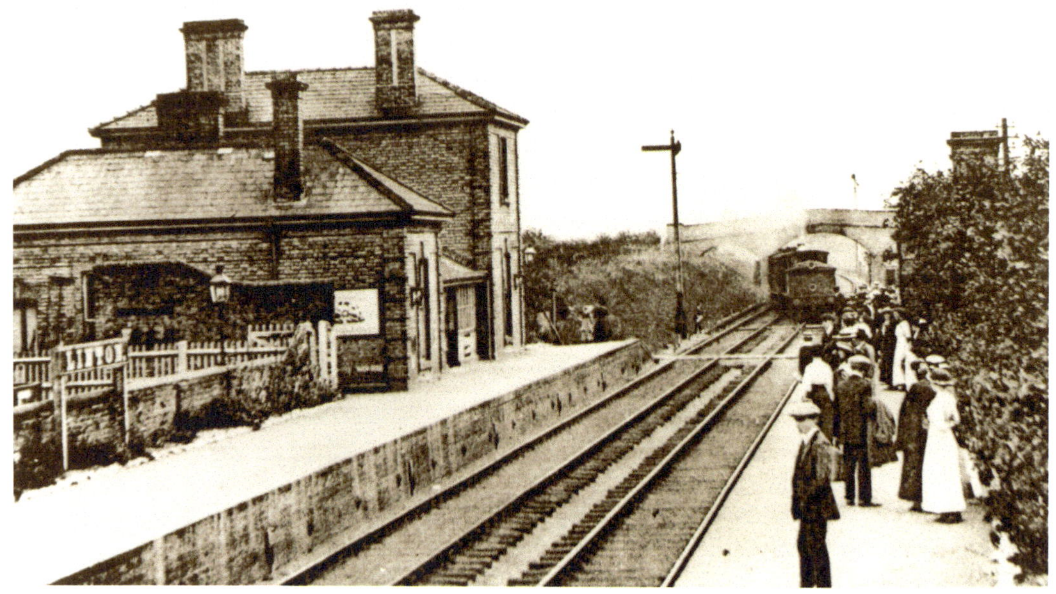

An early Great Eastern view of Linton station, taken from an elevated position as a local passenger service train arrives for Cambridge. There seems to be a healthy amount of passengers awaiting the train, all in period dress. (Lens of Sutton Association)

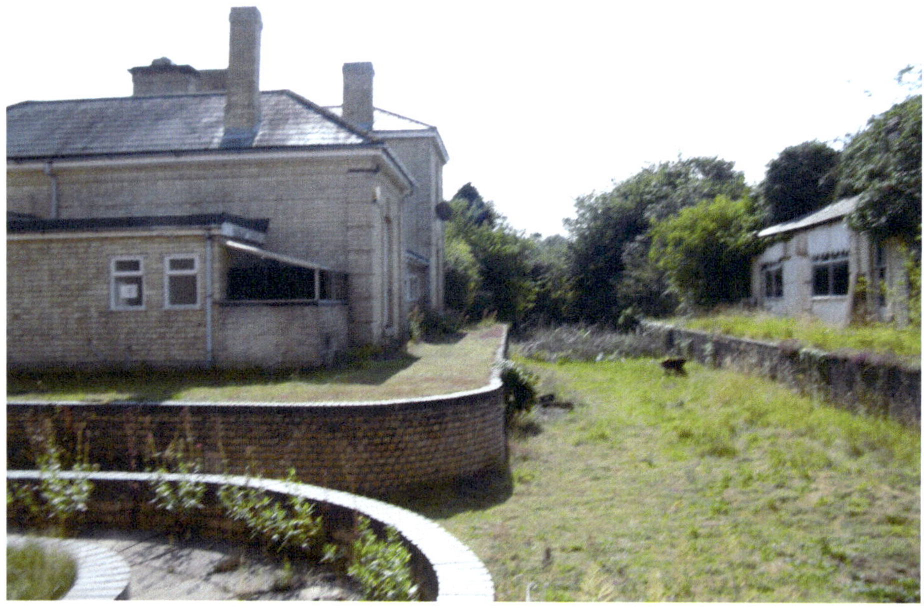

The up platform retains all its buildings, but a new entrance to the track bed has been cut through the old platform wall and a single storey extension has been added to the station buildings. (Paul Lemon)

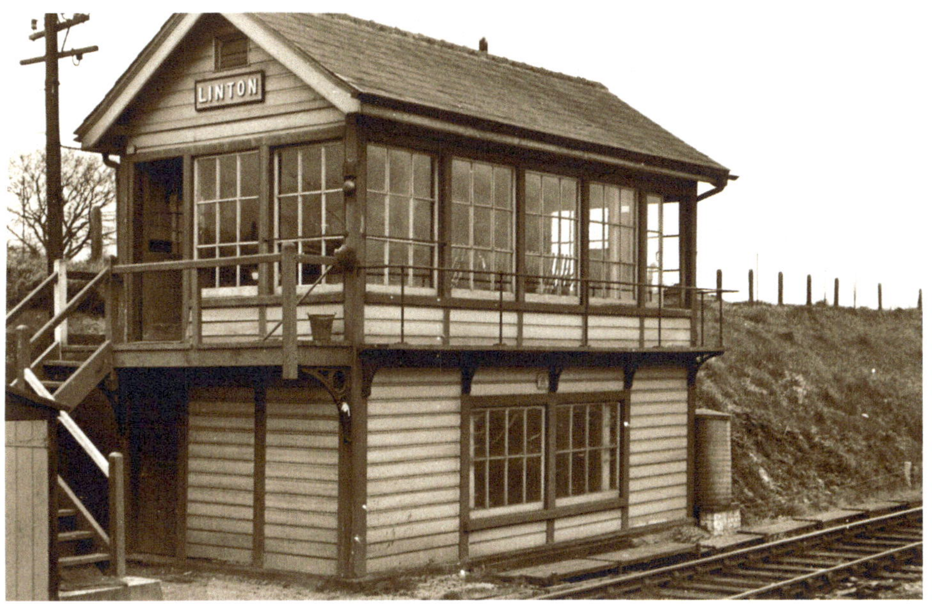

A close up view of Linton signal box, which was located on the down side of the line, at the end of the Cambridge-bound platform. This box dates from the 1889 resignalling of the line and contained a thirty-lever Saxby & Farmer frame, with twenty-three working and seven spare levers at its busiest. By 1896, Electric Tablet working was in use between Pampisford and Bartlow Junction; when Pampisford signal box closed as an economy measure in 1925, the section became Linton to Shelford Junction. Linton signal box remained in use until the line closed completely in 1967. (David Lawrence)

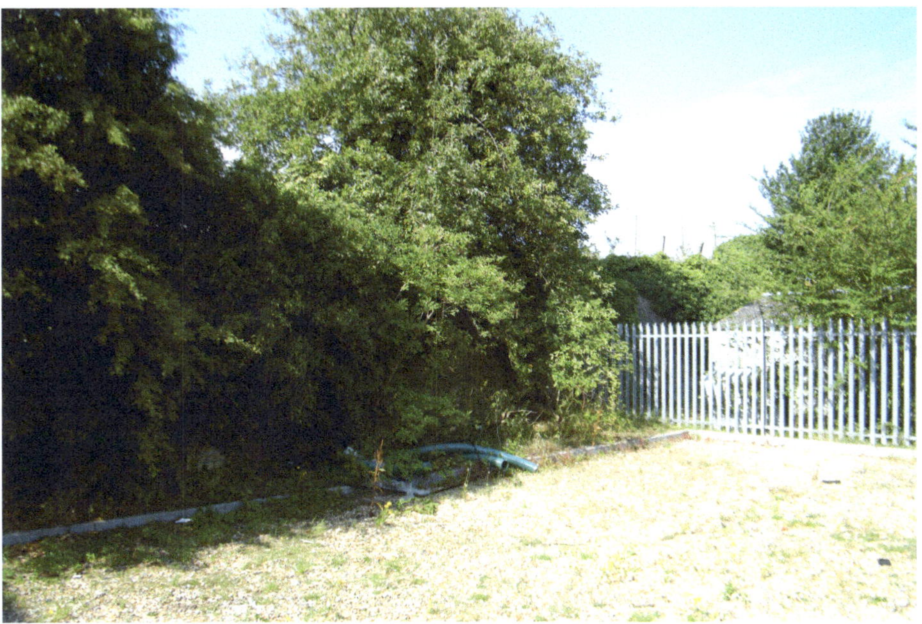

Today, all that remains is the concrete retaining wall hidden under the bushes. In the foreground is a parking area for a new large factory unit. (Paul Lemon)

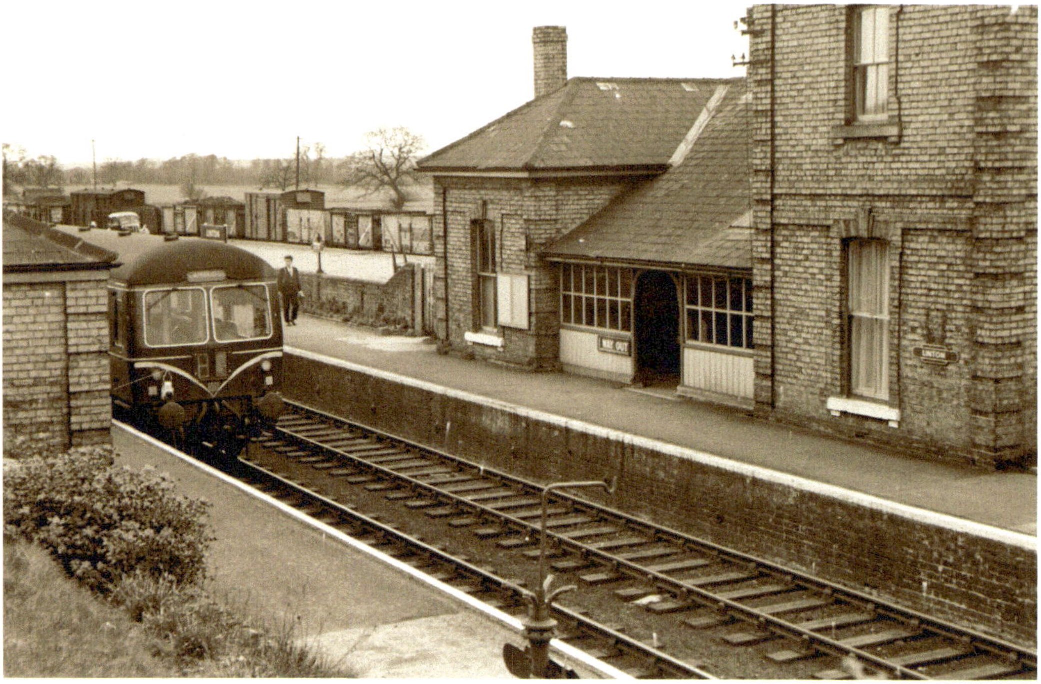

Rear end view of a Craven diesel multiple unit in the down loop at Linton; as can be seen, the main station buildings were on the up side. At this time, there seems to be plenty of wagons in the goods yard – freight facilities were withdrawn from Linton on 12 September 1966. (David Lawrence)

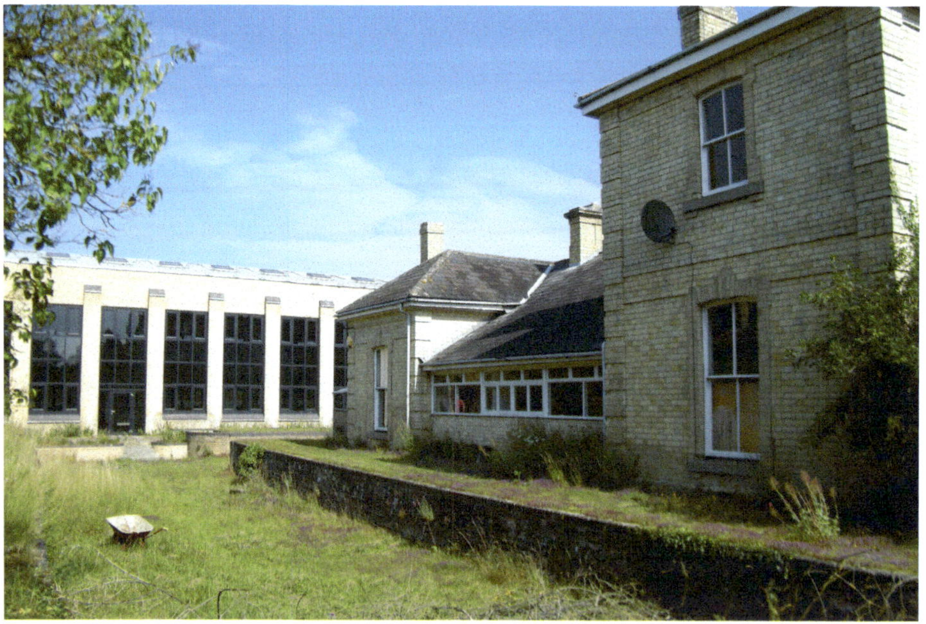

From this angle today, we can see how near the adjacent factory is – the central part of the building has benefitted from new windows. (Paul Lemon)

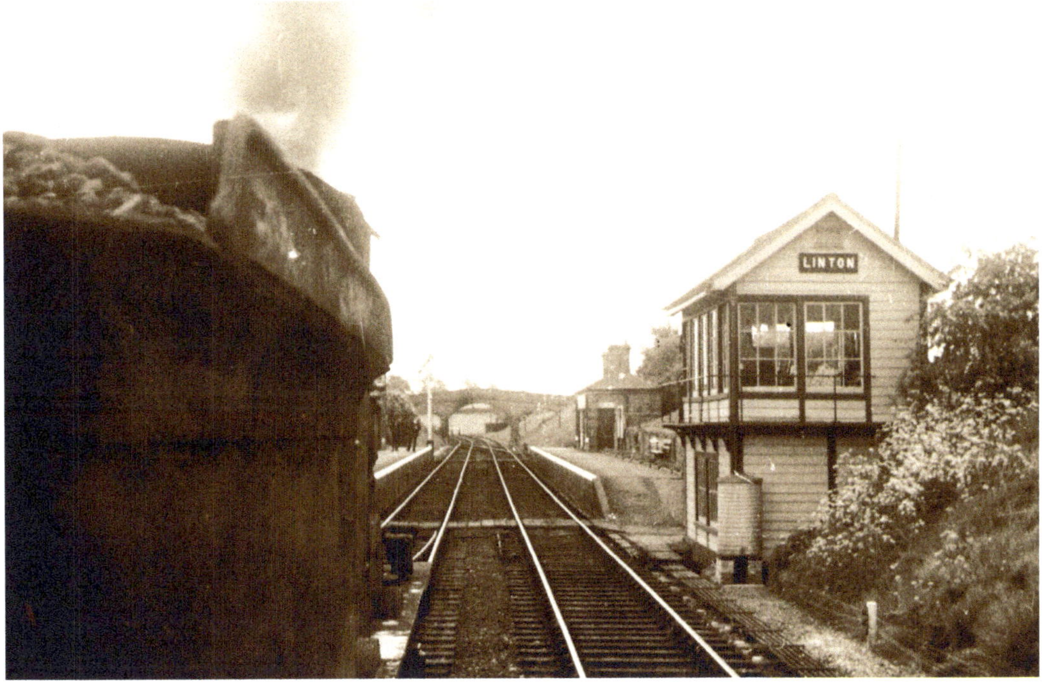

Linton signal box and station as seen from the leading coach of a train hauled by locomotive 62792 on 20 May 1956. The connection to the goods yard can be seen just in from of the engine. (R. C. Casserley)

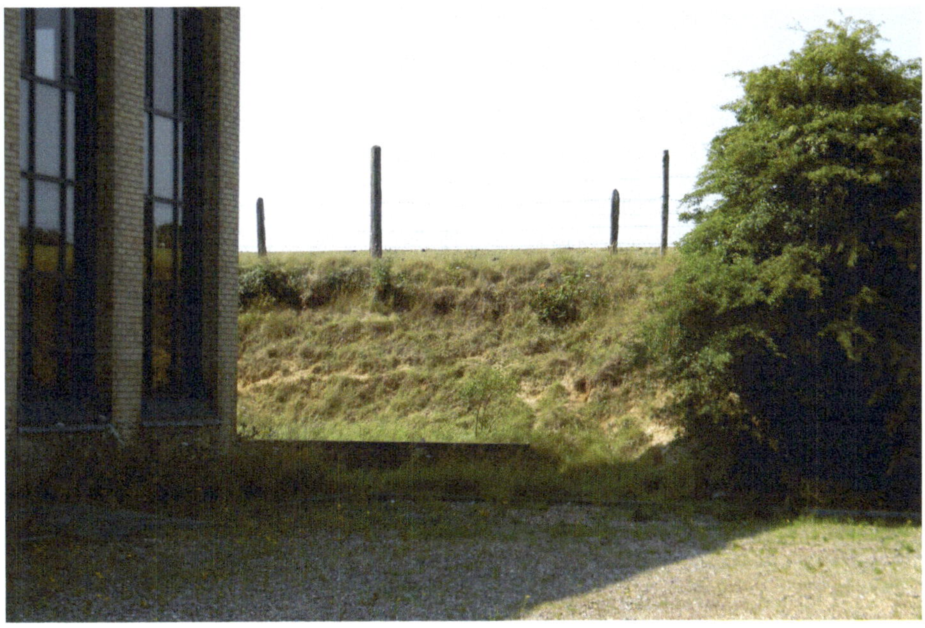

Today, a large factory unit occupies the site. The former boundary posts stand at the top of the edge of the former platform, and part of the brickwork can be seen to the right of the building. (Paul Lemon)

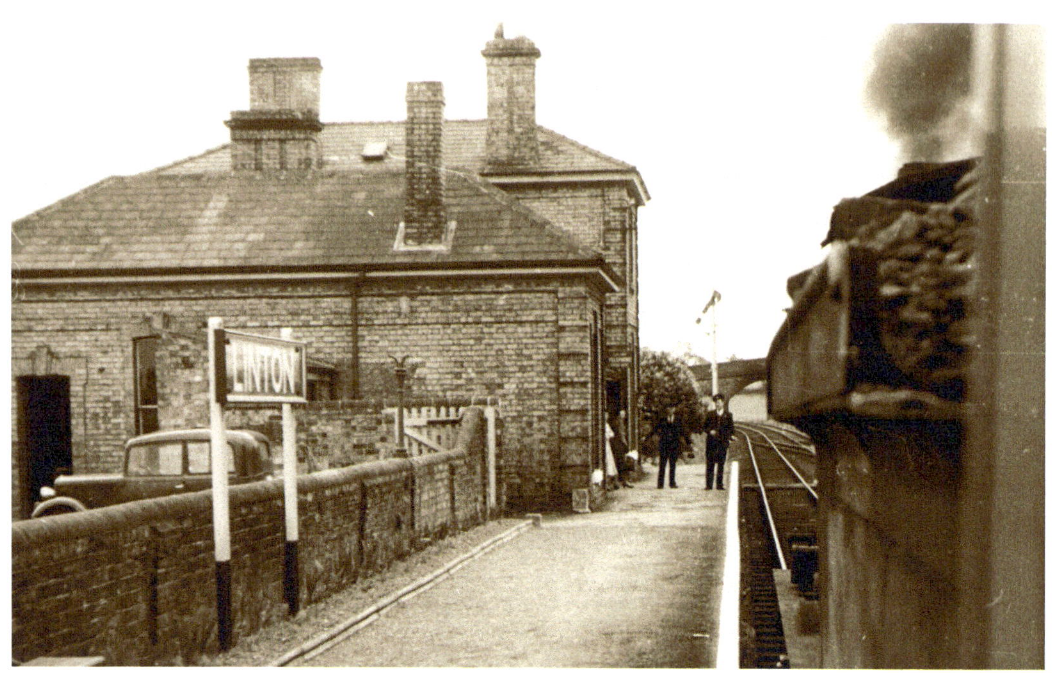

Reflections from the carriage window as a steam-hauled passenger train arrives at Linton – there seems to be a couple of passengers and two station staff. With no train to cross, the signal is off for the train to proceed to Bartlow and Haverhill. (Rail Archive Stephenson)

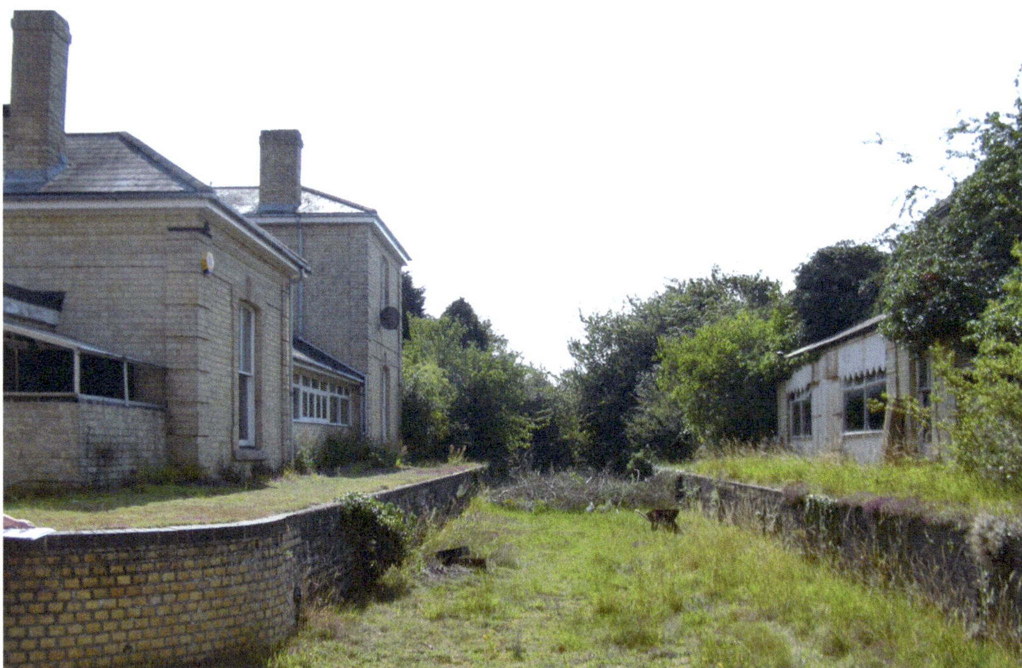

Standing on the old track bed today, the bridge in the distance has gone, as has the signal. Beyond the trees in the distance, the former track bed is buried under a new factory development. (Paul Lemon)

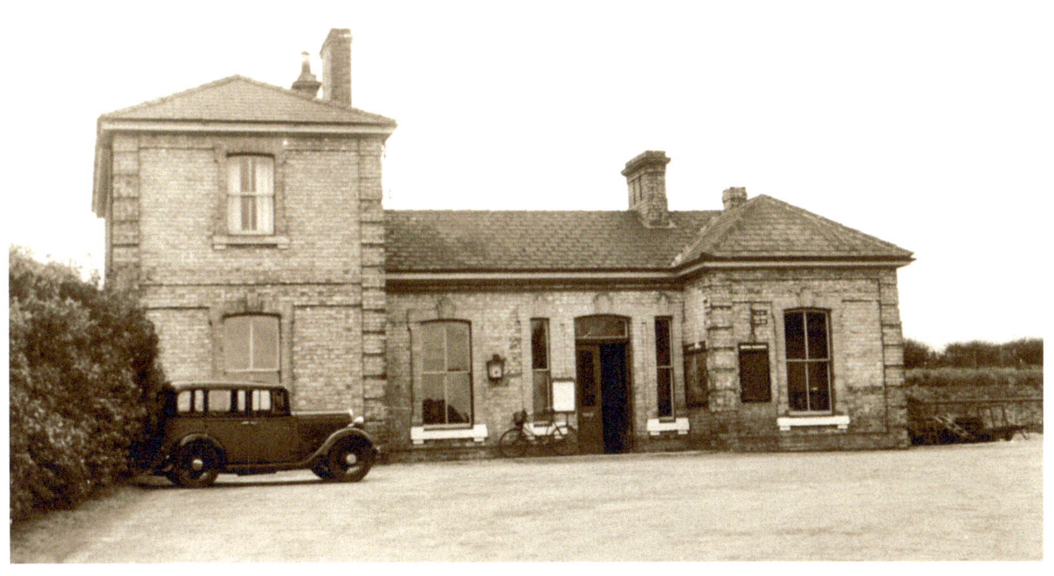

Exterior view of Linton Station as seen on 28 September 1957; the photographer's car is seen parked up, awaiting the next trip. The standard GER buildings of 1865 can clearly be seen – the stationmaster's house was the portion located on the left. (H. C. Casserley)

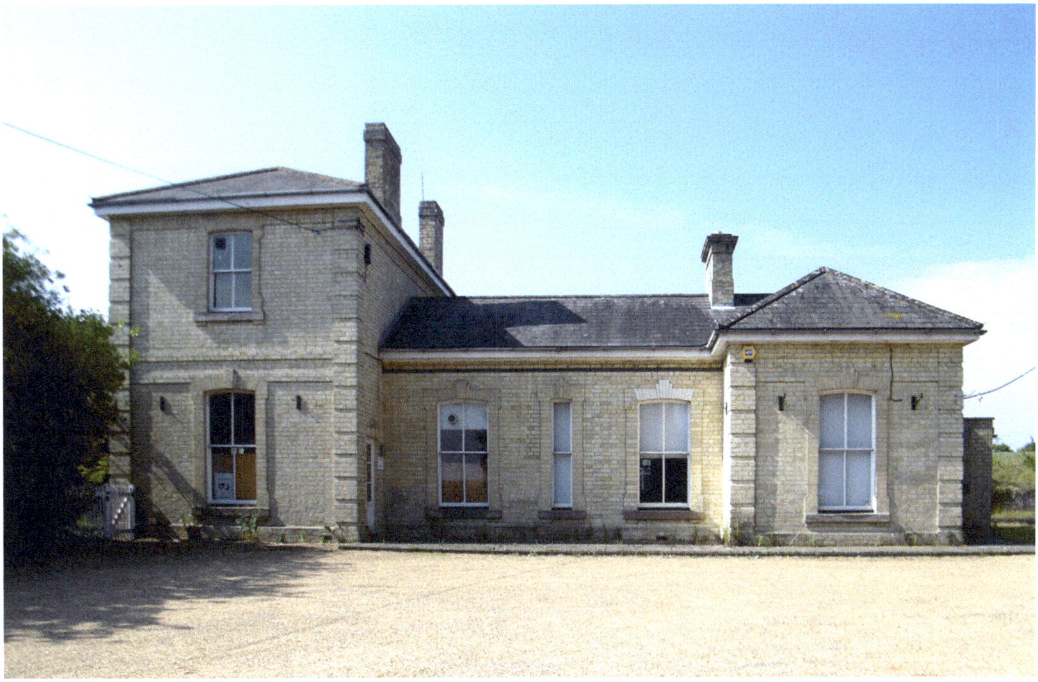

Today, it is hard to imagine that fifty-four years separate these two pictures. Back in 1957, trains had another ten years to run. Today the rail link to Cambridge is sorely missed. (Paul Lemon)

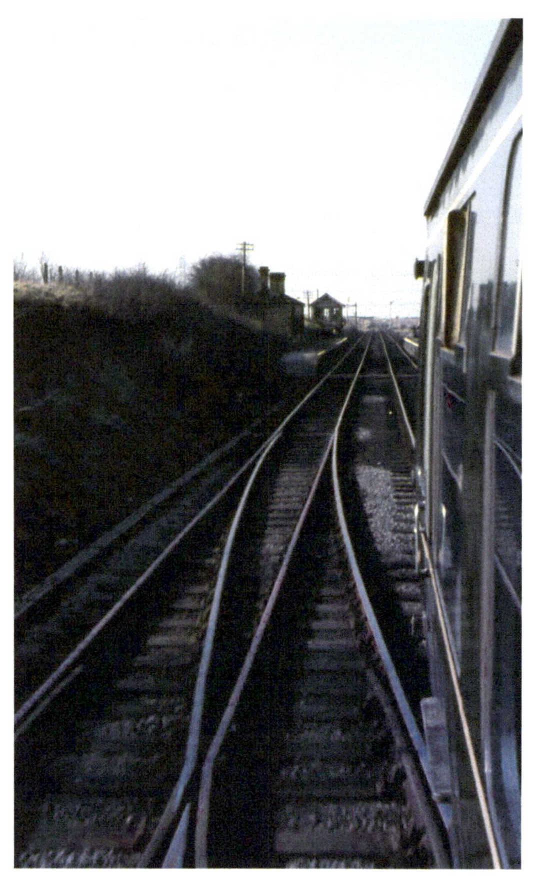

Left: A colour view of Linton station taken from a departing DMU on 4 March 1967, the last day of passenger services over the line. The line on the left formed a long head shunt protected by trap points; a similar arrangement was provided at the other end of the loop. (D. J. Plyer)

Below: A Derby lightweight diesel multiple unit arrives at the up platform at Linton on the same day; it would seem that the photographers outnumbered the passengers. (Stations UK)

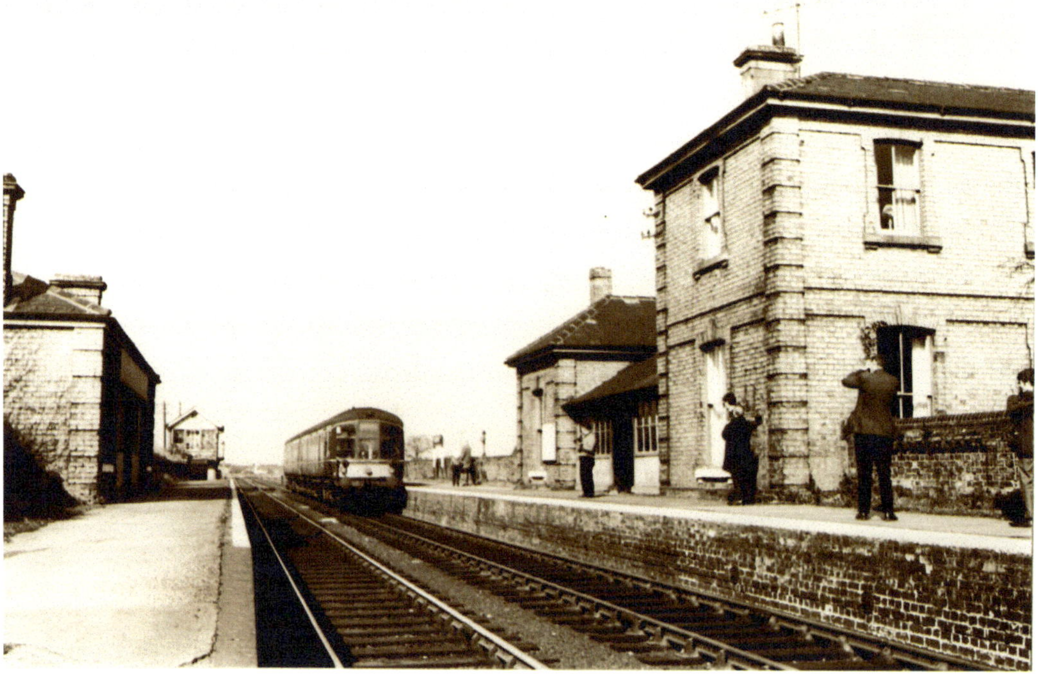

Pampisford

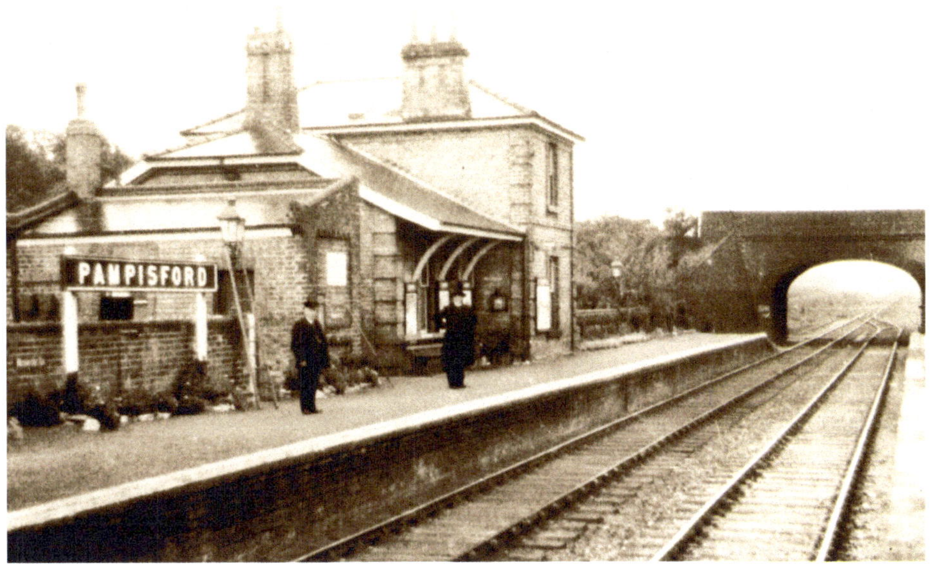

Pampisford station, formerly Abington, some 39 miles from Marks Tey, opened to passenger and freight traffic on 1 June 1865. The main station buildings were on the up side; the station was provided with a crossing loop and was fully signalled in the 1889 resignalling. Electric tablet working was introduced by 1896 between Shelford Junction and Bartlow; both Pampisford and Linton were tablet stations. The LNER closed the signal box and crossing loop as an economy measure in 1925; the former down platform line became a siding. (Stations UK)

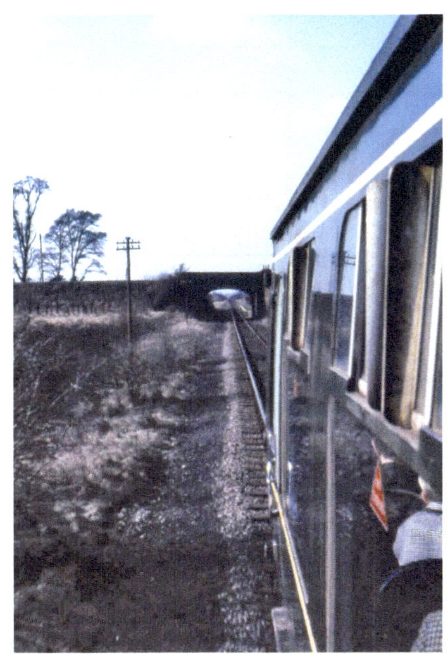

The view from an arriving DMU, looking through the bridge at the approaching station; the whitened edge of the platform can just be made out. (D. J. Plyer)

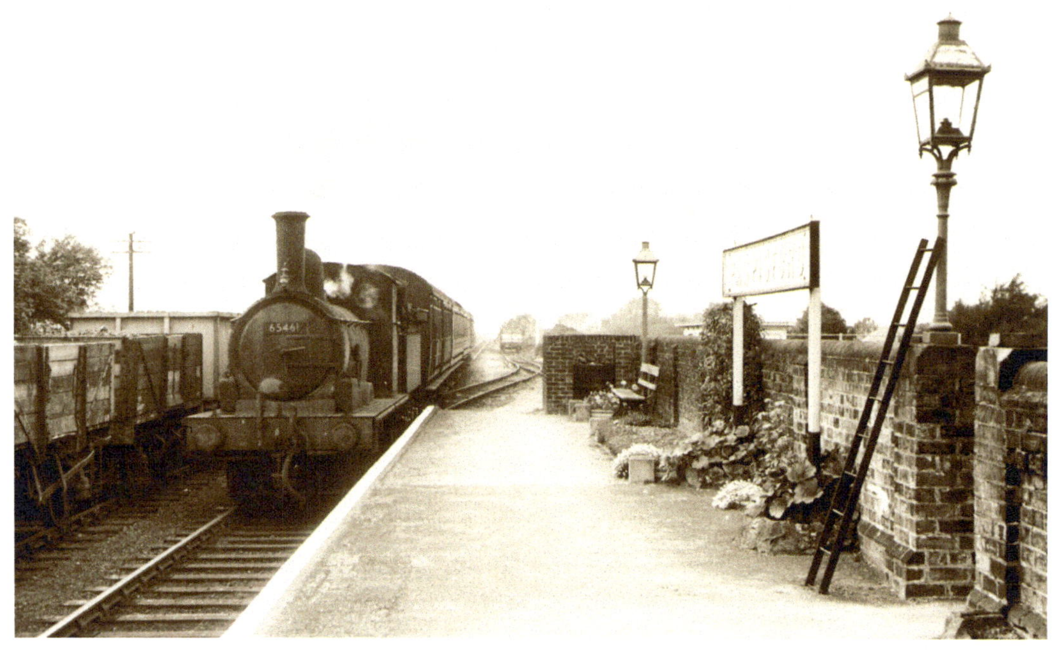

Class J15 locomotive No. 65461 enters the station from the direction of Cambridge. The connection to the goods yard can be seen trailing into the platform line; the former down platform on the right is being used for storage of wagons waiting departure or unloading as appropriate. (H. C. Casserley)

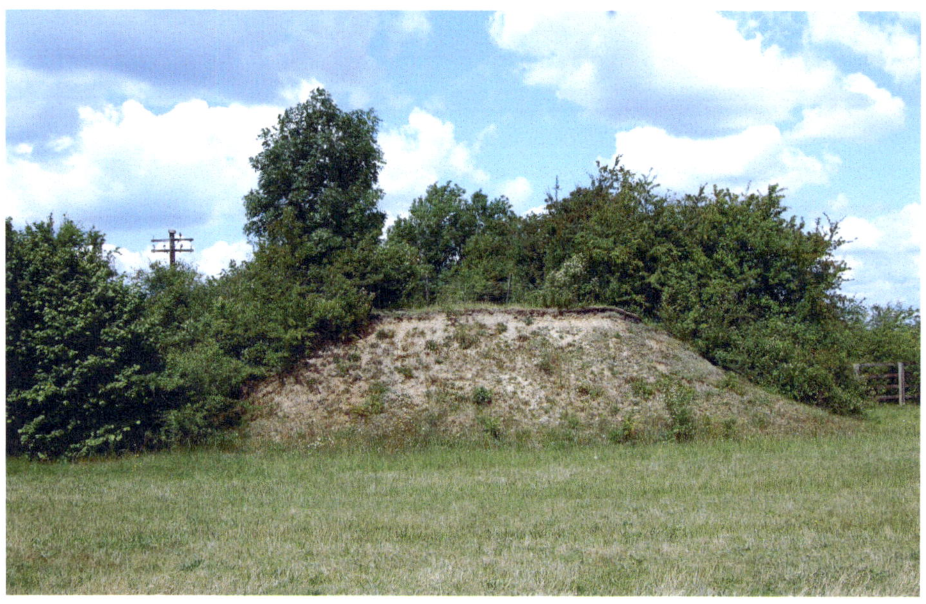

After closure, the station site was used as a building materials recycling depot. Later, parts of the site were given over to industrial use, as well as disappearing under the A11 trunk road dualling. This picture shows the truncated track bed on the Cambridge side of the station. (Ray Bishop)

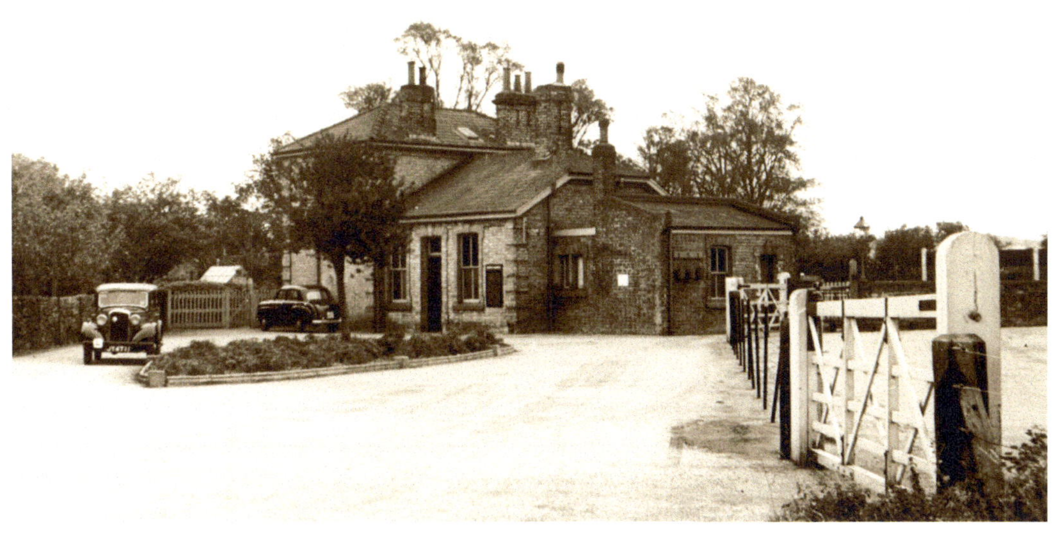

An exterior view of Pampisford station taken from the approach road on 28 September 1958; the photographer's car is again seen parked up, waiting for the drive to the next station. (H. C. Casserley)

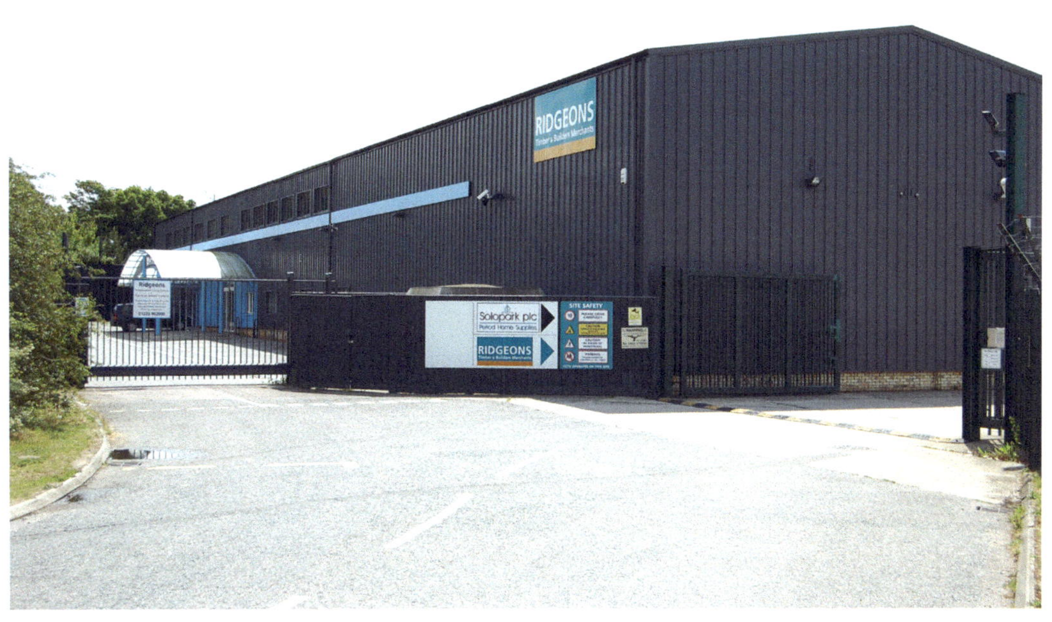

Today, some of the station site has been redeveloped into industrial use; the rest lies under the A11 trunk road. (Ray Bishop)

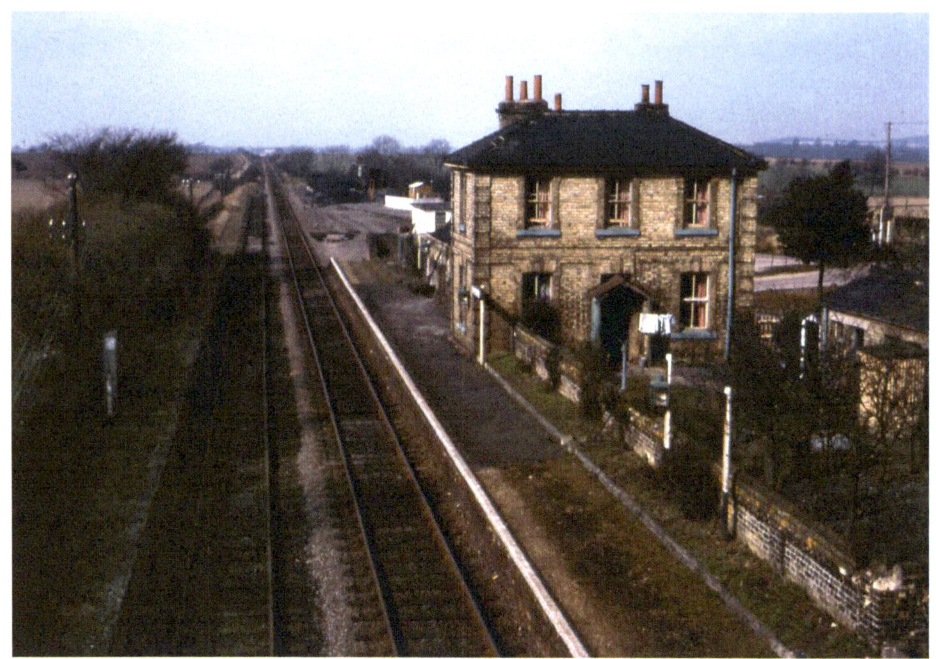

A colour view of Pampisford station taken from the main A11 road bridge over the line. Train services had ceased two days previously; the track in the goods yard had already been lifted, as had the connections to the down siding line. The main line track would remain in situ until late 1969, when it was recovered for scrap. (D. J. Plyer)

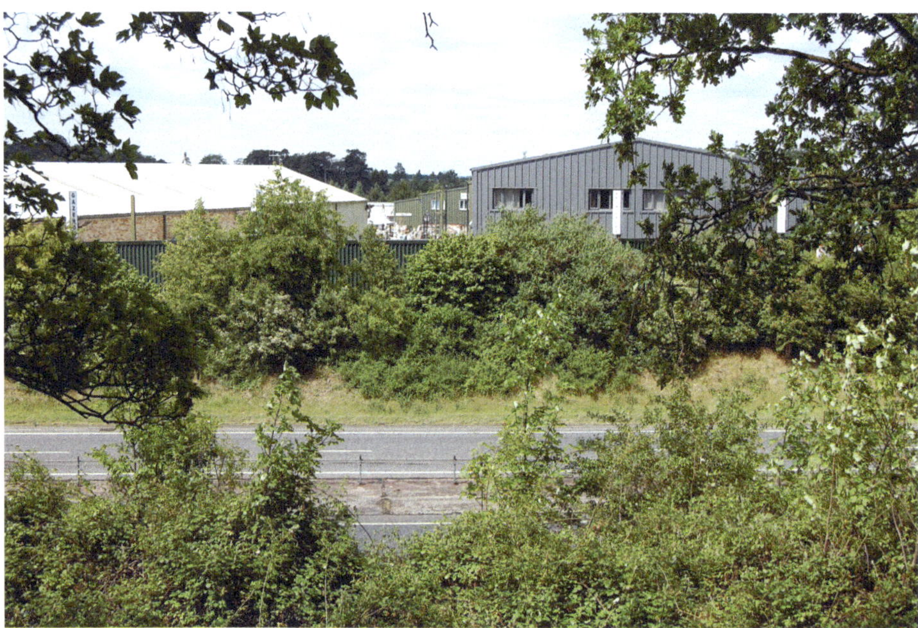

The complete station site was obliterated when part of it was used for the A11 trunk road. The remainder was put to industrial use, and this view was taken from the original road bridge. (Ray Bishop)

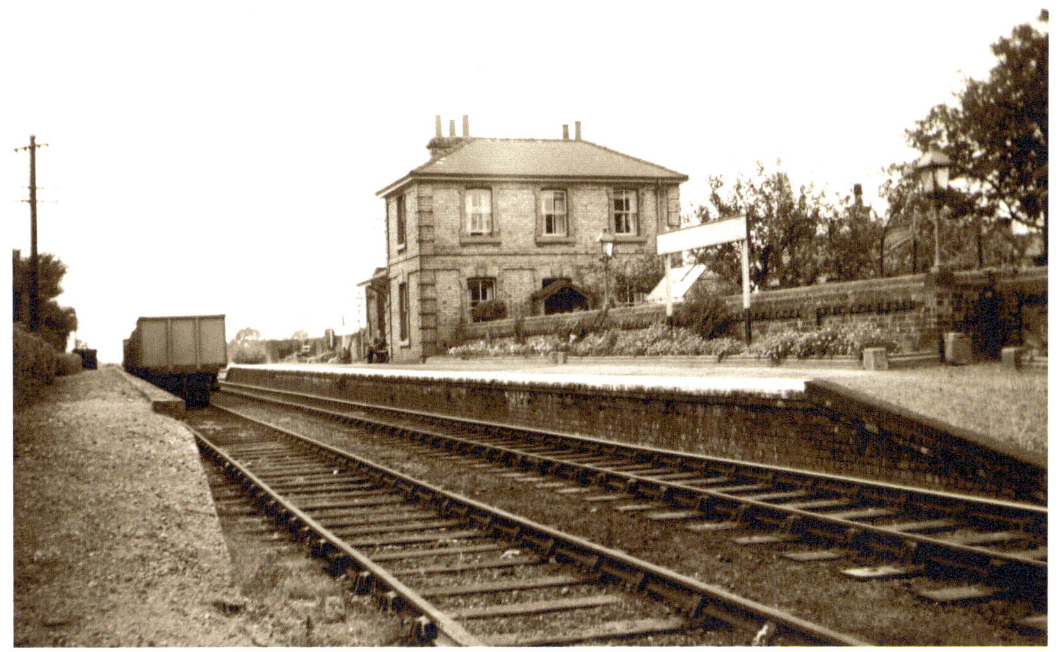

General view of Pampisford station taken from the Colchester end, as seen on 28 September 1957. The former down loop line was in use as a siding for storage of wagons waiting departure.

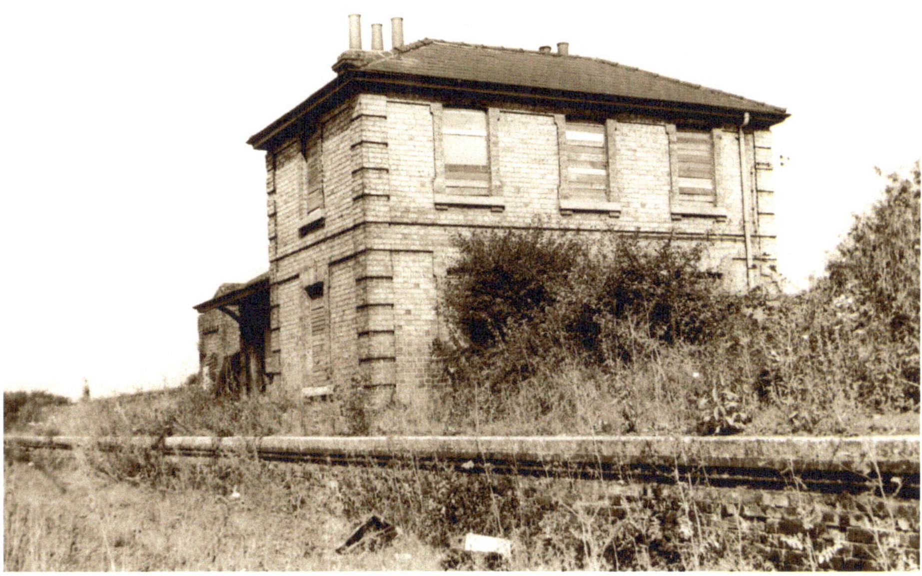

A sad scene some fourteen years later, captured by the same photographer. The station is all boarded up, the track had been lifted and Mother Nature was slowly taking over the site again. The station buildings and yard became a builders' material recycling depot until the former station buildings were obliterated to make way for the new A11 dual carriageway. (Both R. M. Casserley)

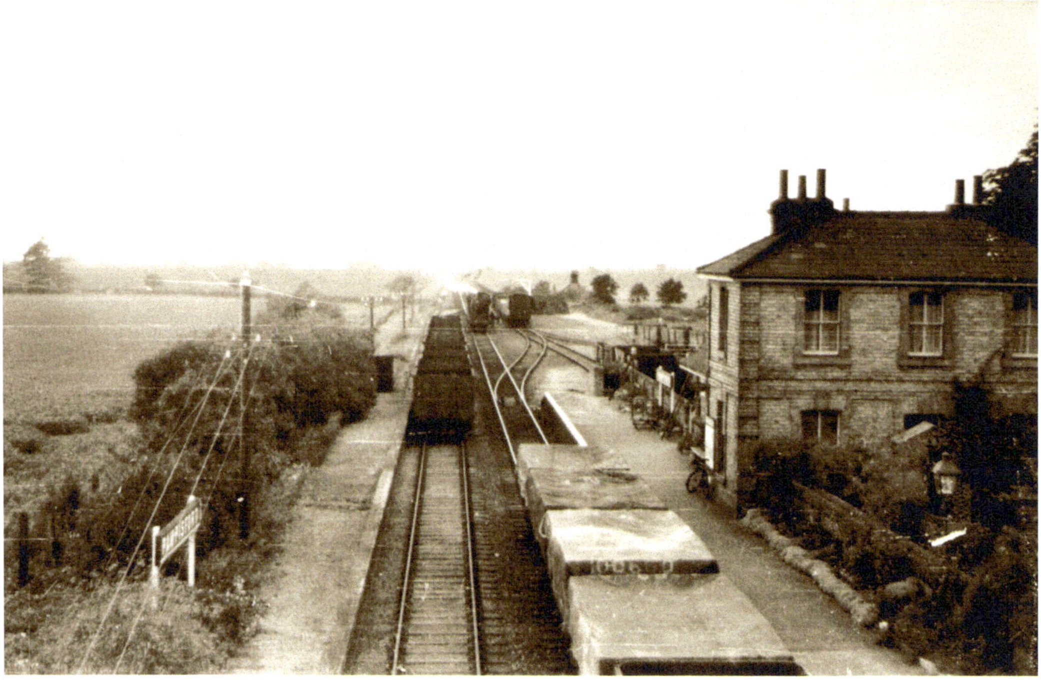

An overall view of the station taken from the road bridge in about 1936, during the LNER era. A locomotive can be seen shunting wagons and making up the outgoing train; the former down platform can clearly be seen on the left, together with the old-style station name board. (Stations UK)

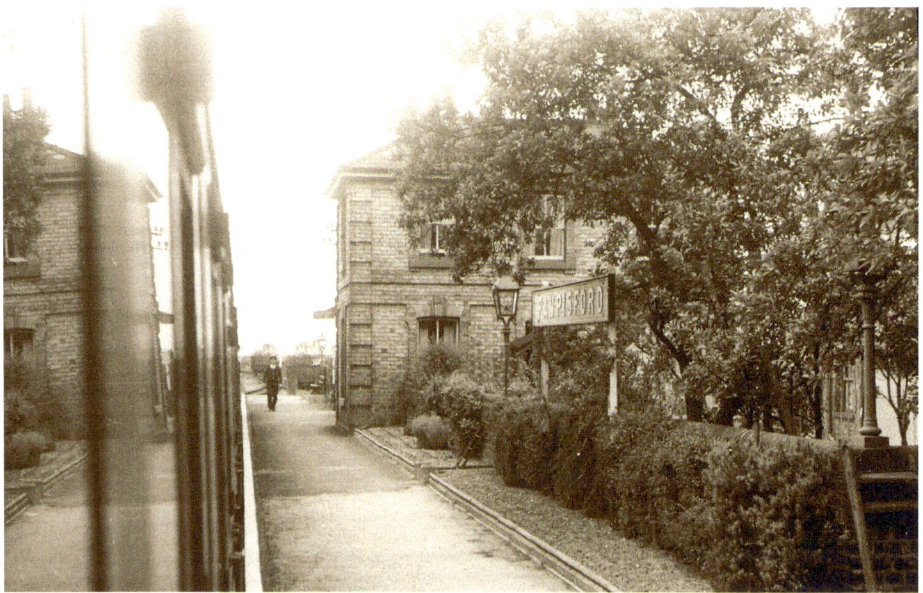

The main station buildings at Pampisford, taken from a carriage window of an arriving train. Today, both these views have been lost forever under the A11 dual carriageway. (R. M. Casserley)

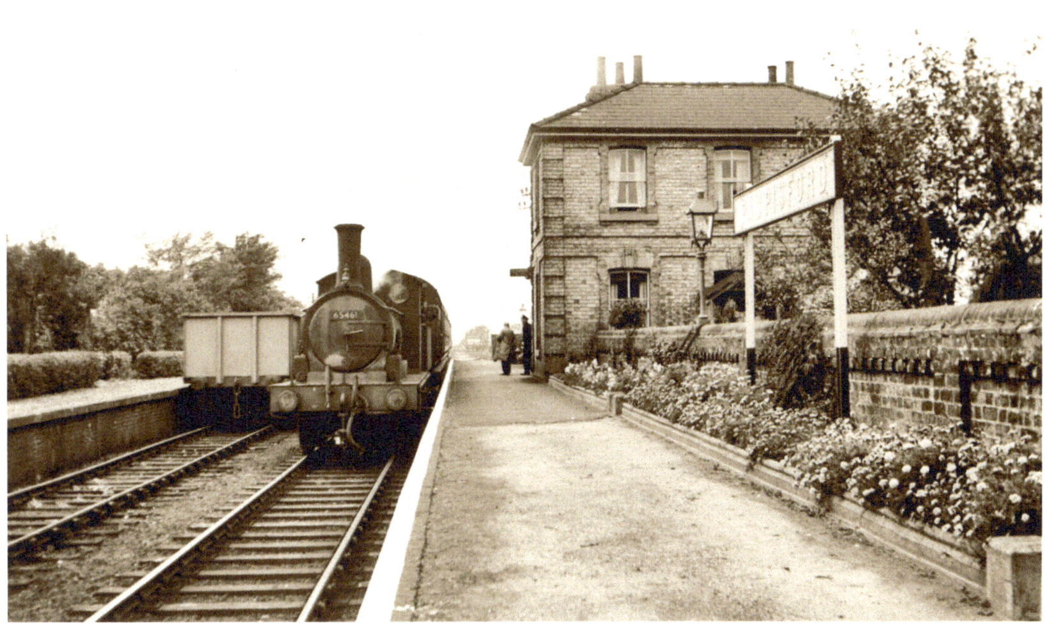

The 13.35 Cambridge to Colchester passenger train stands at Pampisford, hauled by locomotive type J15 number 65461. Note the well-kept flower beds – no weeds or litter, as would be the norm these days. (R. M. Casserley)

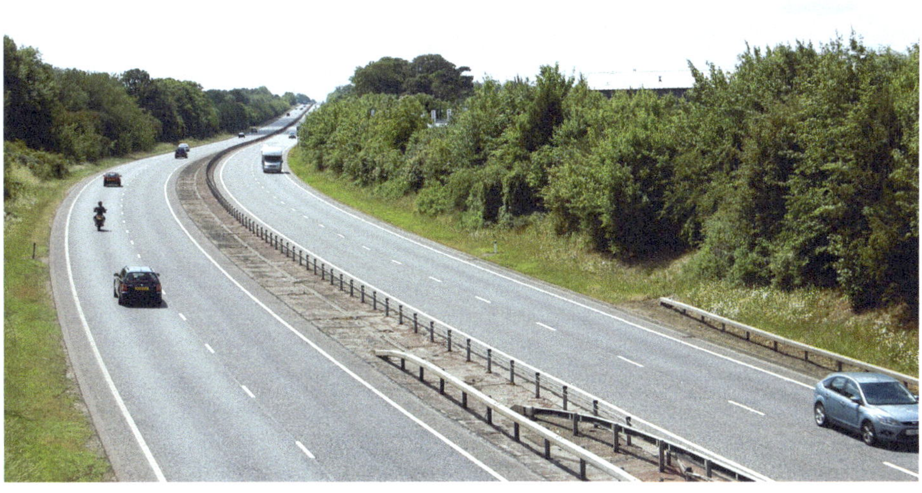

Today, no railway, just the A11 dual carriageway. The station used to stand in the middle of the right-hand carriageway; part of the former goods yard is now a retail park. (Ray Bishop)

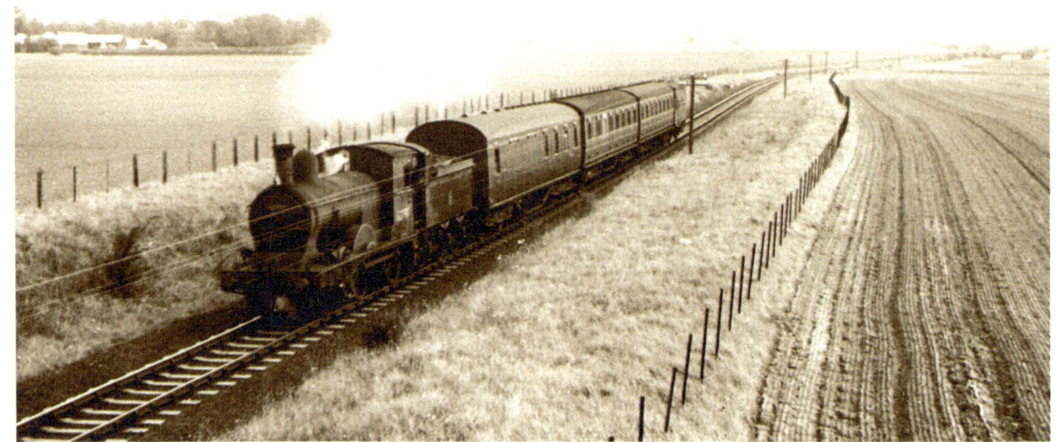

Class E4 number 62797 is seen near Pampisford with the 11.36 Colchester to Cambridge passenger on 5 October 1957, with a train consisting of a full brake coach, two passenger coaches and a van on the rear. The E4s had given sterling service on the local branch lines around Cambridge; the last members of this class would be withdrawn soon after diesels took over the passenger and freight workings in 1959. (H. C. Casserley)

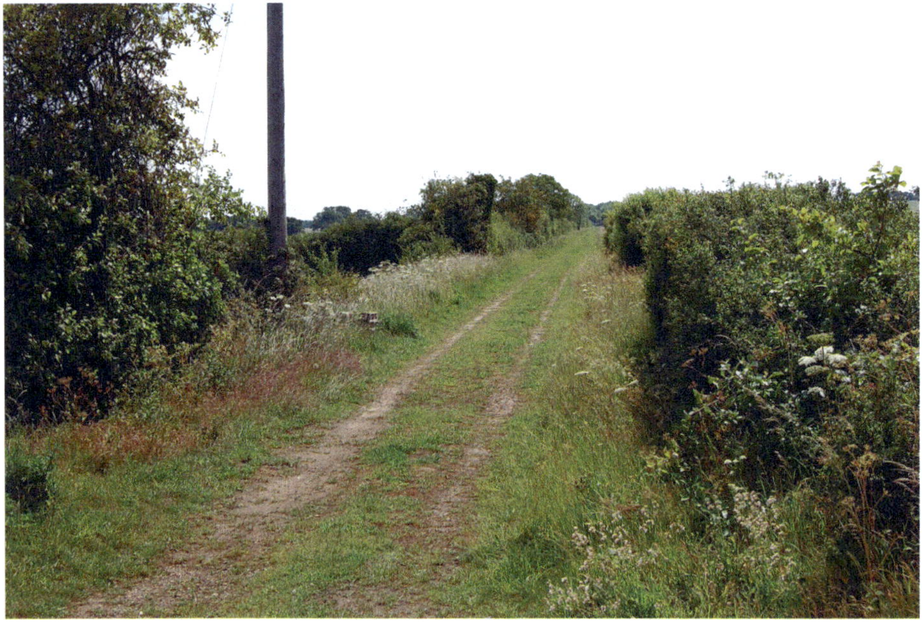

Today, the abandoned track bed is seen disappearing out of view, having been used by the local landowner as an access between fields. Due to the open nature of the surrounding land, the track bed is relatively free of trees and bushes. (Ray Bishop)

Shelford

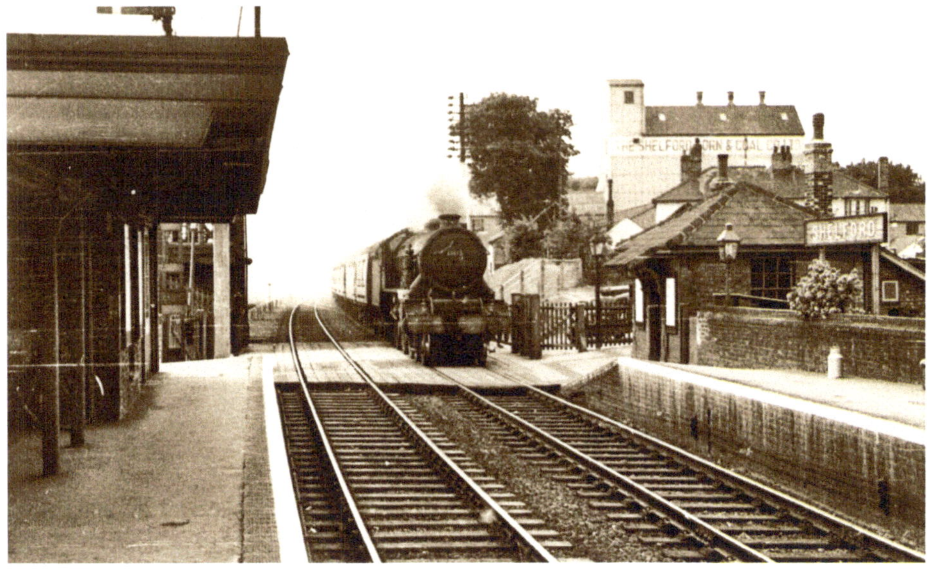

Up platform view taken during 1954 as locomotive No. 61692 enters the station on a down main line service to Cambridge. The level crossing was located immediately at the London end of the platforms; the signal box was on the up side, opposite the main station buildings. (Stations UK)

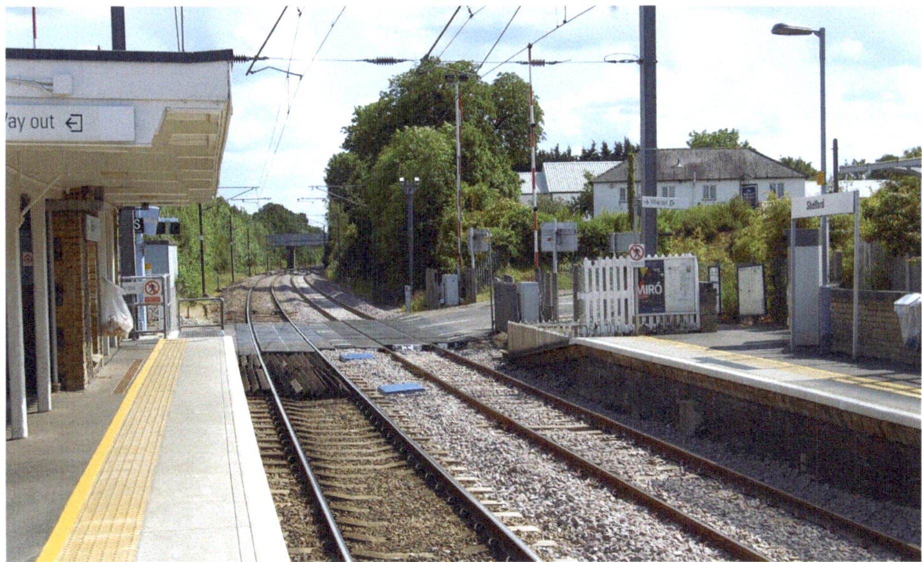

Today, we still have the main line railway providing an electrified commuter service to Cambridge and London. Note that the mill in the background of the previous picture has been demolished, as has the small brick building at the end of the down platform. (Ray Bishop)

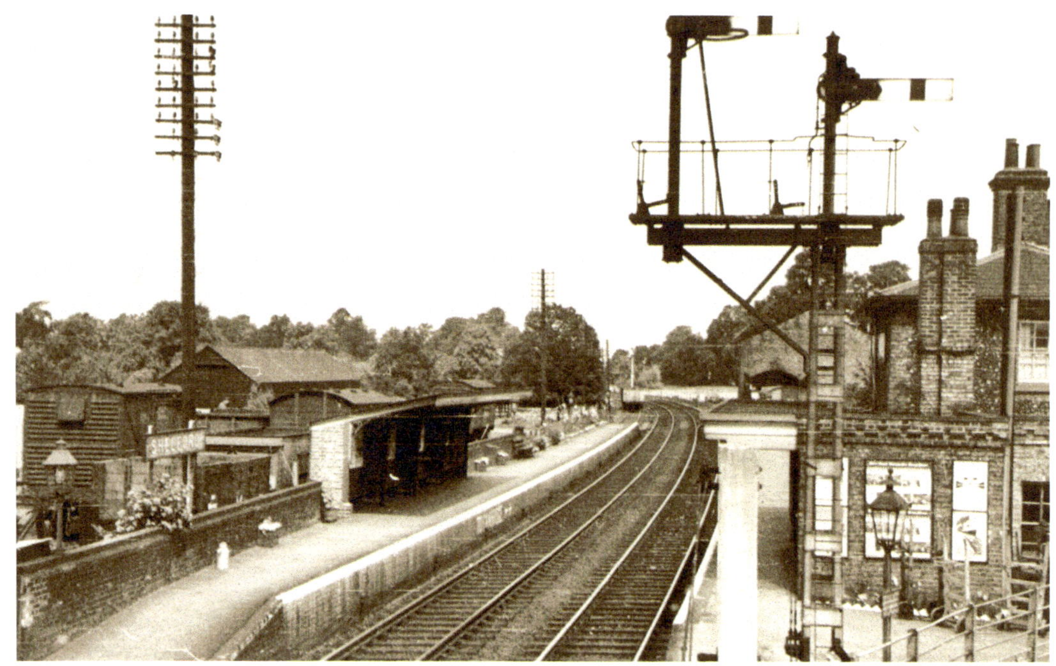

Elevated view of the station taken in 1954, looking north. The large bracket signal controlled access to the Stour Valley line, which ran parallel with the up main line for a short distance before curving away to the south-east. All the goods facilities were situated to the north of the station. (Stations UK)

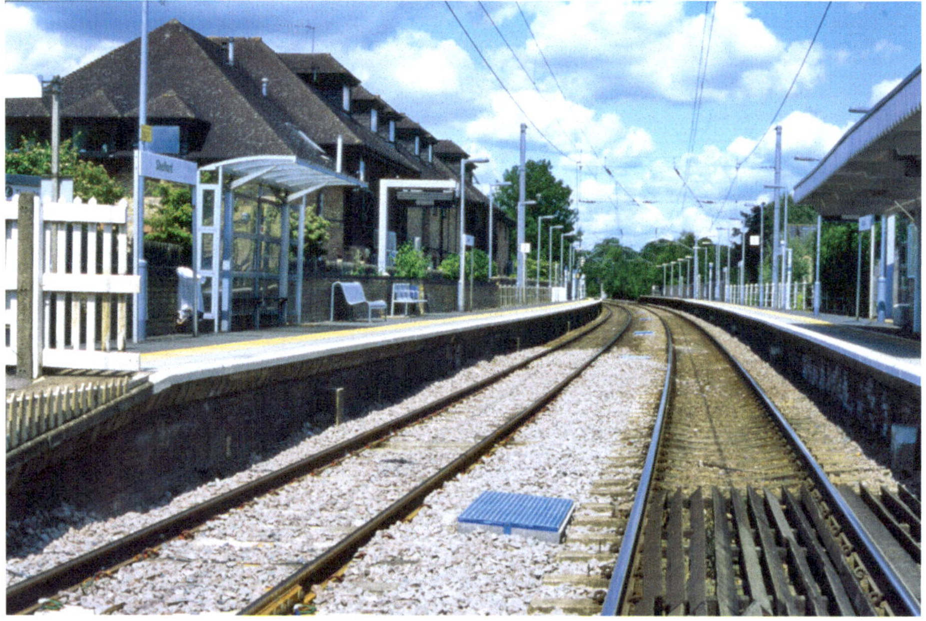

A similar view, looking north from the level crossing. Shelford station benefitted from the electrification of the line from Bishop's Stortford and resignalling in the 1980s; the station platforms were also extended to take eight-coach EMU trains. (Ray Bishop)

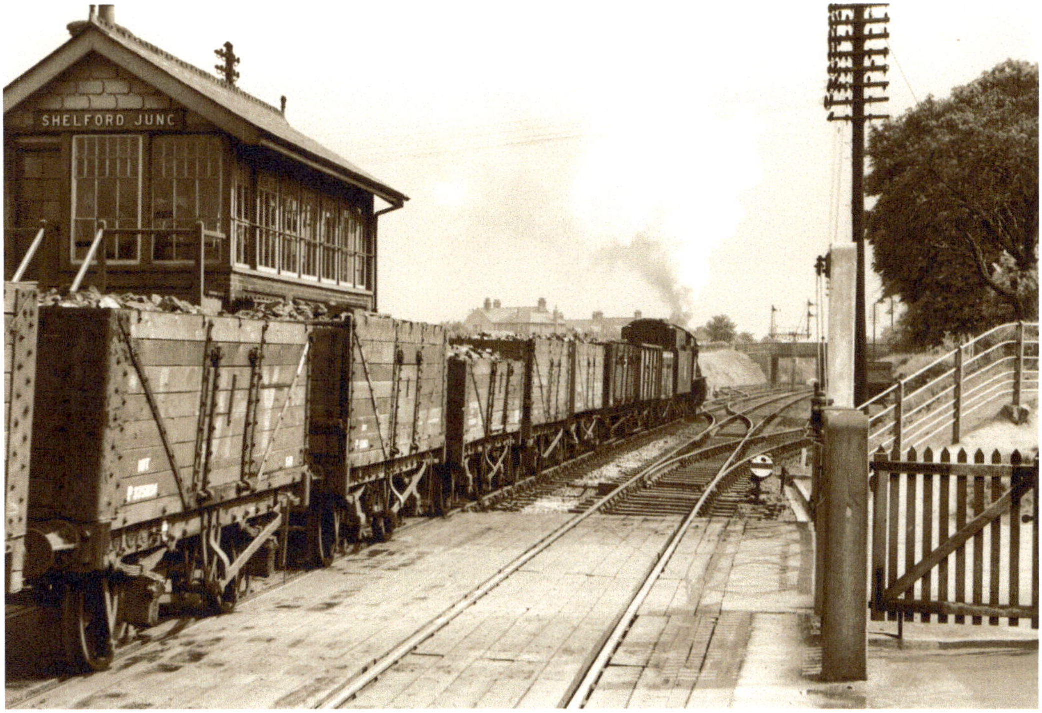

A heavy, steam-hauled coal freight train heading south through Shelford. The signal box contained a thirty-six-lever McKenzie & Holland lever frame and in the 1950s thirty-five levers were working and only one spare; by January 1966, this changed to twenty-four working and eleven spares. The signal box survived in a much reduced form until the early 1980s, when it was closed under the Cambridge area Resignalling. (R. E. Vincent/Transport Treasury)

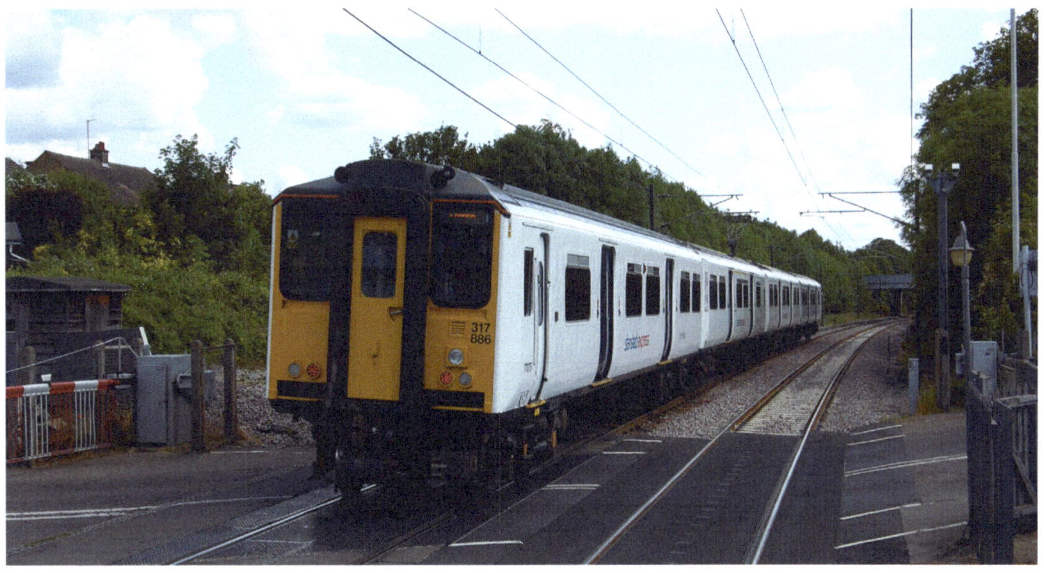

Today, electric multiple unit 317886 departs south from Shelford over the level crossing; the signal box is long gone, but the bridge in the distance is common to both pictures. (Ray Bishop)

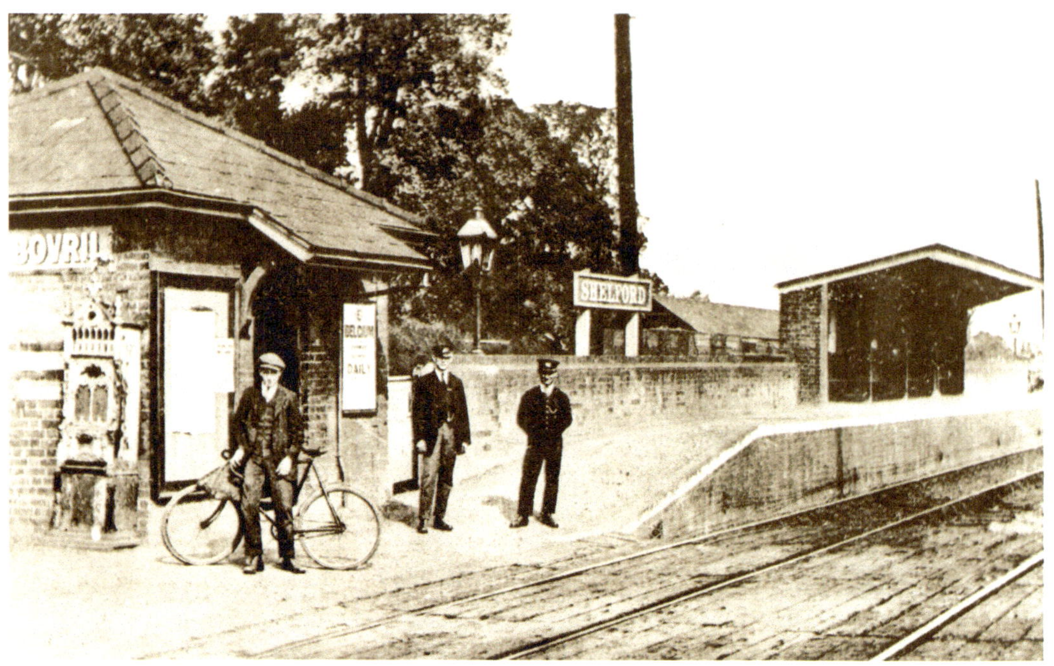

An early Great Eastern Railway view of the down platform and some station staff. Note the old adverts and what looks like an early vending machine next to the small building, by the man with the bike. (Lens of Sutton Association)

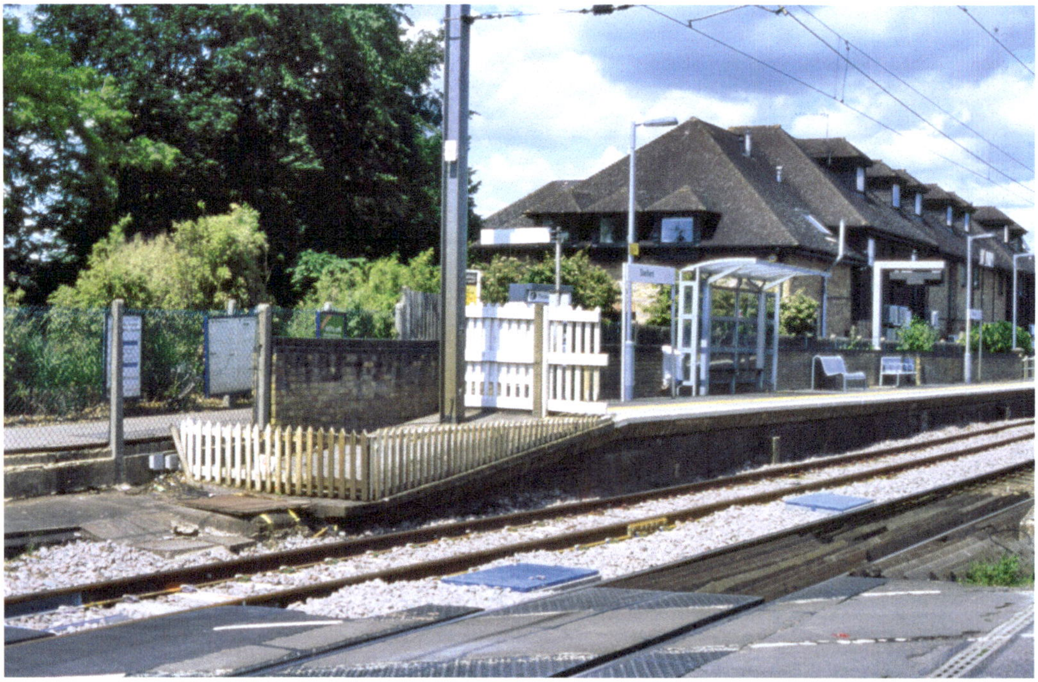

Today, the small building has been demolished in favour of a passenger exit clear of the crossing. A modern bus-type shelter has replaced the old structure seen in the top picture. (Ray Bishop)

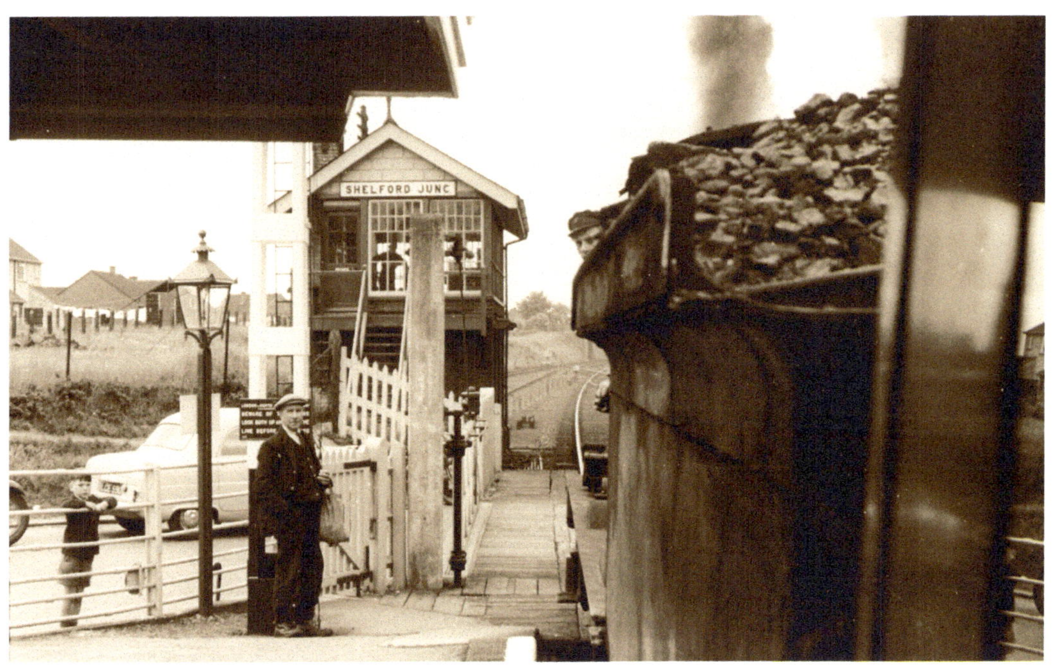

Locomotive 62792 on the 11.05 Cambridge to Colchester passenger service stands at Shelford awaiting the right away. This view was taken on 26 May 1956; the photographer was leaning out of the front coach to capture this image. (H. C. Casserley)

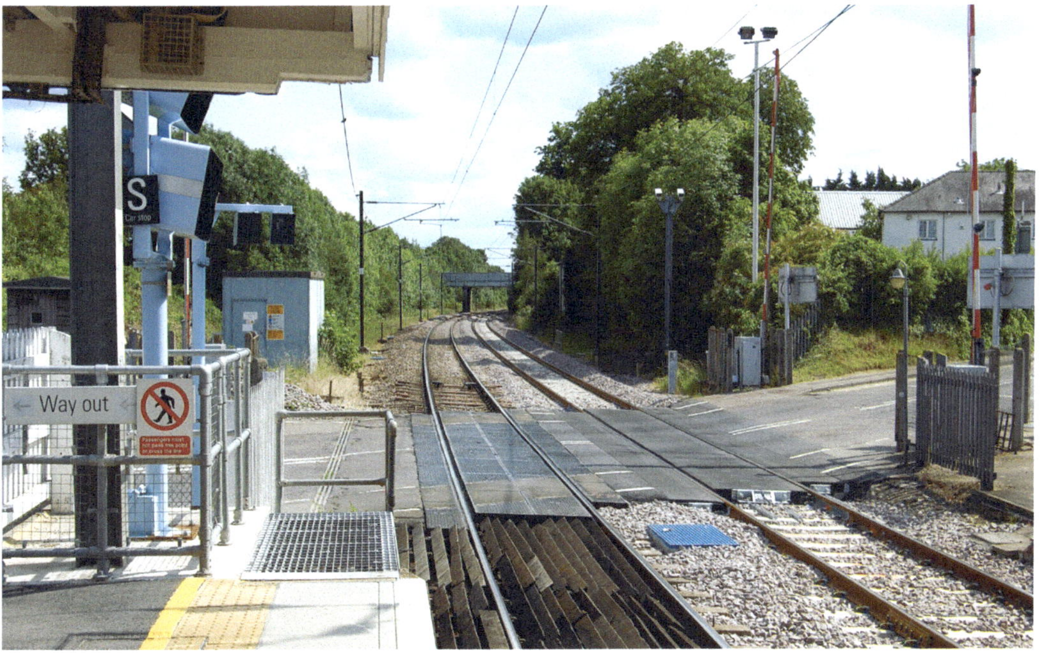

Today's view, minus signal box, is taken from nearly the same position, featuring the monitors aiding the driver to see if all is clear when he shuts the doors of the train; a line-side building stands on the site of the signal box and houses signalling equipment. (Ray Bishop)

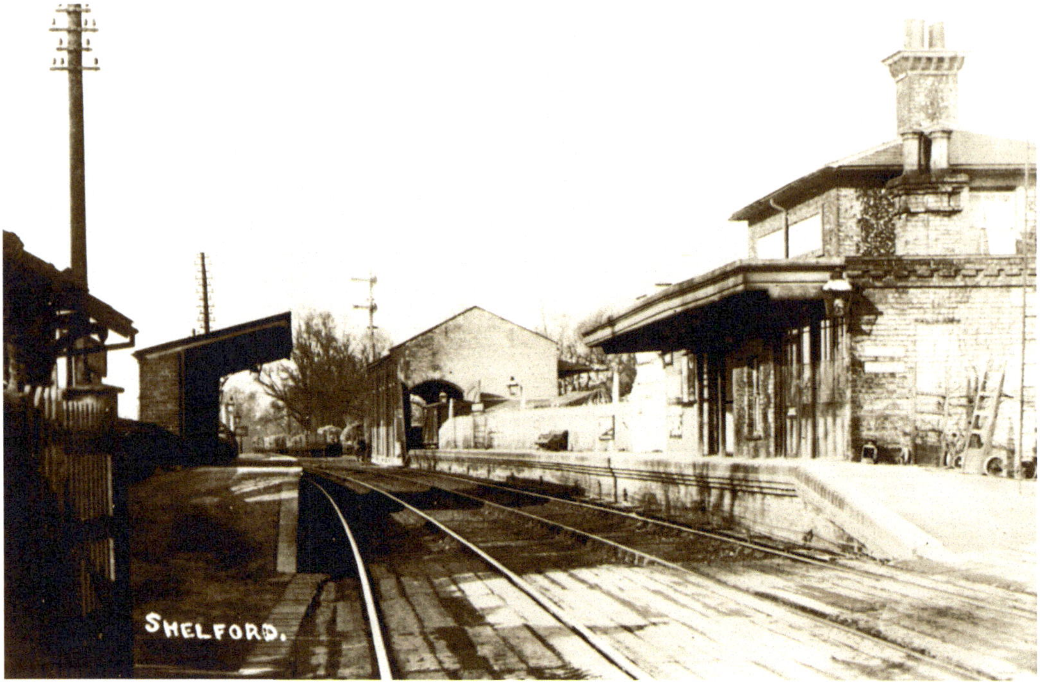

An old postcard view of Shelford station taken from the level crossing in around 1910 with the main buildings on the right and the goods yard in the distant. (Stations UK)

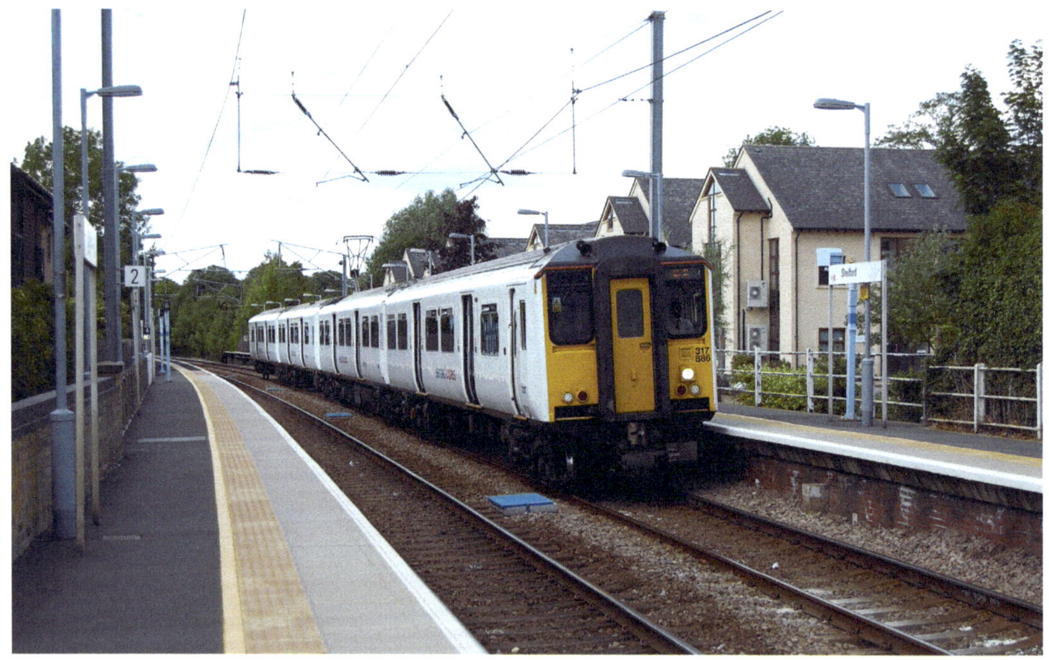

Today, a Class 317 EMU arrives in the up platform; houses have been built on the former goods yard. Since the top view was taken, the station has benefitted from new electric lighting and platform extensions. (Ray Bishop)

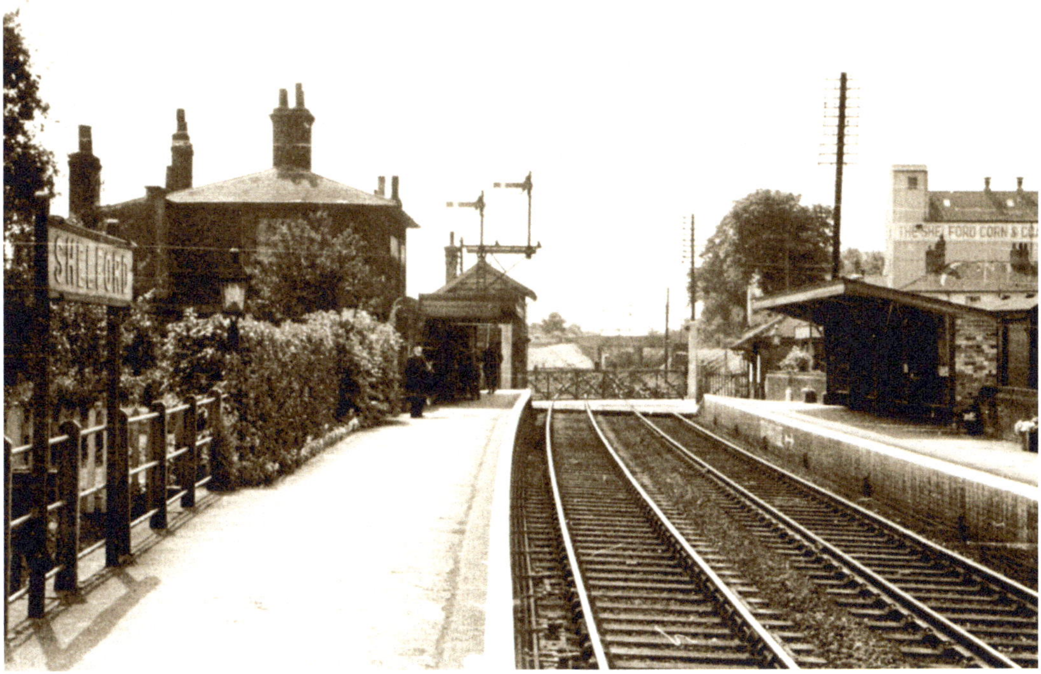

Shelford station as seen from the up platform looking south towards the level crossing. The left-hand semaphore arm on the large bracket signal controlled access to the Stour Valley line. This view was taken in 1954. (Stations UK)

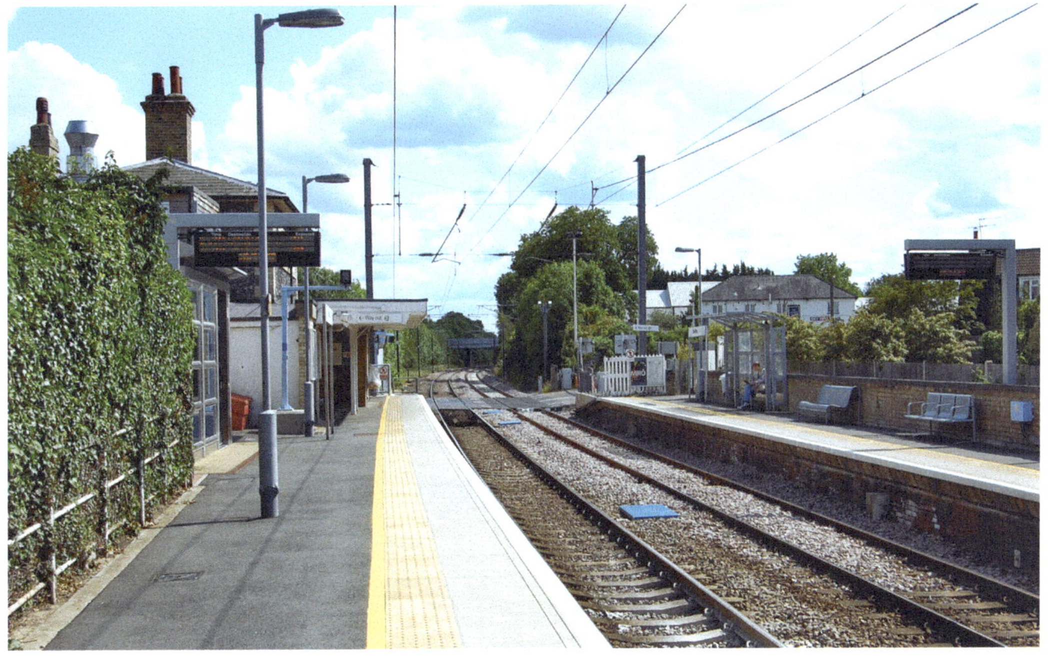

A similar view today shows the station buildings, a waiting shelter and a train indicator board displaying the next train. (Ray Bishop)

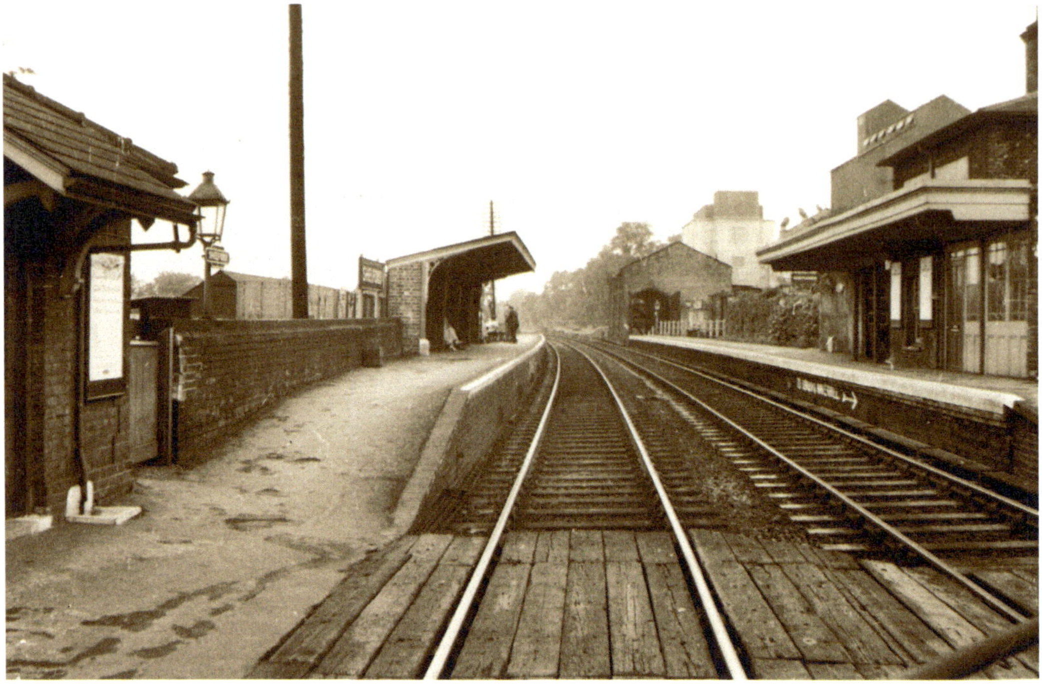

A general view taken from the level crossing at Shelford, looking northwards towards Cambridge, in 1958; the goods yard and shed are on the up side and the main station buildings are located on the up platform. Back in 1958, the road surface over the level crossing was made of timber. (Stations UK)

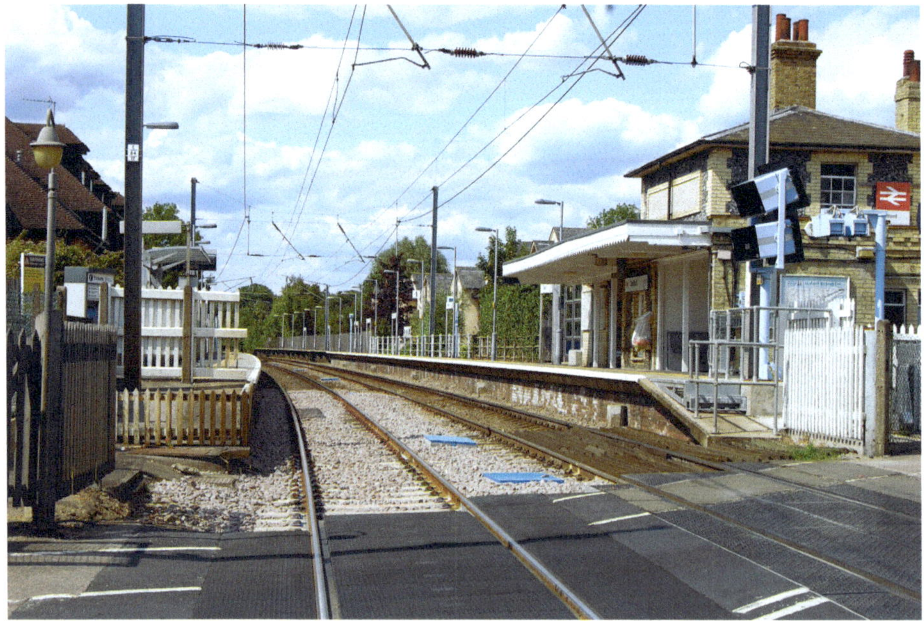

Today, the same view shows a modern road surface on the crossing and modern housing replacing the goods yard. The platform extension can be clearly seen. (Ray Bishop)

Bartlow (Branch)

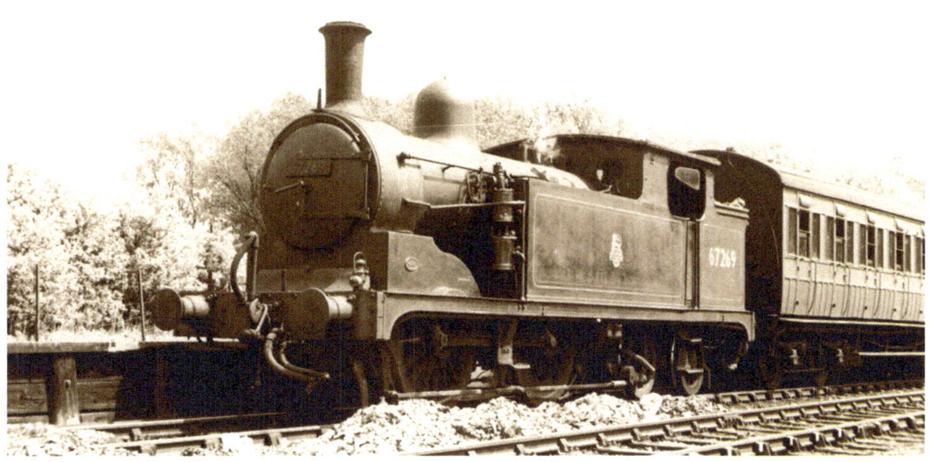

LNER Class G5 locomotive No. 67269 stands at the branch platform at Bartlow, waiting its return working to Saffron Walden and Audley End; the pile of clinker dumped next to the engine indicates that this was a favorite spot for the fireman to clean the fire. This view was taken on 26 May 1956. (H. C. Casserley)

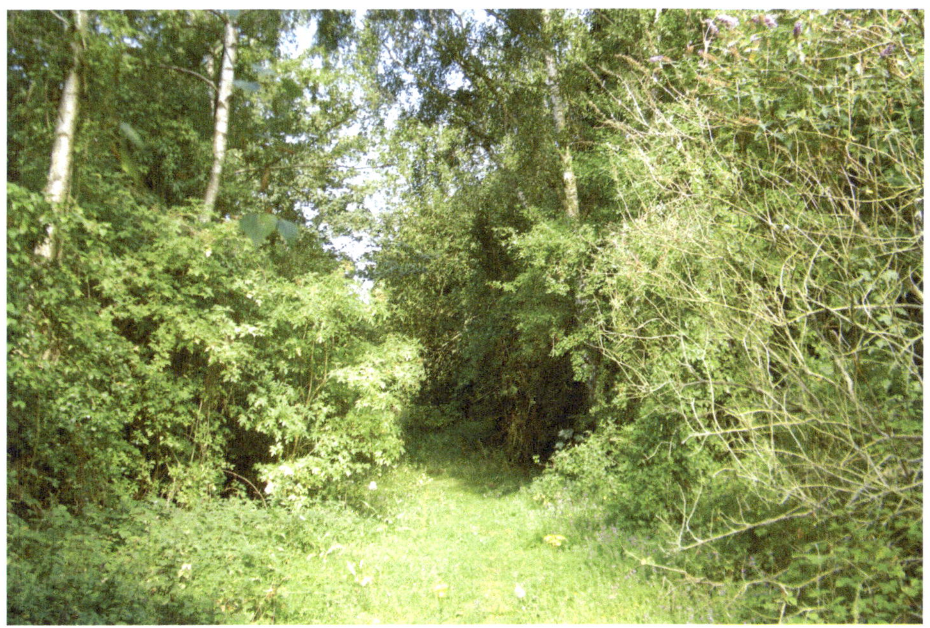

Standing among the trees today, the branch platform is hidden away behind the trees on the left. For many years, the ash and clinker ballast helped keep the weeds at bay. (Paul Lemon)

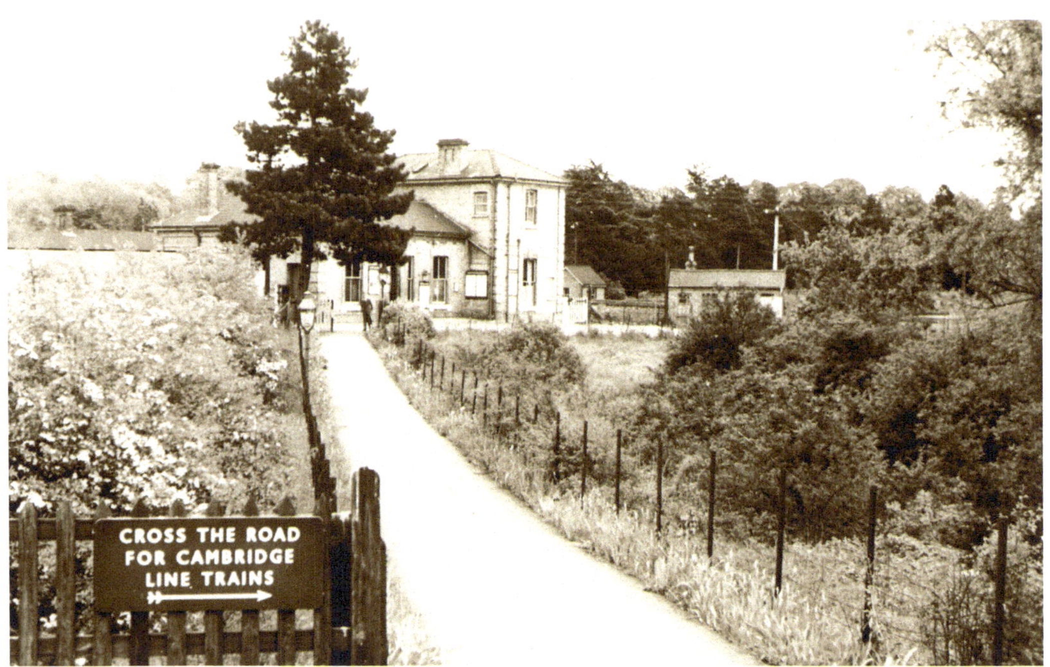

A view from the branch platform across the connecting footpath to the main station; the main station buildings were on the down platform at Bartlow. A simple waiting shelter was all that was provided on the branch platform, together with a couple of oil lamps to illuminate things on dark winter nights (H. C. Casserley)

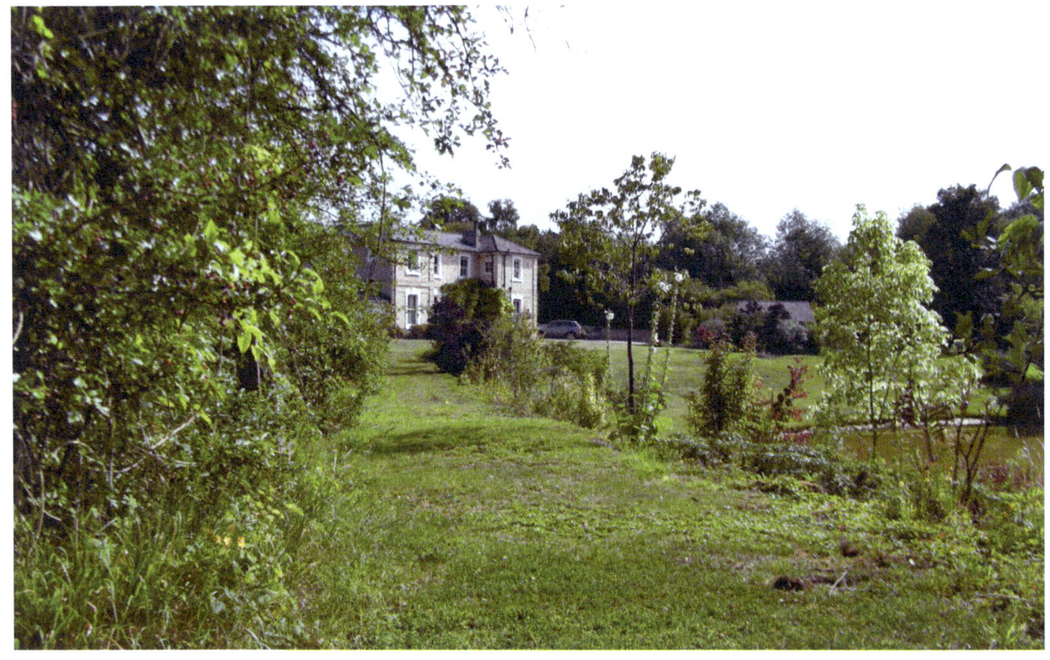

Today, the footpath still exists, albeit grassed over; the extended station buildings can clearly be seen. (Paul Lemon)

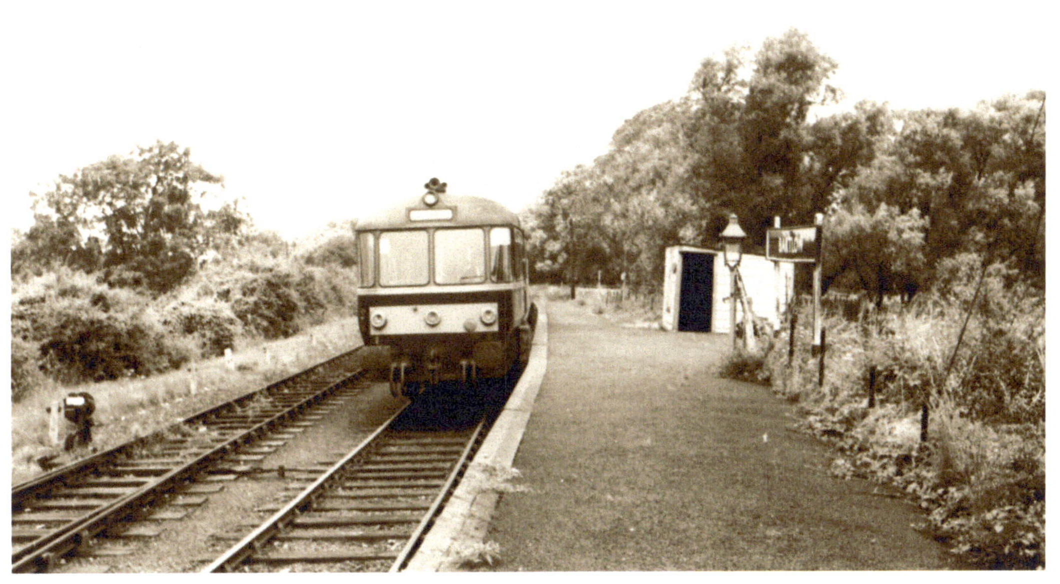

A Waggon und Maschinenbau four-wheeled diesel rail bus stands at Bartlow branch platform, waiting for any potential passengers and departure time in the spring of 1964, just a few short months before closure. (Stations UK)

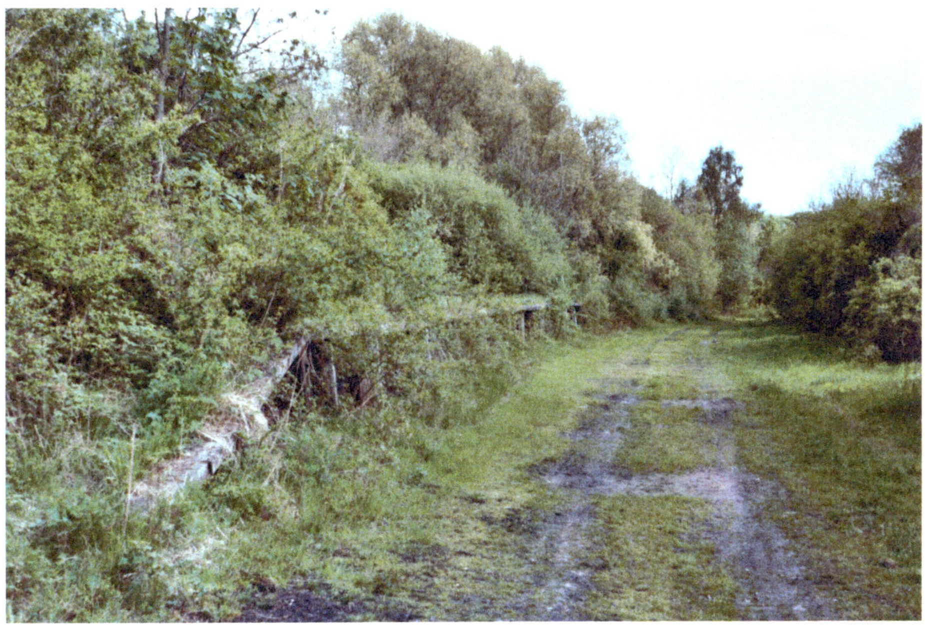

Nearly twenty years later, looking in the opposite direction, we see the remains of the branch platform heavily overgrown with bushes and trees. The track bed remains reasonably clear, as it was used at this time by the local farmers as an access to their fields. (Andy T. Wallis)

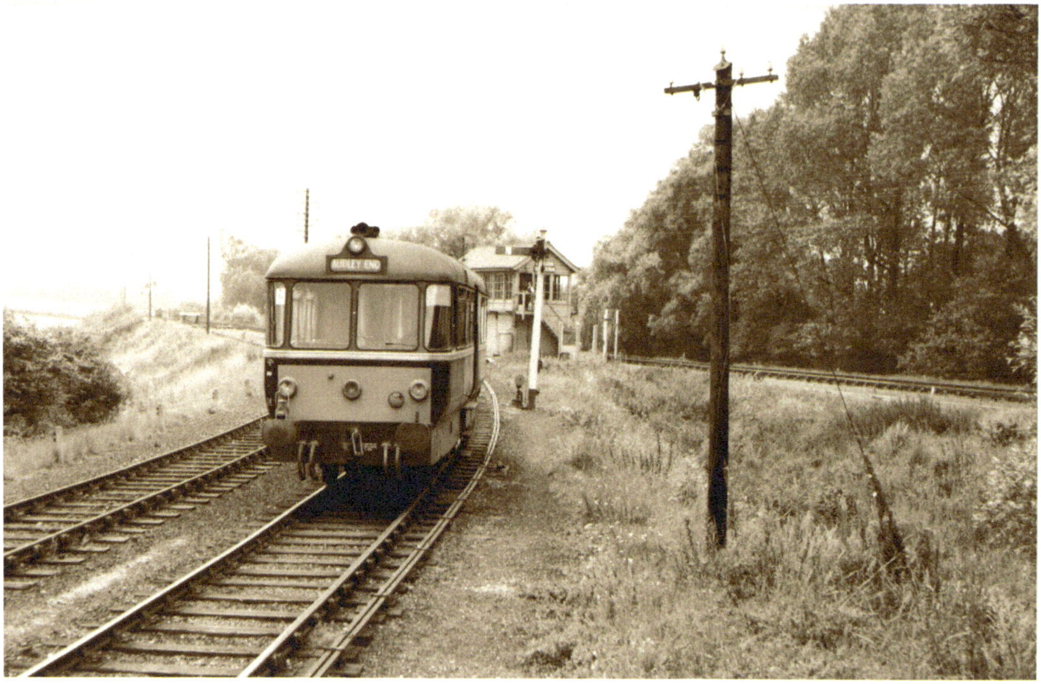

During the rail bus era, two services a day were extended from Bartlow through to Haverhill. Here we see one of the services arriving at the branch platform at Bartlow, having just reversed off the main Stour Valley line. (Dr I. C. Allen/Transport Treasury)

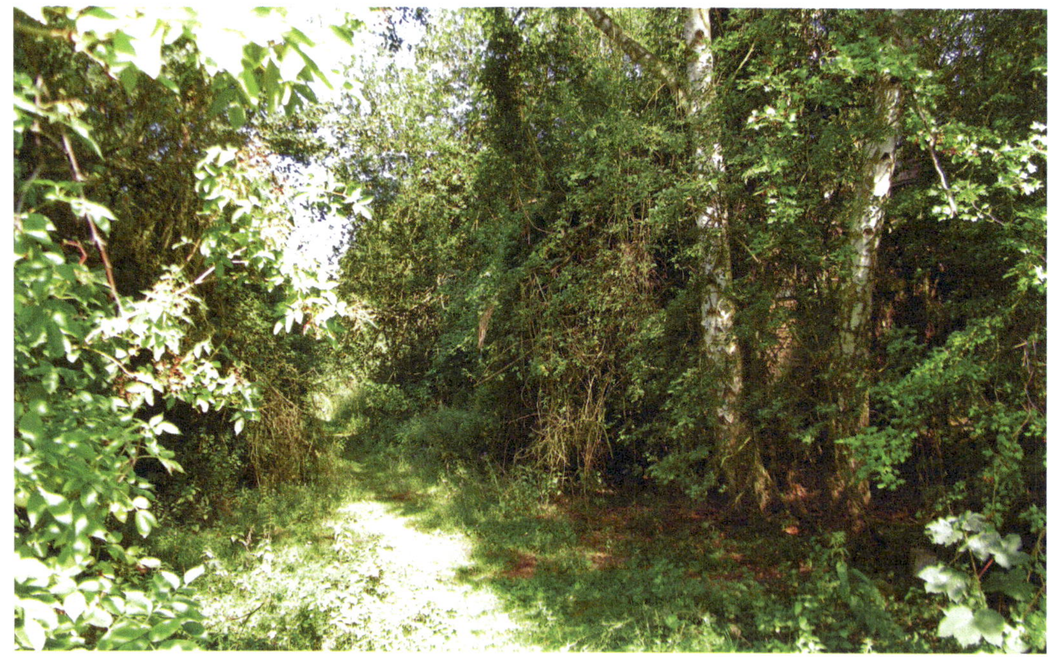

The whole area today has been taken over by trees; the left hand edge of the formation can still be seen under the bushes in the lower view. (Paul Lemon)

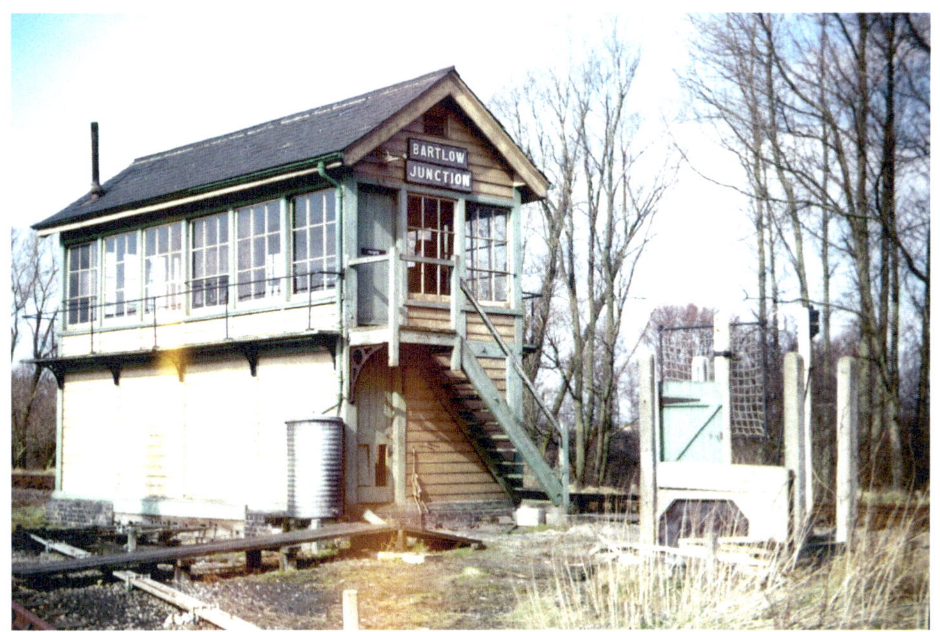

A close-up of Bartlow Junction signal box as seen in 1967, shortly after it had closed; the signal box was situated in the gap between the branch and main line and was equipped with a Saxby & Farmer thirty-eight (later thirty-nine) lever frame with thirty working and eight spare levers, later thirty-three working and six spare after the station signal box was abolished. (N. L. Cadge)

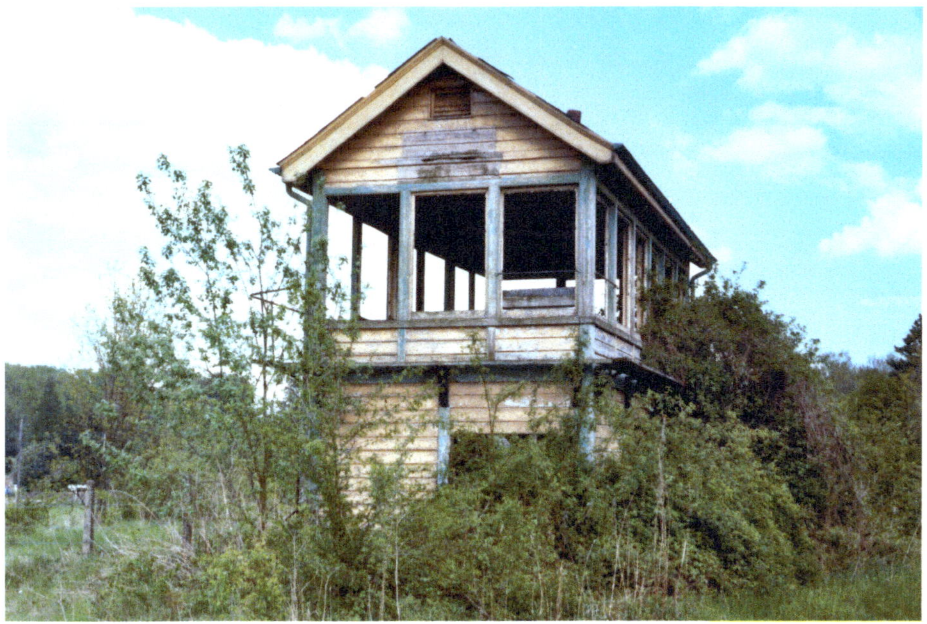

The derelict signal box survived for many years after closure, and by the late 1980s it was completed hidden by trees and shrubs; this view was taken in 1983. The shell lasted well into the 2000s, but finally the roof collapsed into the interior of the building. (Andy T. Wallis)

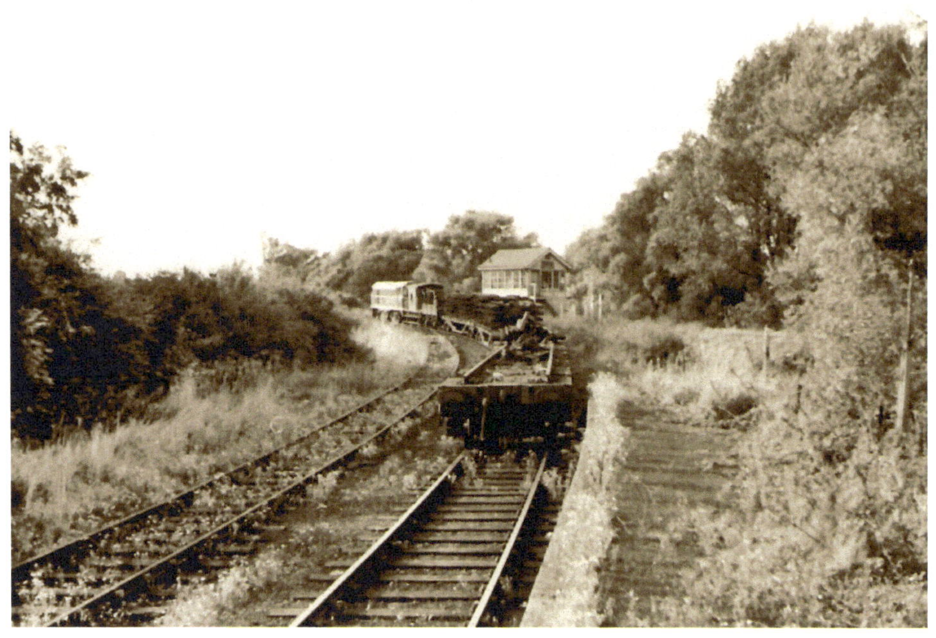

During the summer of 1968, the branch track was lifted by contractors and we see a Class 31 diesel and a demolition train leaving the branch with another load of rails and sleepers in the high summer of that year. After three and a half years, nature was already reclaiming the old branch platform. (Brian Barham)

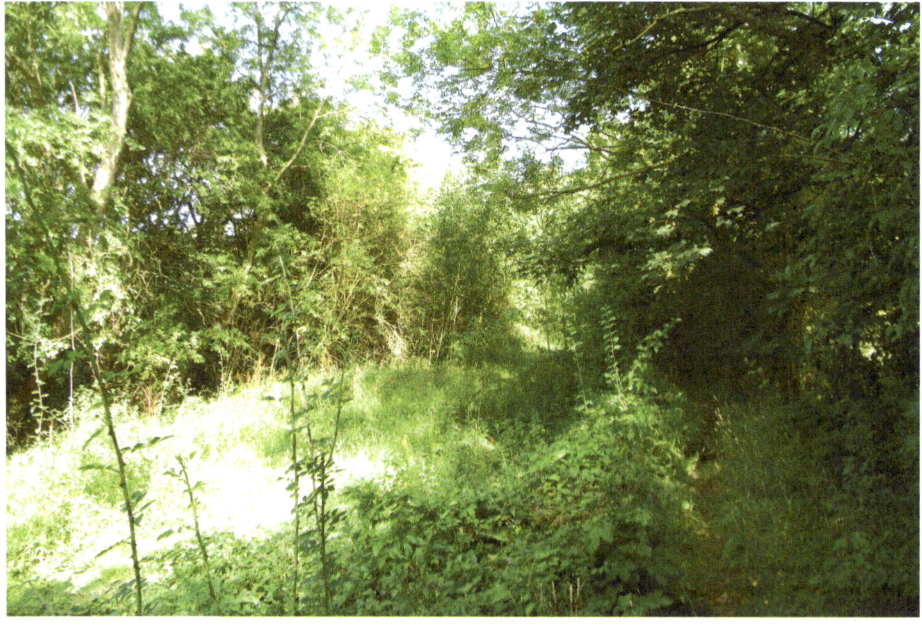

Standing in the same position, looking towards the junction, the trees dominate the view. The raised part of the platform still exists, although the wooden retaining walls have mostly rotted away. (Paul Lemon)

Ashdon Halt

Right: Locomotive N7 69690 makes a spirited start away from Ashdon Halt in the late 1950s; these locomotives had replaced the earlier GER/LNER G5 tank engines and their old rolling stock on the branch in October 1956. In 1958, the N7s and their Gresley push/pull sets started working through to Haverhill. The halt was not that near to the hamlet it was supposed to serve, being reached by a narrow lane from the main road. (G. E. Buncombe)

Below: On 9 February 2007, some fifty years after the previous picture, the track bed is being used as a farmer's access. The platform still exists, with the old carriage body located on it, although in a dilapidated state. (Paul Lemon)

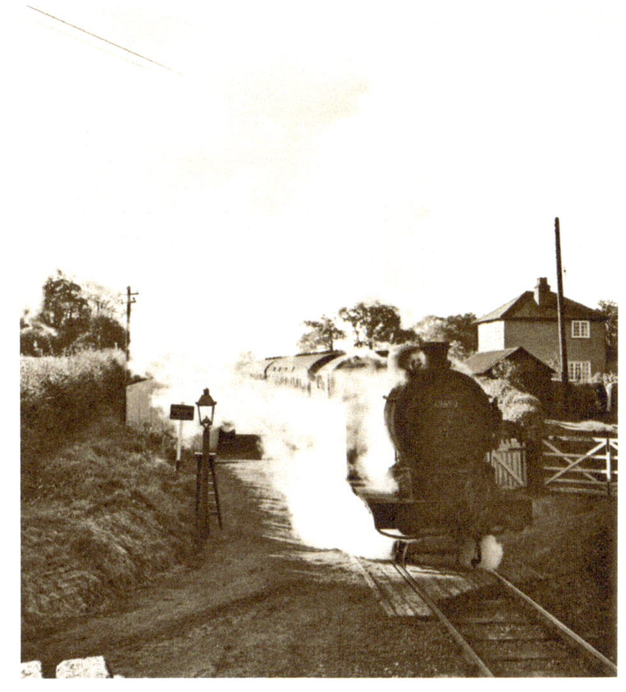

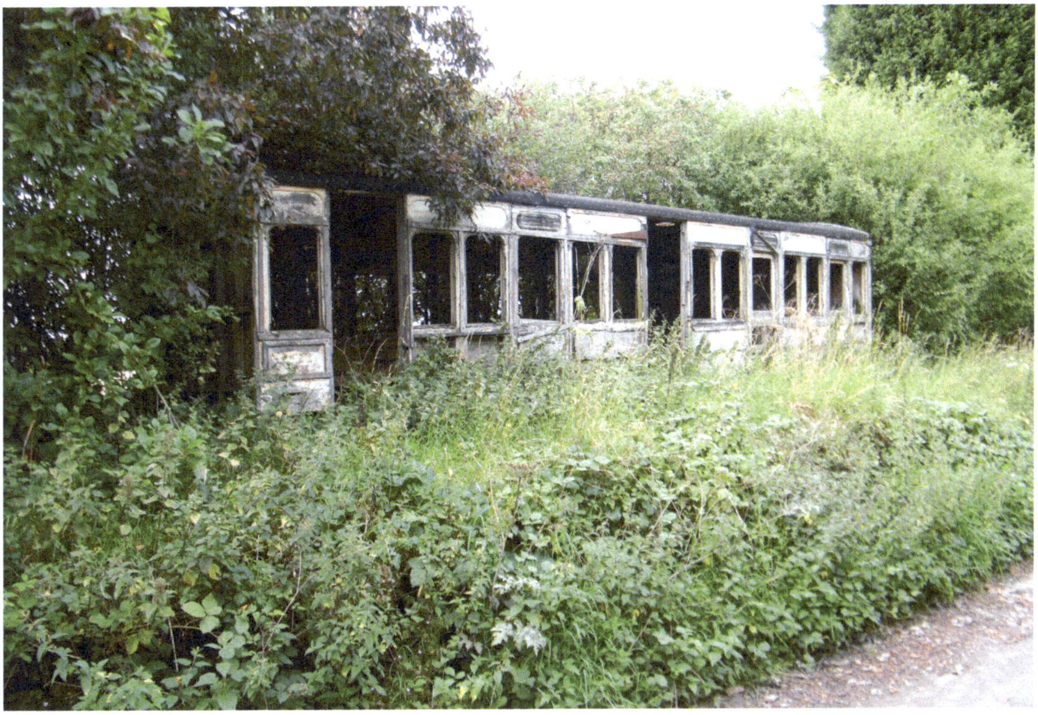

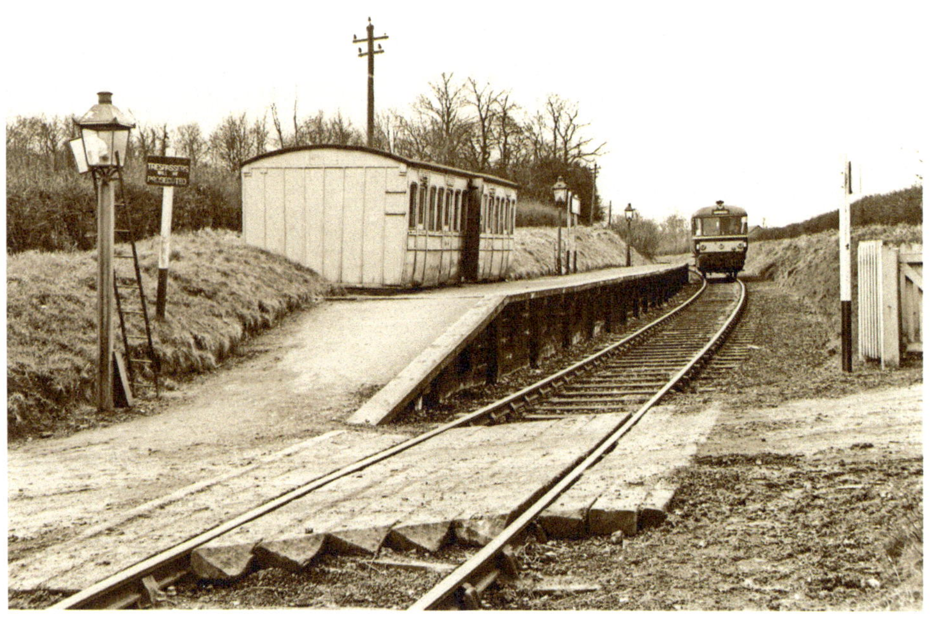

On 7 July 1958, diesel rail buses replaced the steam push/pull working on the branch. Five vehicles built by the German firm Waggon und Maschinenbau were allocated to this and other branches. A rail bus is seen arriving at Ashdon Halt on route to Bartlow and Haverhill. (G. E. Buncombe)

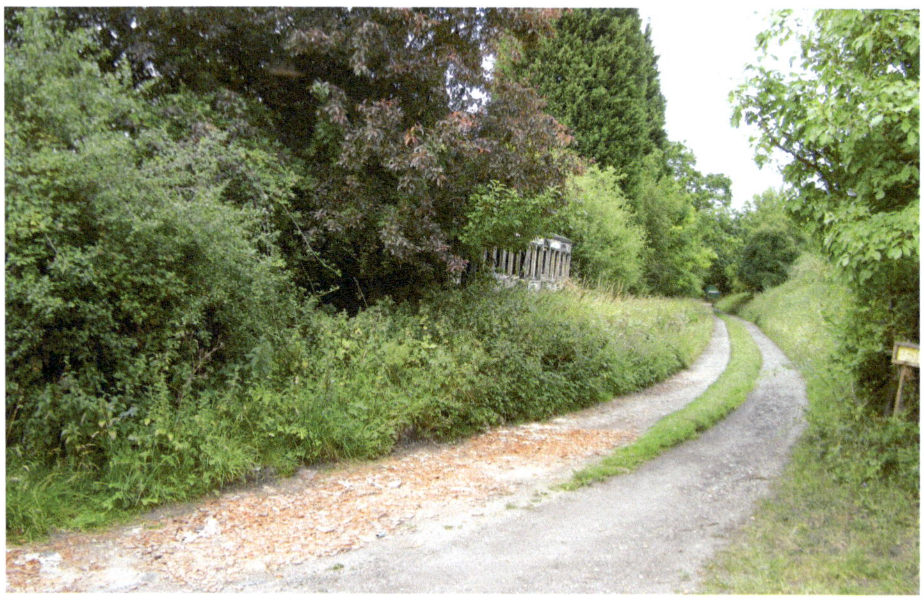

A near-replica of the above picture shows the former track bed curving and climbing away from the old halt, with the derelict coach body parked on it among the trees and shrubs. (Paul Lemon)

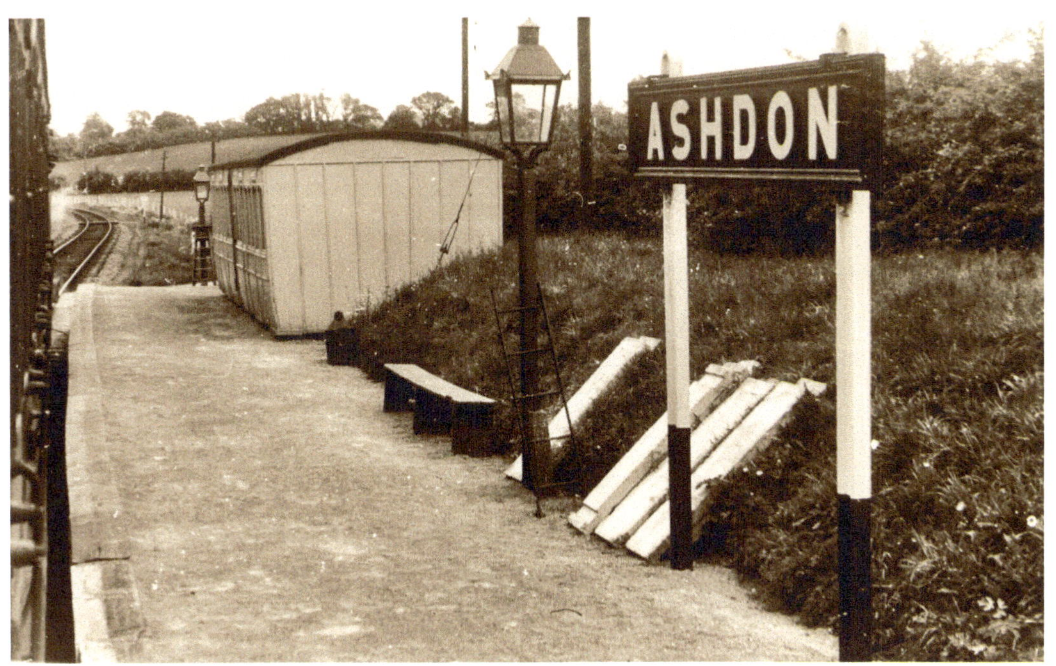

A neat and tidy Ashdon Halt viewed from a train window on 26 May 1956. The halt was of simple construction, with a timber face and edge with ash and clinker surface. Accommodation was provided using an old grounded coach body. Two oil lamps and a name board completed the layout. (R. C. Casserley)

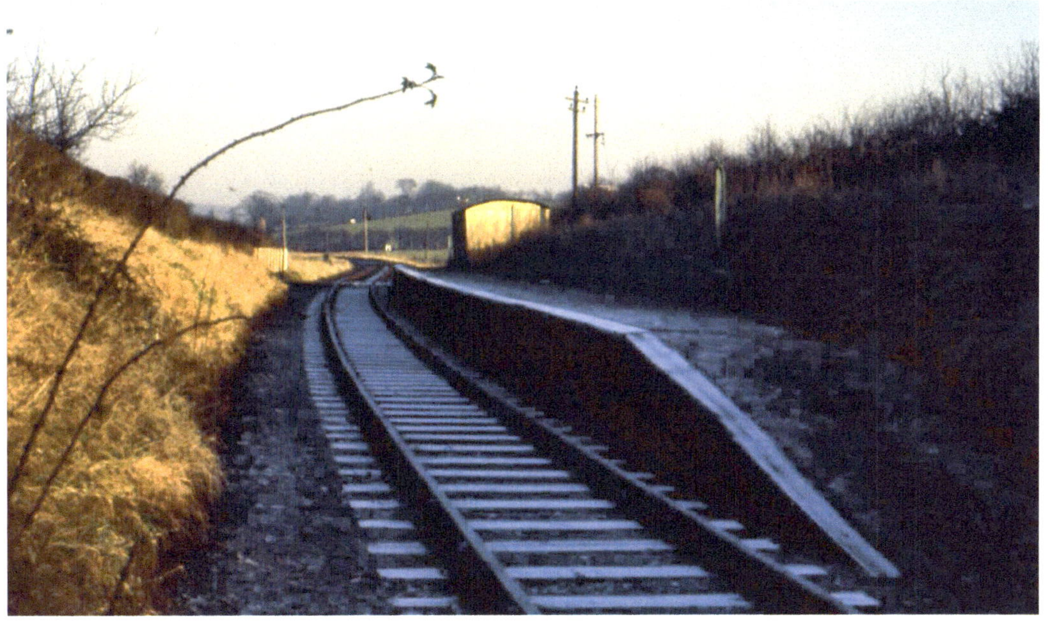

On a bright, cold December day in 1965, the line was still intact, having closed completely a year before. It was to be another eighteen months before the scrap man started to dismantle the line. (D. J. Plyer)

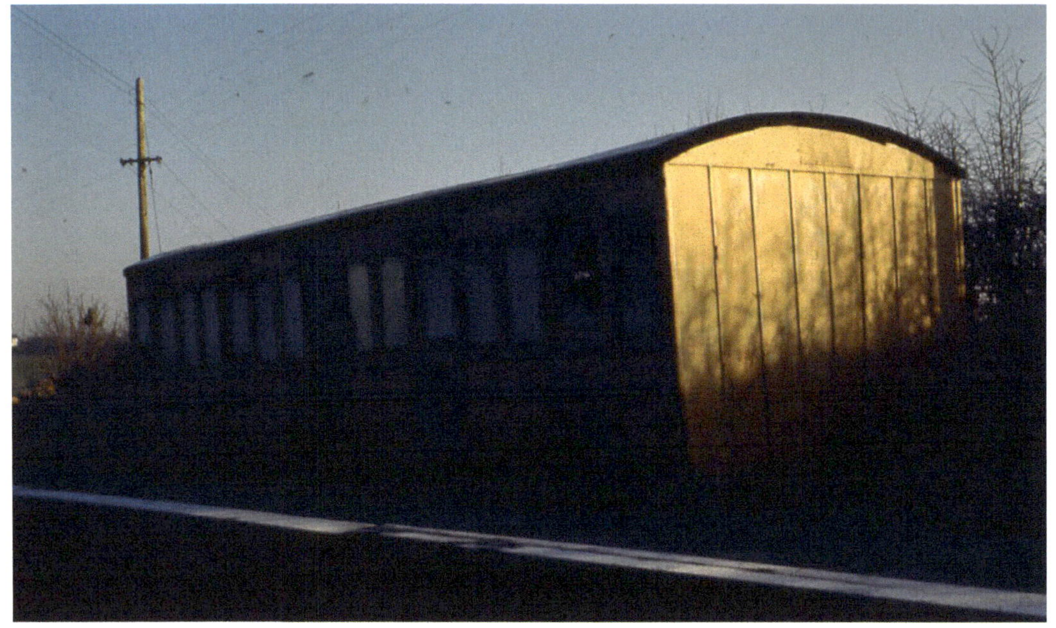

A close-up of the old Great Eastern Railway grounded coach body used as passenger waiting accommodation at Ashdon, as seen on 26 December 1965, a year after the line had closed completely. (D. J. Plyer)

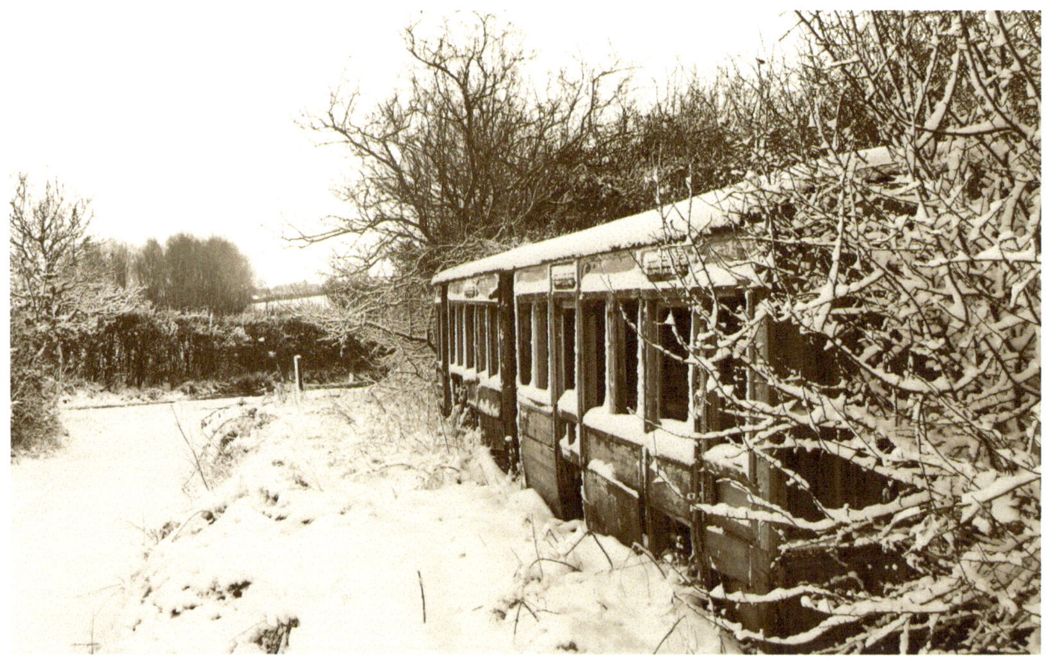

Some forty-four years later, in snowy conditions, we see the old coach body still in situ, but minus all the glass in its windows; vegetation has completely taken over the old platform. The track bed was in use as an access road; beyond the hedge, the track bed has been ploughed into the surrounding farmland. (T. Stephens)

Acrow Halt

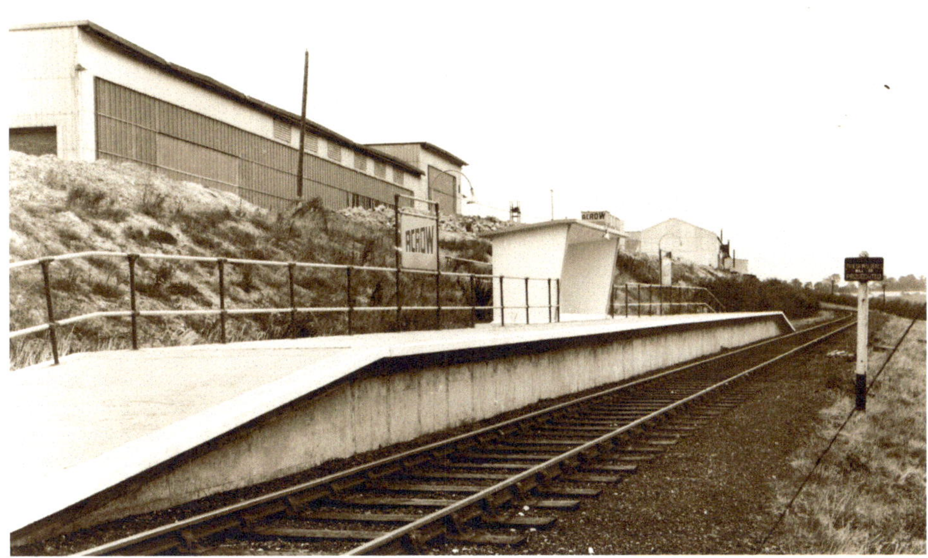

Acrow Halt was purpose-built by the adjacent engineering company for use by its employees; the platform and waiting shelter were constructed from concrete. The halt opened on 25 March 1957 and closed with the withdrawal of the passenger service on 7 September 1964. (Lens of Sutton Association)

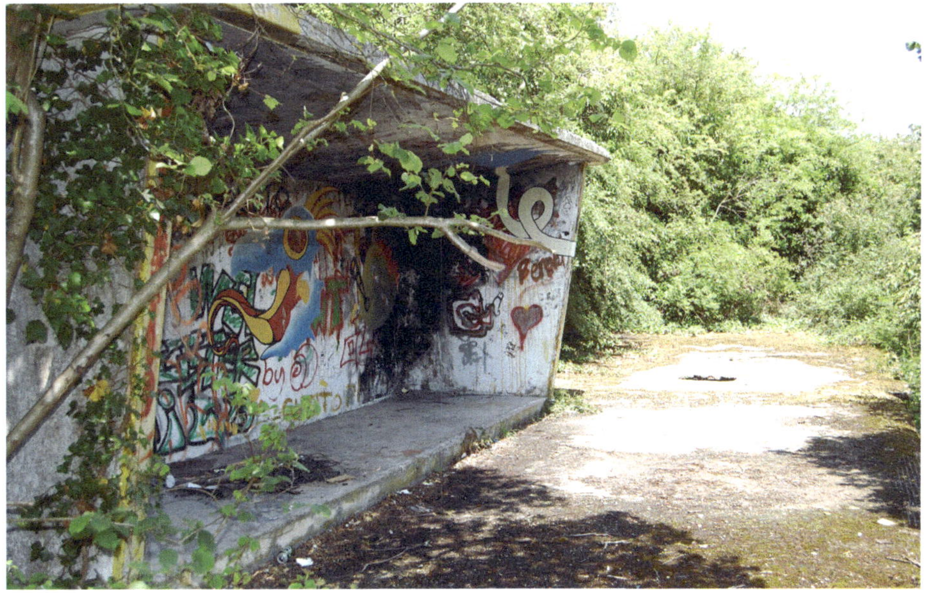

Today, among the trees and bushes, the waiting shelter and platform still exist, obviously used by the local 'art brigade' as a practice site. (Ray Bishop)

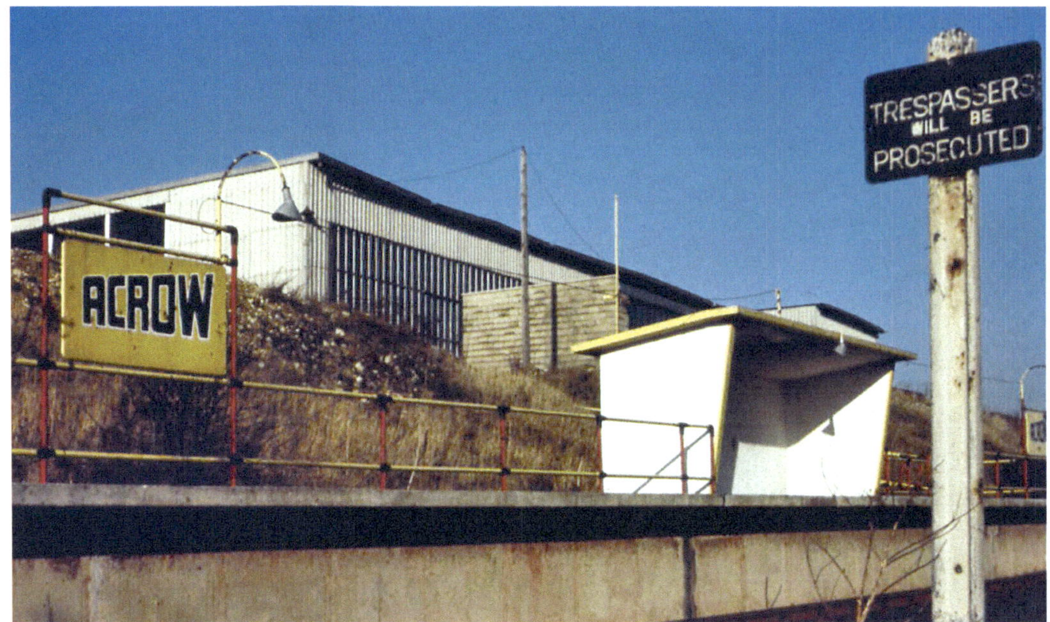

A rare colour photograph of Acrow Halt taken on 26 December 1965, a year after the line had closed completely. The concrete waiting shelter can be clearly seen, with the Acrow's Engineering works in the background, as can the 'Trespassers will be Prosecuted' sign in the foreground. Freight trains had ceased to run some twelve months earlier and it would be another thirty months before the demolition trains commenced their task. (D. J. Plyer)

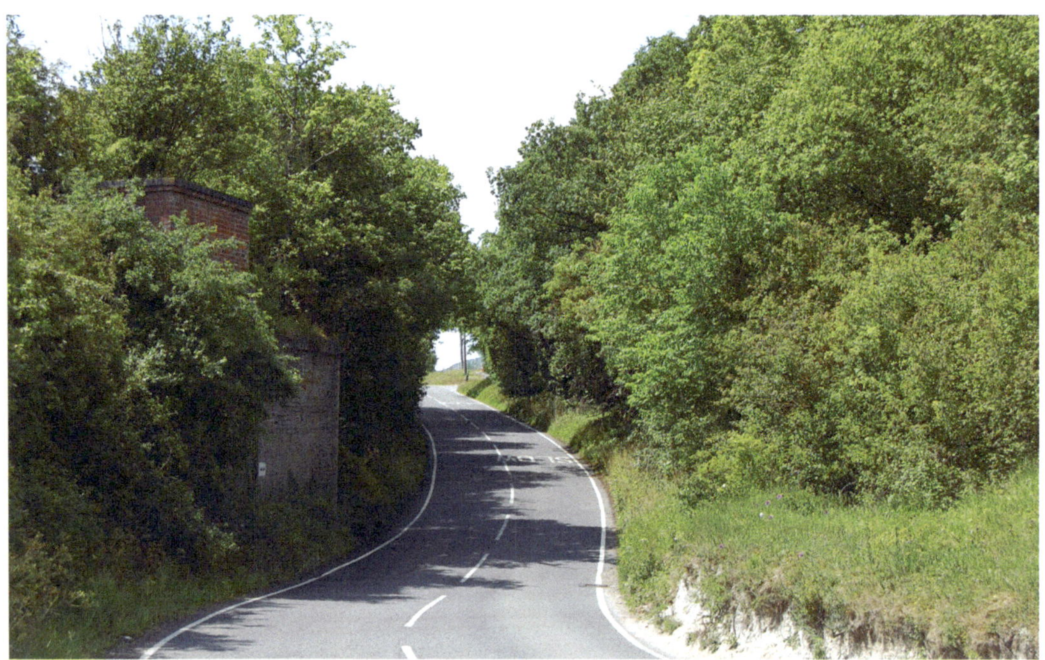

Today, the above view is totally obscured by trees, so we see the remaining bridge abutment. The halt was on the right, in among the trees. (Ray Bishop)

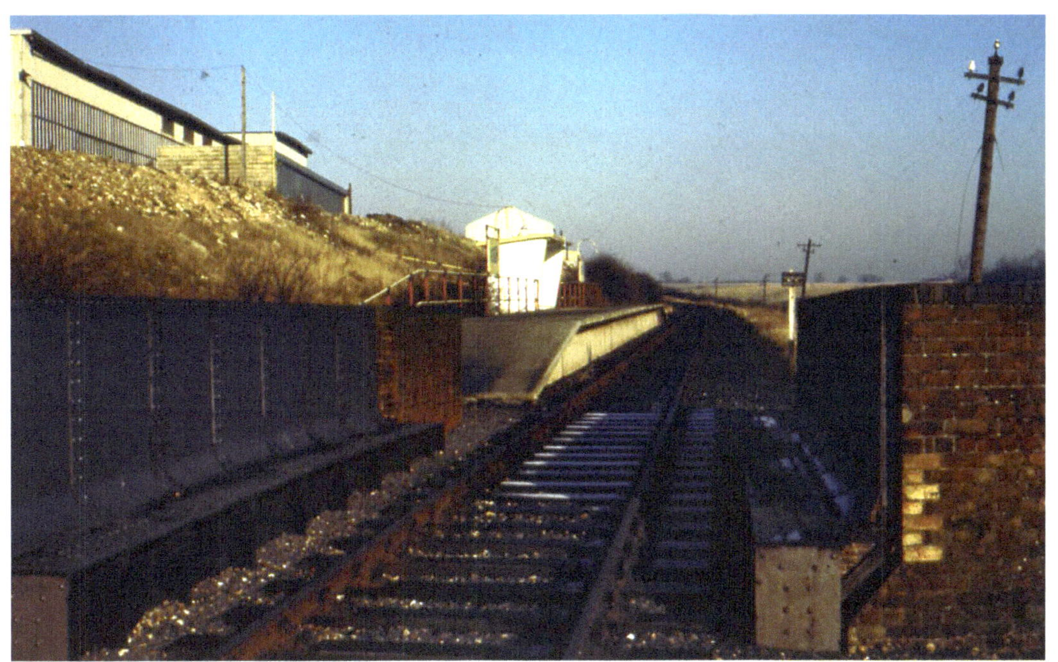

Acrow Halt, viewed from the other side of Ashdon Road bridge; the track by this time was well rusted, having not seen a train for some twelve months. A private siding serving the works trailed into the single line on the Bartlow side of the halt; at this point the line was climbing a gradient of 1 in 75. (D. J. Plyer)

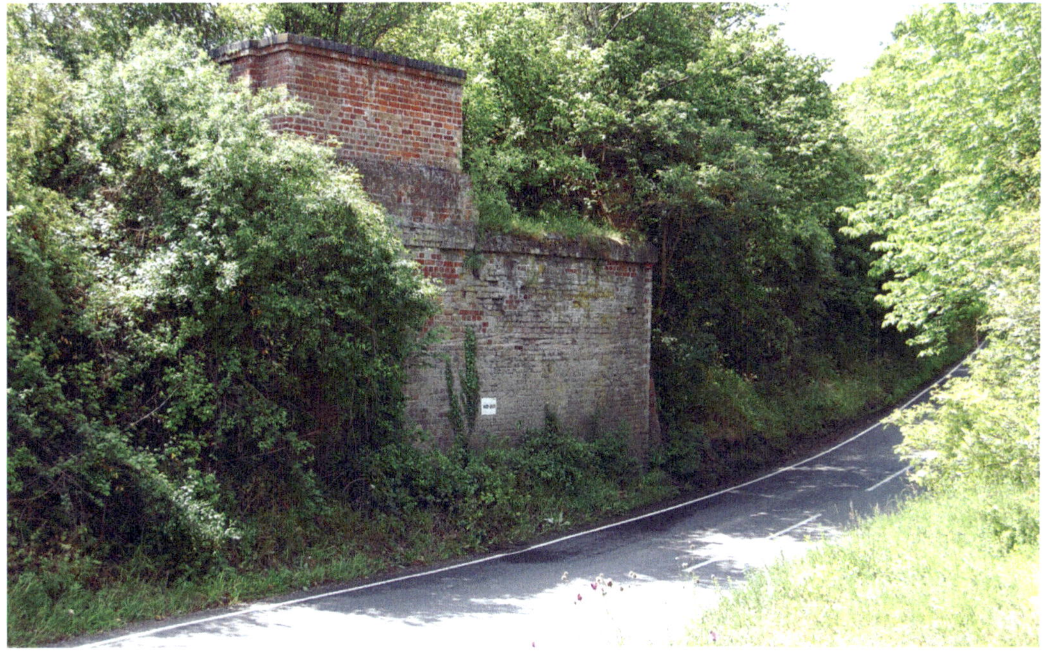

A close-up of the abutment which is all that remains of the bridge mentioned above. (Ray Bishop)

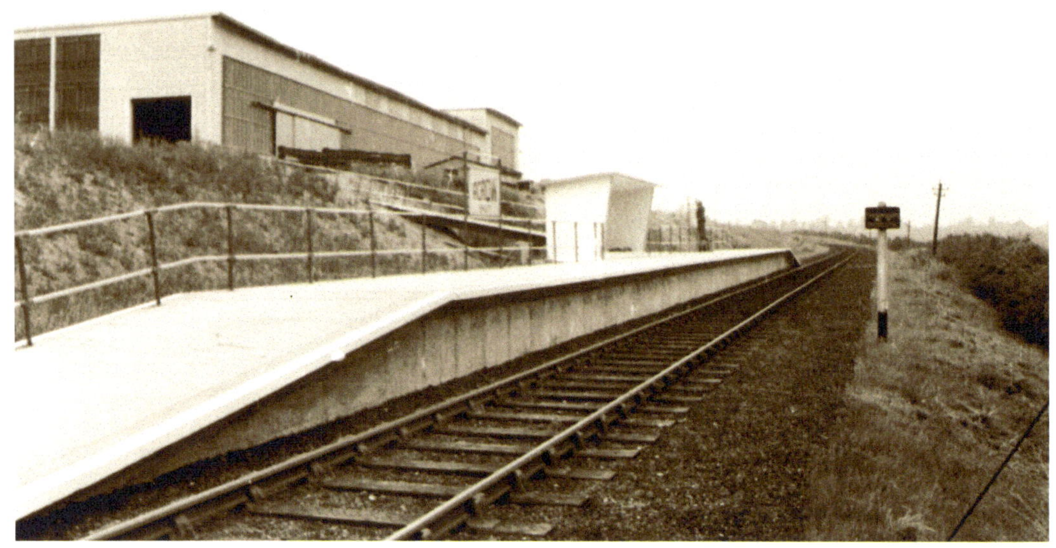

Another view of the halt taken in 1958, this time from the line side, looking up the gradient towards Bartlow; the use of concrete in the construction gives the halt a nice, clean appearance. (Stations UK)

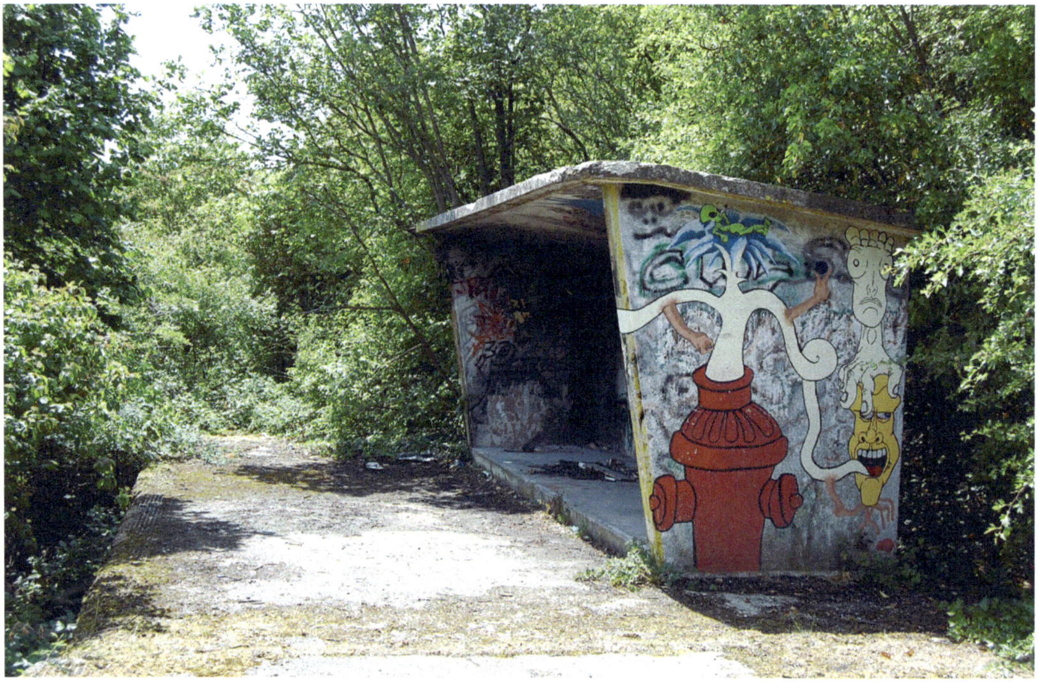

Today, with care, one can stand on the crumbling remains of the old platform; in this view, looking towards Saffron Walden, the local graffiti artists have been hard at work. (Ray Bishop)

Saffron Walden

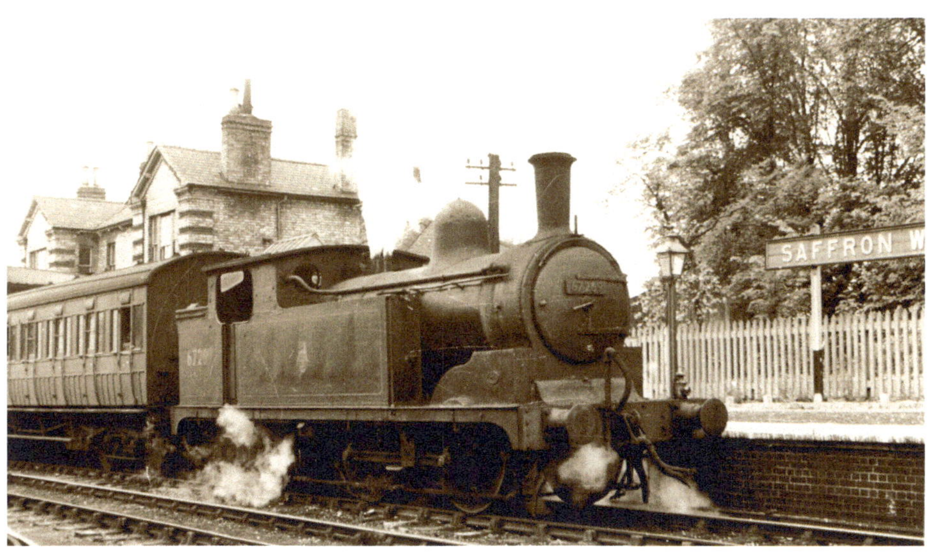

Originally designated North Eastern Class 'O' and designed by Wilson Worsdell, these 0-4-4 tank engines eventually migrated south under the LNER and were designated Class G5 and successfully worked the Saffron Walden branch, working from July 1951, when push/pull working was introduced on the branch. Locomotive 67269 is seen waiting to depart from Saffron Walden in May 1956. (R. M. Casserley)

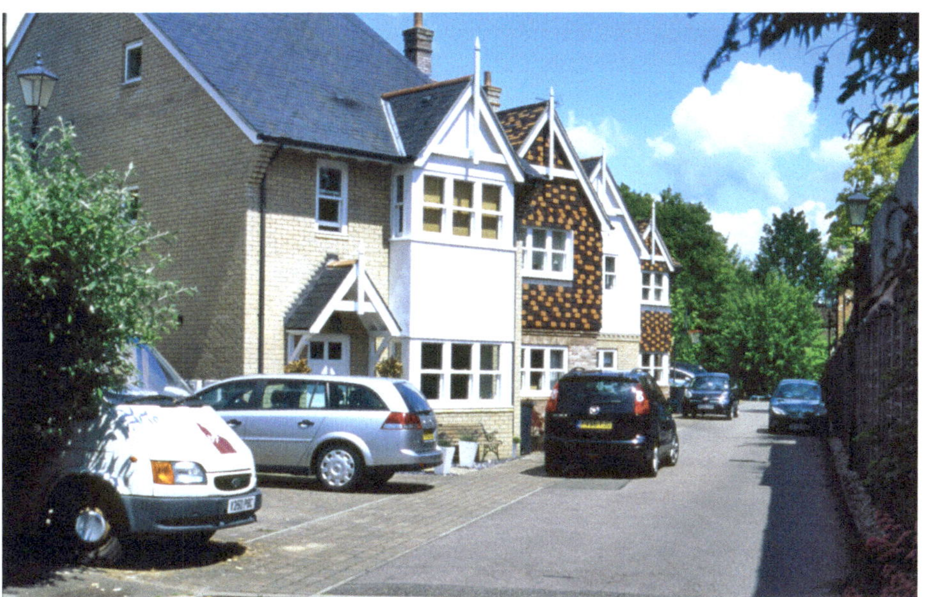

Today, the whole station site has been given over to a new housing development; previously the station site had been used as a car sales and service area. (Ray Bishop)

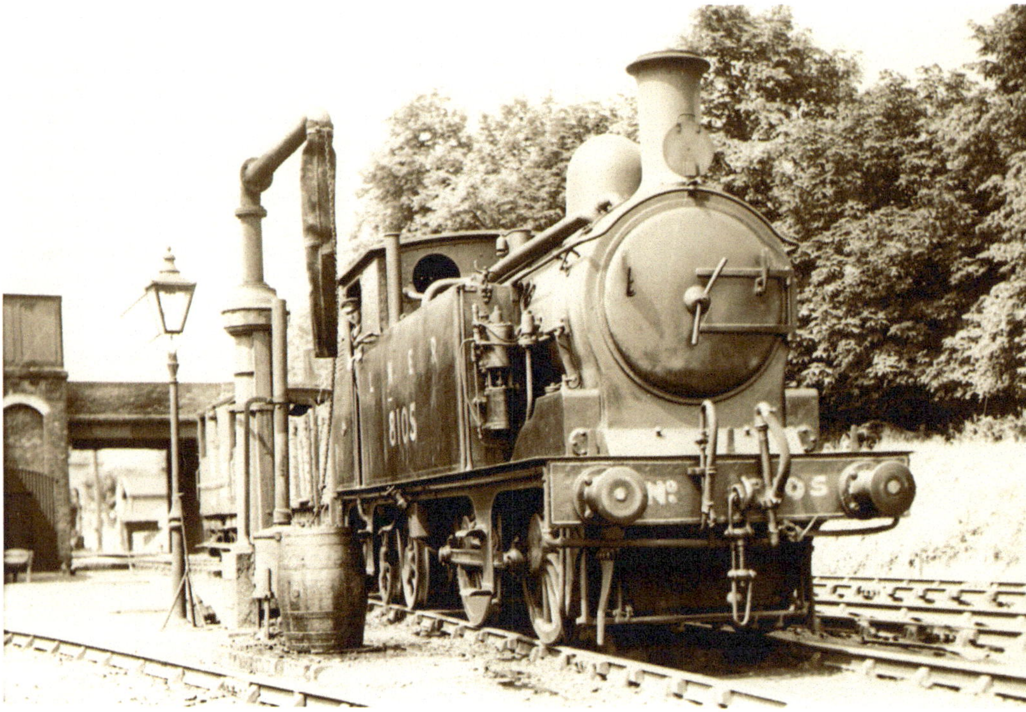

Locomotive Class G4 number 8105 shunting coal for the loco department at Saffron Walden on 27 June 1936; the G4s took over the branch workings from 1928, displacing the unpopular F4 and F5 2-4-2 tanks. (H. C. Casserley)

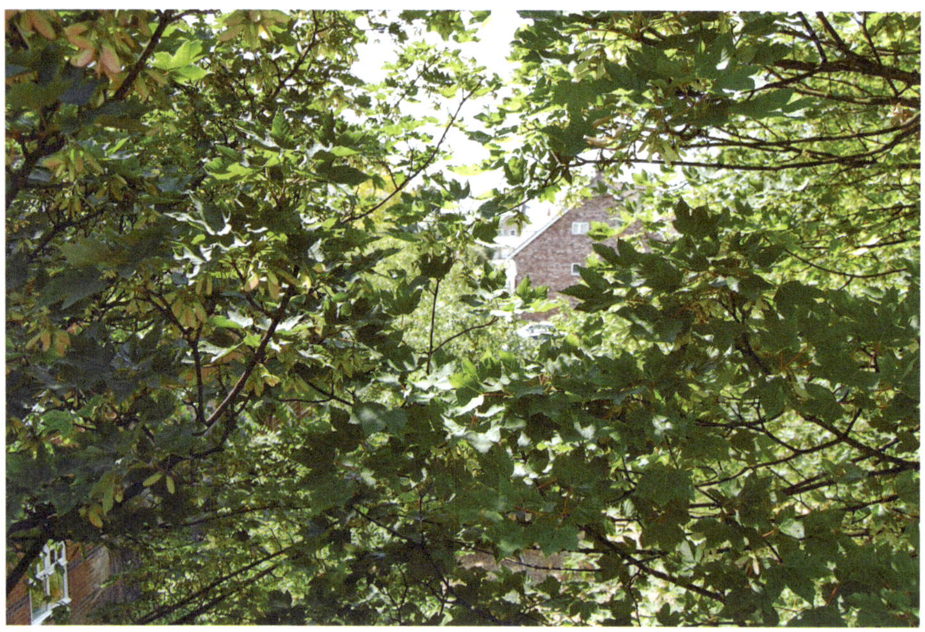

Due to access not being available, this view is taken from the bridge seen in the upper view, looking through the blanket of trees at the new housing development. (Ray Bishop)

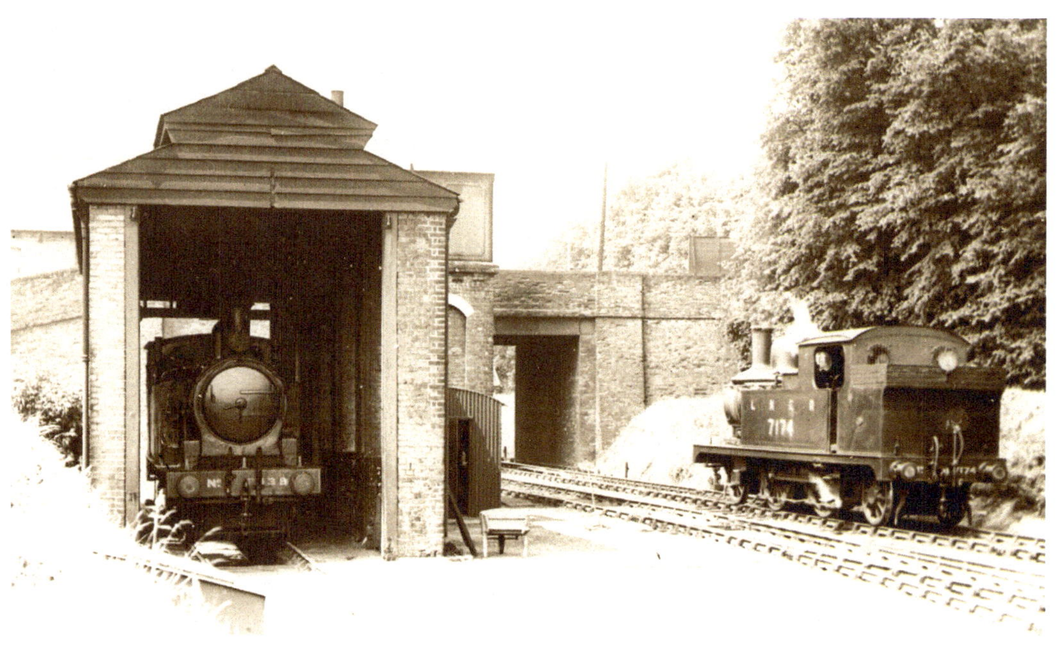

Locomotive G4 8139 is seen in the shed while locomotive F4 7174 passes light engine towards the station. The G4s were withdrawn in the late 1930s to eventually be replaced with Ivatt-class C12 4-4-2 tank engines. Eventually, four locomotives of this class were allocated to the branch duties. (H. C. Casserley)

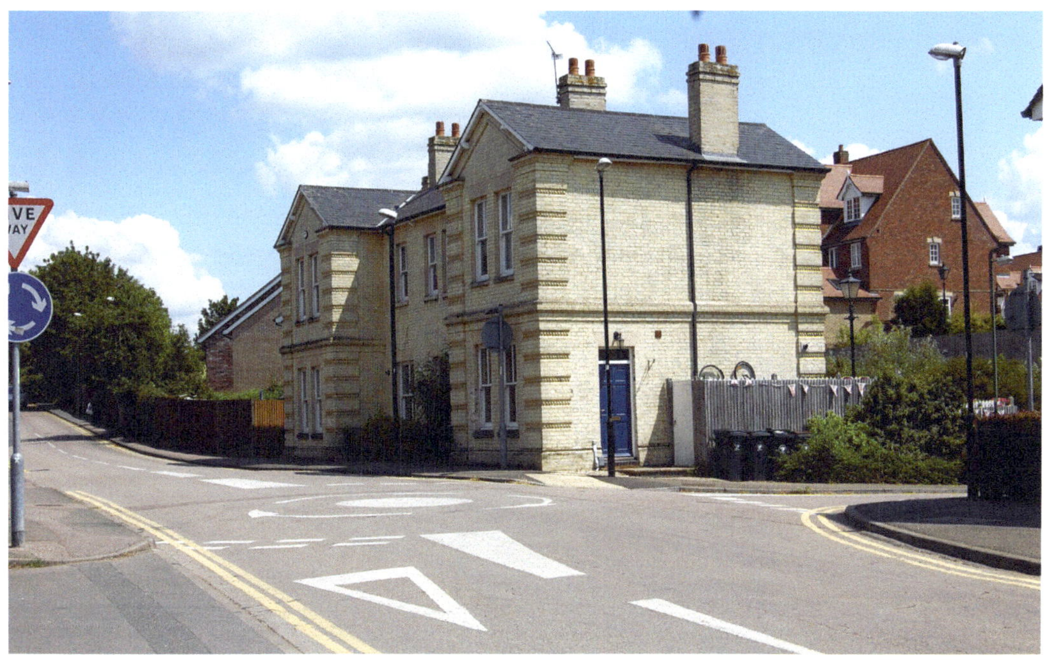

As an alternative to another picture of trees, this view is of the station buildings, taken from the access road. A new roadway was created to serve the new houses – it is seen to the right of the main buildings. (Ray Bishop)

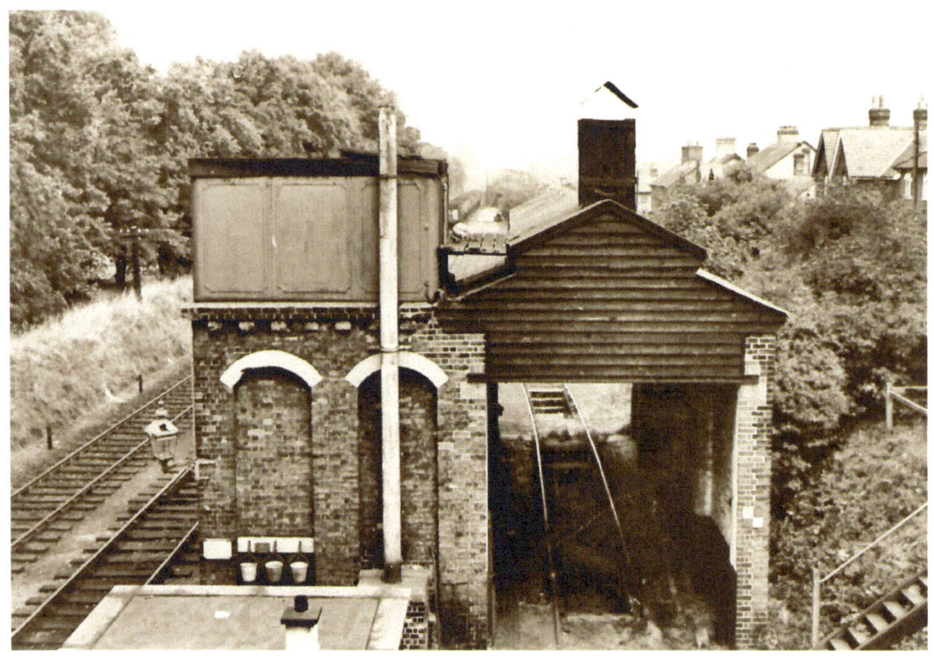

Saffron Walden locomotive shed and motive power depot buildings, including a large water tank, as seen from South Road bridge on 5 September 1964, the last Saturday that passenger trains ran over the branch. Diesel rail buses had replaced steam in 1957. (D. J. Plyer)

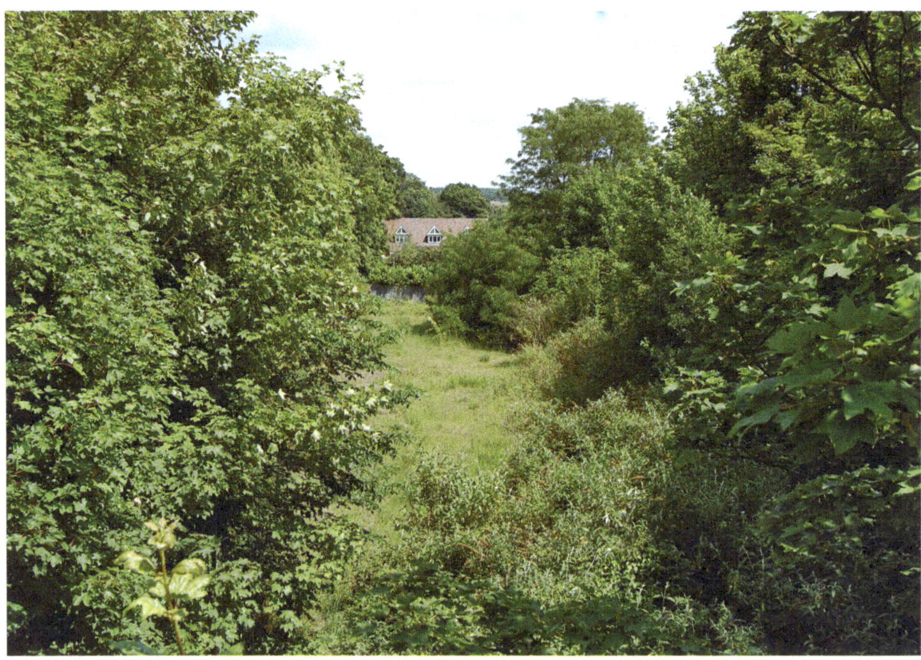

Today, the view is of trees and shrubs, with a house in the distance that appears to be built on the track bed, in contrast to the scene behind the cameraman, where all the available land has been turned over to housing. (Ray Bishop)

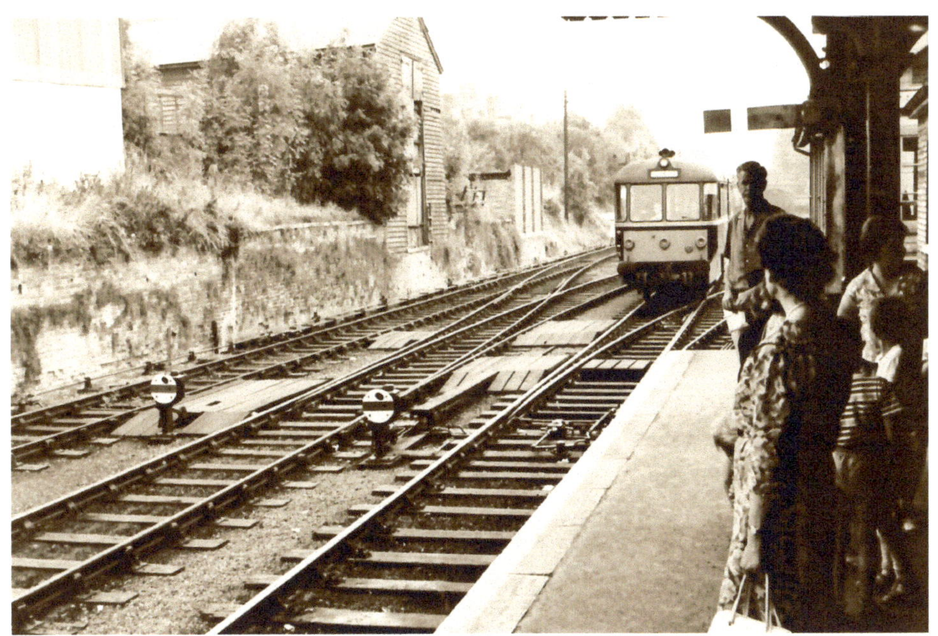

A diesel rail bus is seen arriving at Saffron Walden on the final Saturday of the passenger service. The branch passenger service had been doomed once the Beeching Report had been published on 27 March 1963. There followed the TUCC enquiry into the closure proposals and a date of 2 March 1964 was advertised by BR for closure, but this had to be postponed as the TUCC report had not been seen by the Minister. A new closure date was announced once ministerial permission was given to the closure on 21 May that year – this was 7 September 1964. (D. J. Plyer)

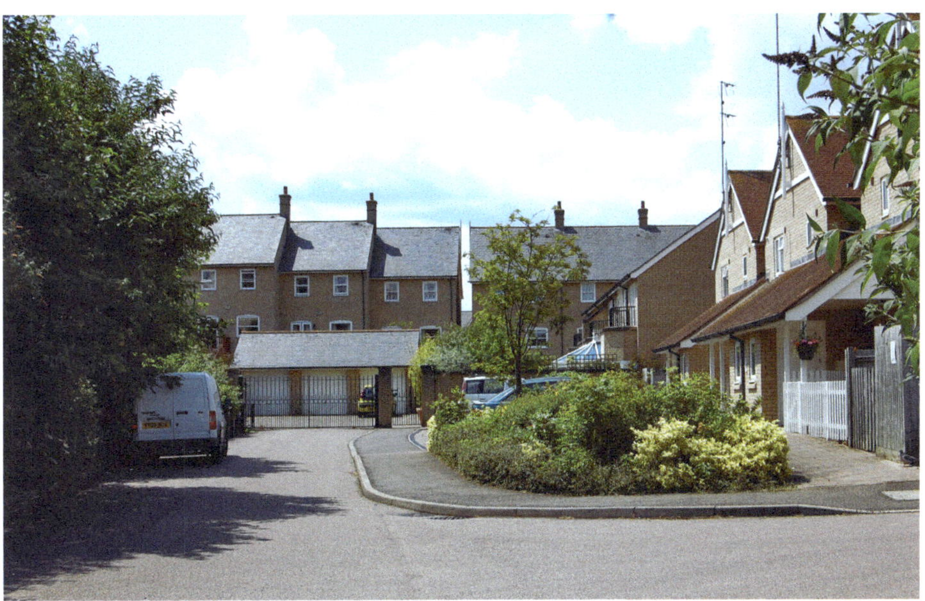

Today, a similar view is of houses; the station is off-camera to the right, and the wall to the left is common to both pictures. (Ray Bishop)

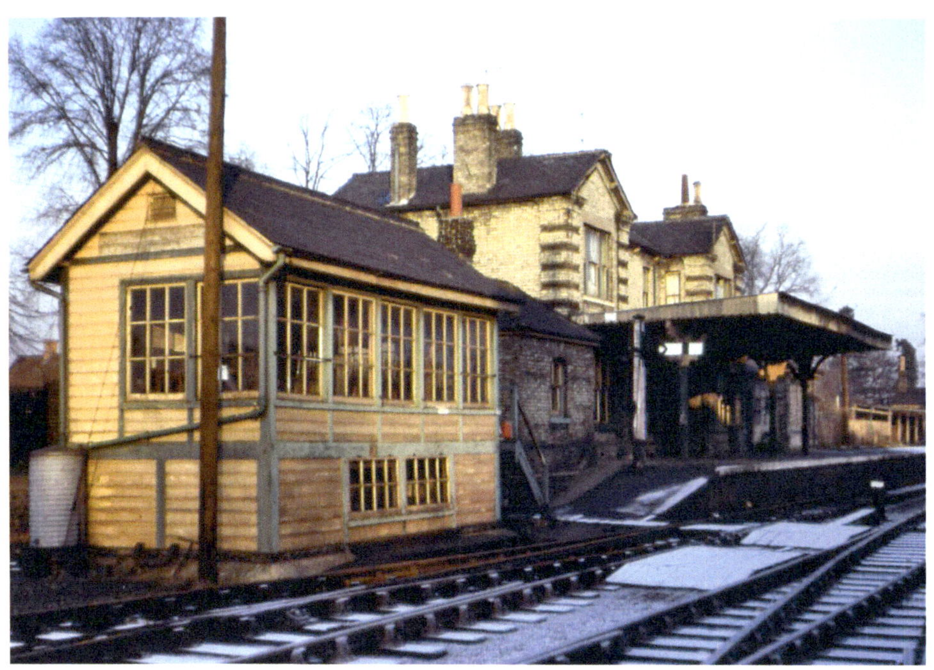

Close-up of the wooden station signal box and station buildings and canopy, as seen on 2 January 1965. The signal box contained a thirty-two-lever Saxby & Farmer lever frame with twenty-six working and six spare levers; the signal box remained open until the total closure of the line on 28 December 1964. (D. J. Plyer)

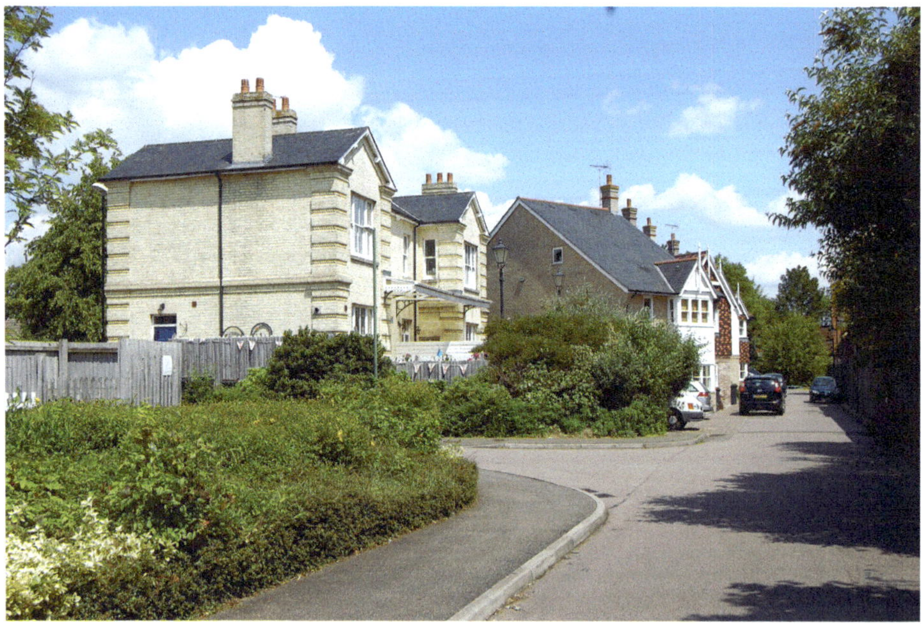

Some 46 years after the previous picture, the station buildings have been tastefully converted into private houses, minus a couple of chimneys and the original canopy. An access road to the houses now runs down part of the former track bed. (Ray Bishop)

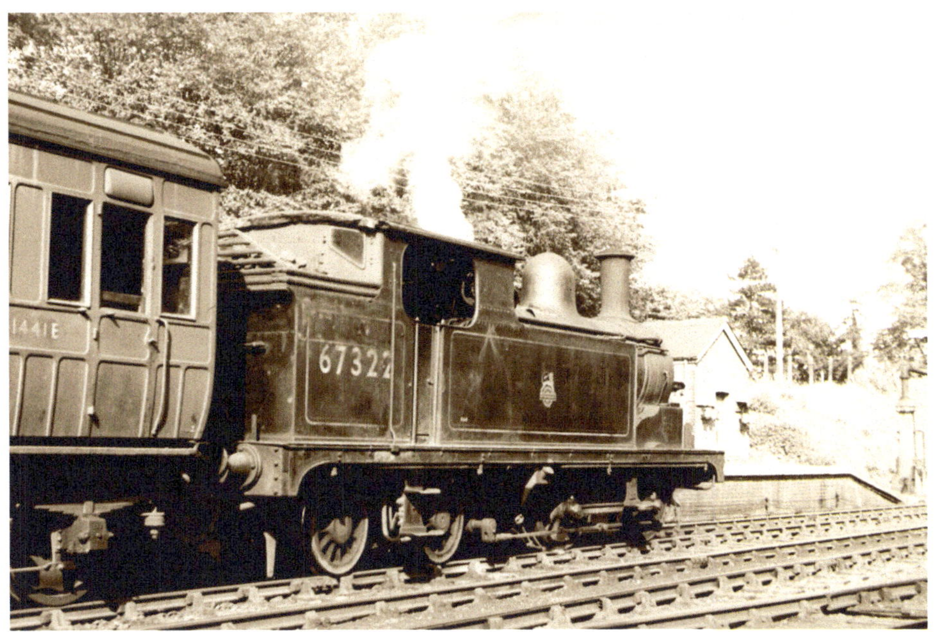

Locomotive Class G5 number 67322 stands at Saffron Walden a month before it was withdrawn and replaced with the 0-6-2 N7 tanks. The reign of the N7s was to be short, as they were replaced in turn by diesel rail buses from July 1958. However, they saw occasional service when the rail buses broke down, which was often in the early days. (H. C. Casserley)

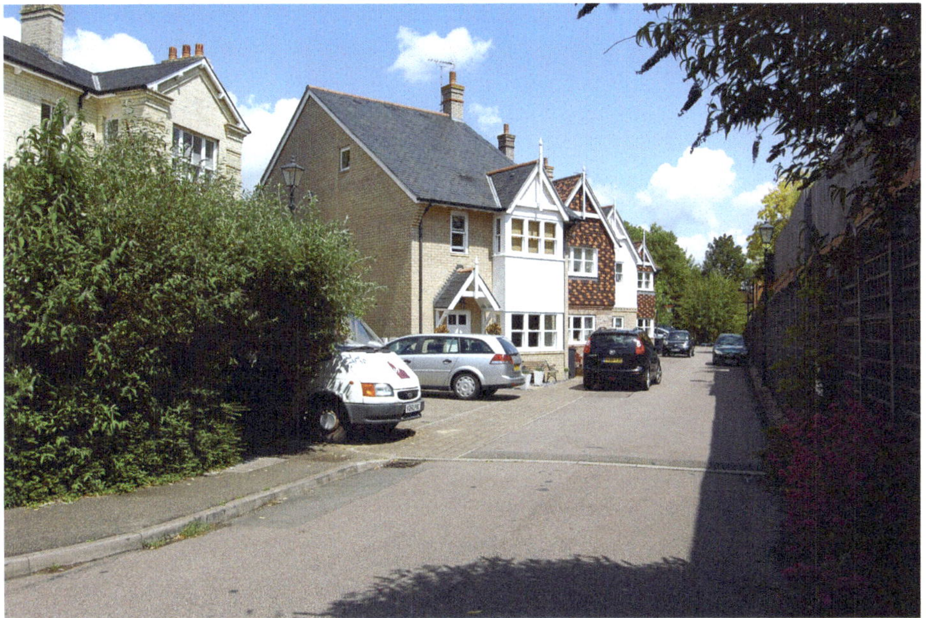

The house to the left of the car in the centre of the picture would be where the old platform was located, as seen in the picture above; on the left can be seen part of the old station building. (Ray Bishop)

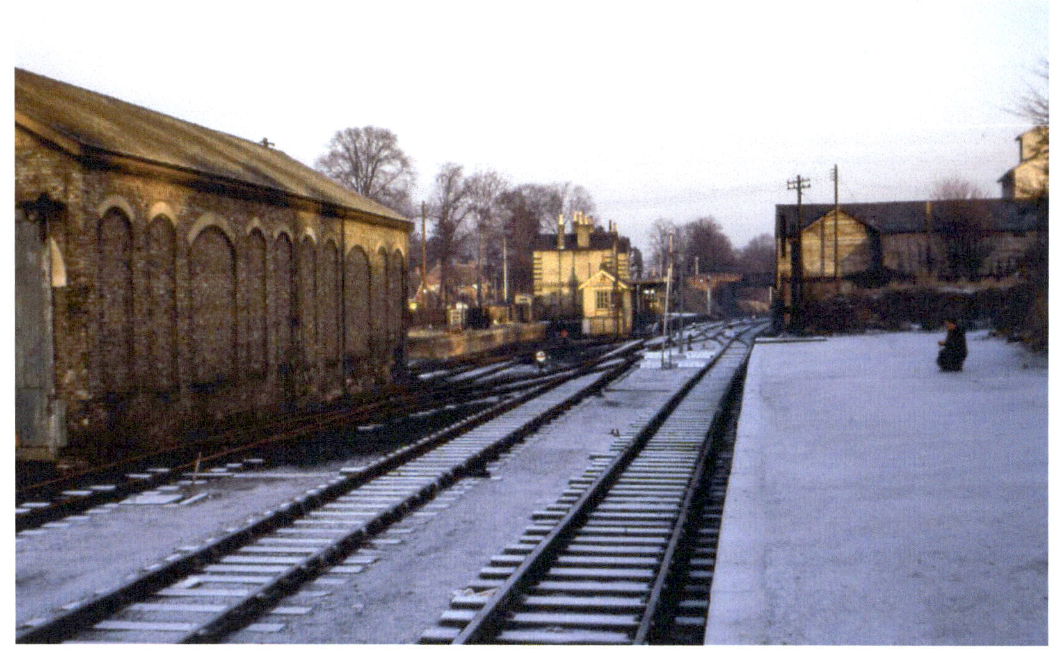

A sad scene at Saffron Walden after total closure, taken on 2 January 1965, just a few days after the last freight service had run. It was to be over three years before the track was recovered and the land sold off for other uses. (D. J. Plyer)

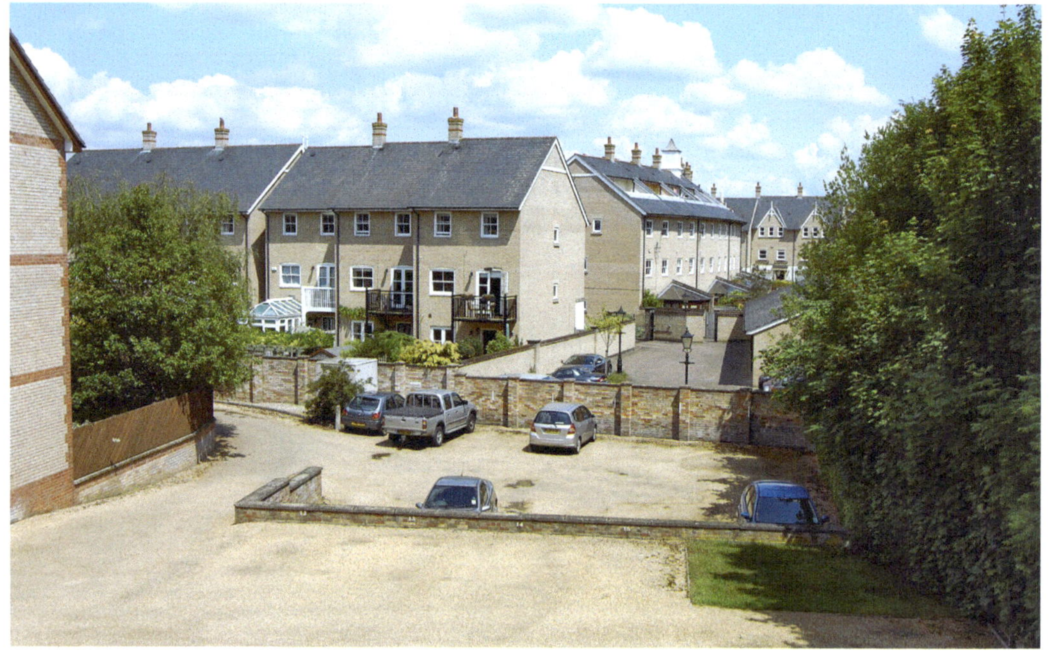

Today, the view from Debden Road Bridge shows the housing development occupying all of the former station and goods yard site; the former station buildings are hidden by the new houses. (Ray Bishop)

Audley End

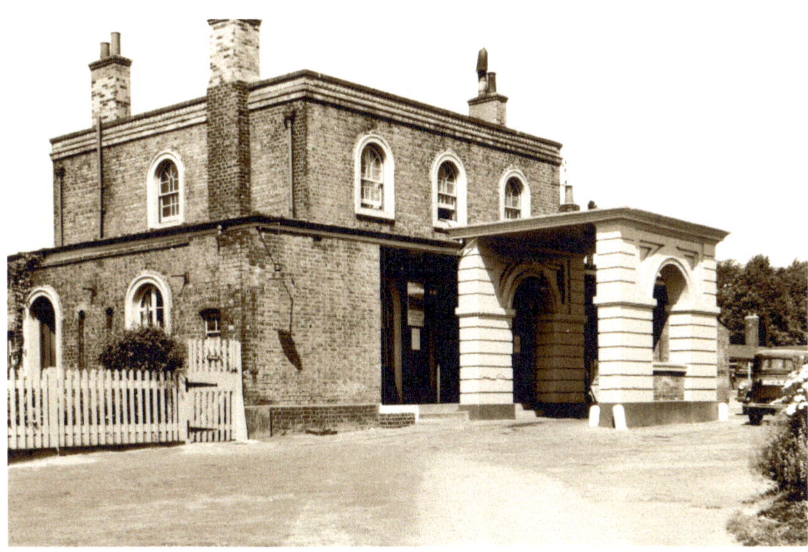

The impressive main station buildings at Audley End as seen on 1 August 1955; this building contained the booking hall and office, as well as the stationmaster's accommodation, and is located on the main up platform, across the car park from the branch platform. (Brian Connolly)

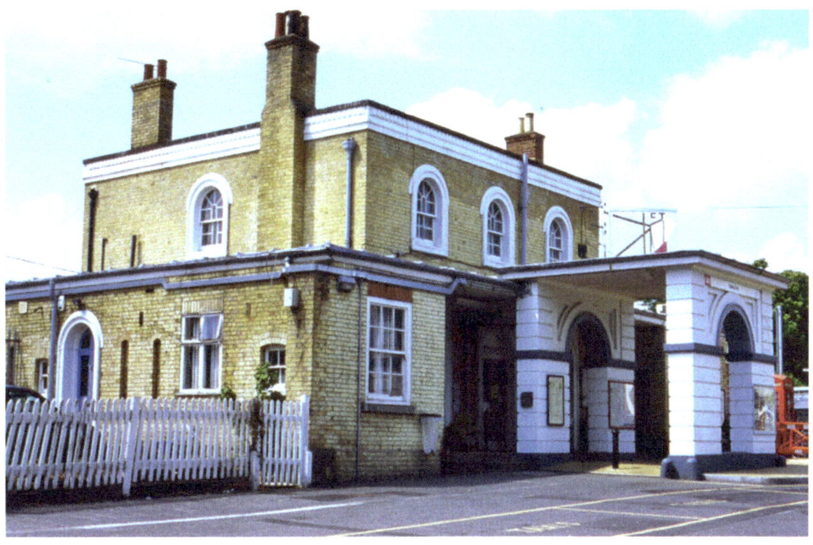

Fifty-six years later, and the main buildings at Audley End are in excellent condition, doing what they were originally designed for. Over the years, the arched windows on the left-hand extension have been replaced and an additional one added to the front of that room; the covered entrance now serves foot passengers only. (Ray Bishop)

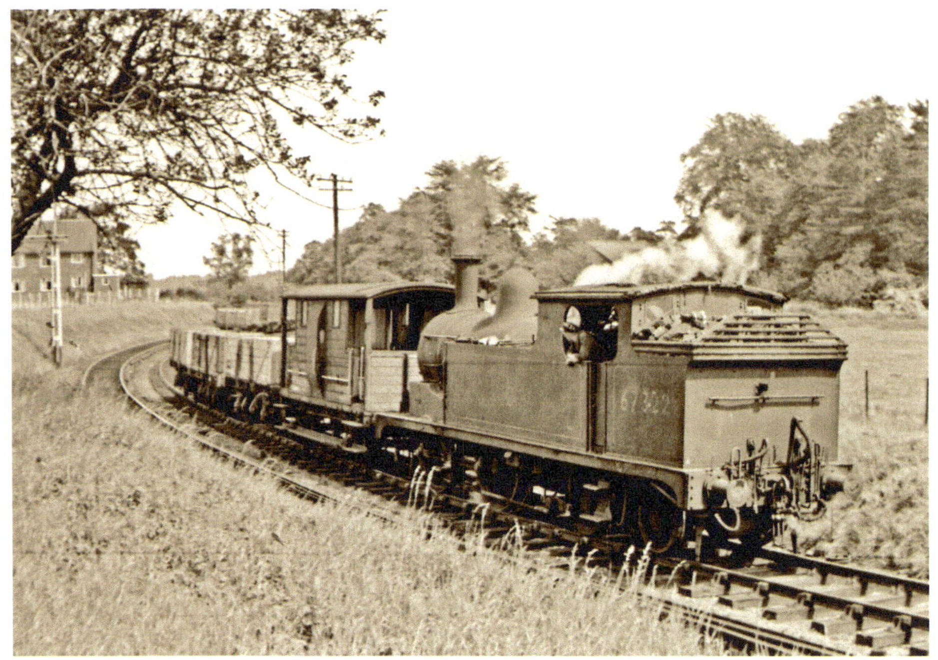

Former North Eastern Railway Class O 0-4-4 tank engine, later classified Class G5 by the London & North Eastern Railway, number 67322 is seen shunting at Audley End with the branch freight; this view was taken on 8 August 1956. The G5s continued to work the branch until October 1956, when they were replaced by Class N7 locomotives; the three G5s were scrapped a short while later. (Brian Pask)

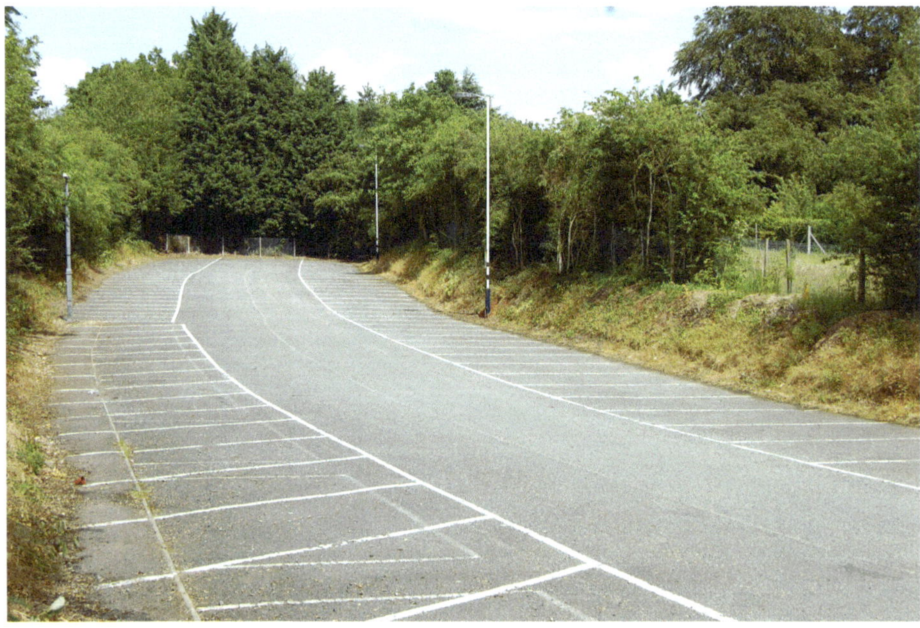

After the branch track and sidings were recovered, the spare land was turned into a car park, which on weekdays is full to capacity; this view was taken in June 2011. (Ray Bishop)

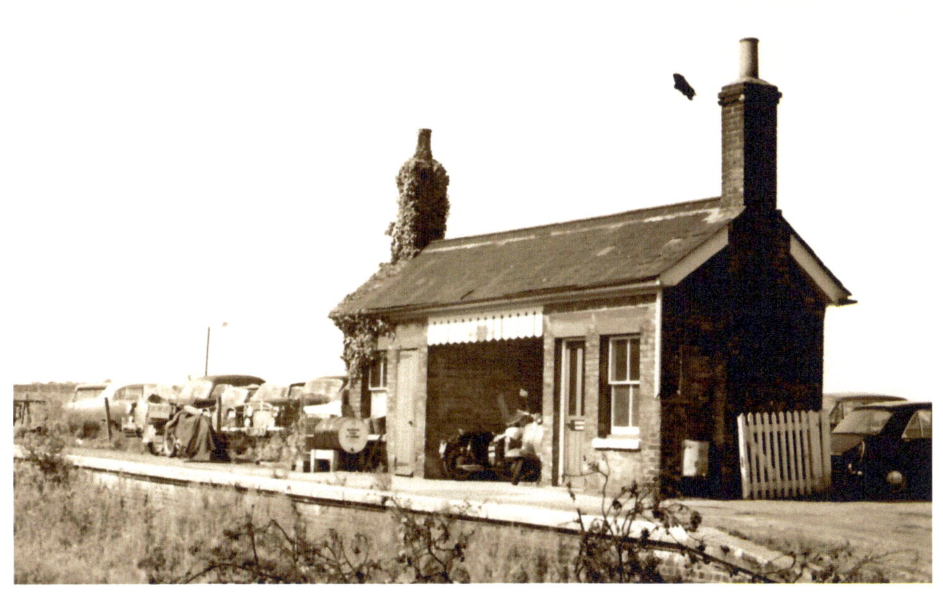

The branch platform building, after the track had been removed but before the car park was extended over the former running line and sidings; the waiting shelter found use as storage for motorcycles. This view was taken on 16 August 1968. (D. J. Plyer)

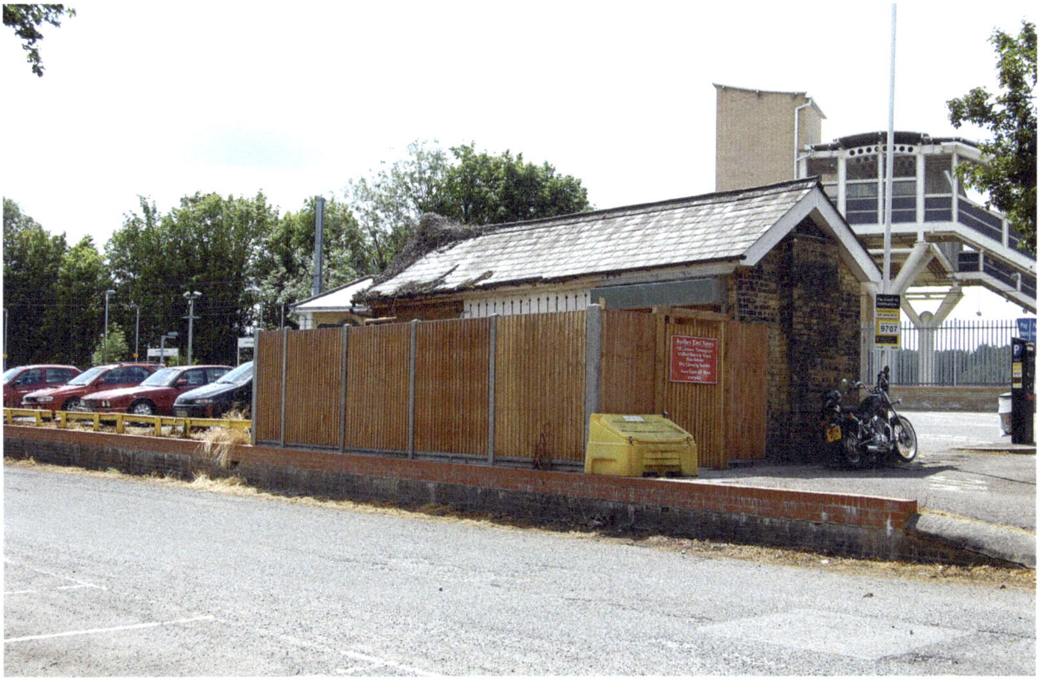

The former branch station building, minus its chimneys, has been turned into a small coffee shop, serving the thirsty and hungry commuters. In the background can be seen the new lifts recently installed to allow disabled access to the platforms. (Ray Bishop)

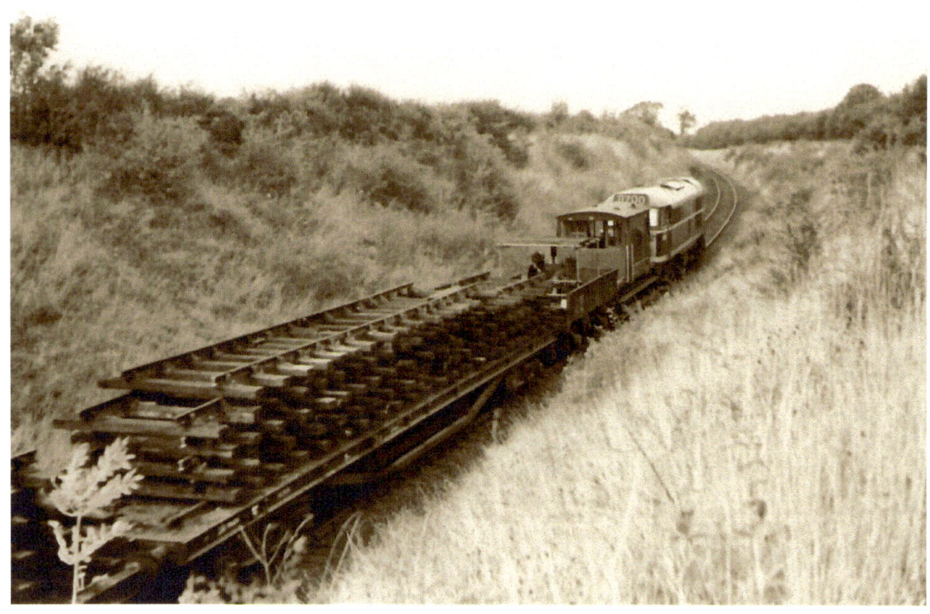

The End
Another load of recovered rails and sleepers departs from the Saffron Walden branch during the summer of 1968. The track panels were loaded onto rail vehicles using a crane fitted with caterpillar tracks; the train is being hauled by a Class 31 diesel. (Brian Barham)

Acknowledgements

Special thanks to Ray Bishop and Paul Lemon for the provision of the modern images, and to Brian Pask, Derek Plyer, Tim Stephens and Richard Casserley for all their help with the archive material and access to their photographic collections. Thanks also to all the other photographers and organisations that have provided views from their collections. Special thanks to the owners of the former stations at Bartlow, Sturmer and Stoke-by-Clare for allowing photographs to be taken of their properties.

Printed and bound by CPI Group (UK) Ltd, Croydon, CR0 4YY
16/07/2026
02169566-0005